Back to the Land
The Pastoral Impulse in England, from 1880 to 1914

Back to the Land

The Pastoral Impulse in England, from 1880 to 1914

Jan Marsh

Quartet Books
London Melbourne New York

First published by Quartet Books Limited, 1982
A member of the Namara Group
27/29 Goodge Street, London W1P 1FD

British Library Cataloguing in Publication Data

Marsh, Jan
    Back to the land.
    1. Country life–Great Britain–History–
    19th century
    I. Title
    941'.009'734   S522.G7

    ISBN 0-7043-2276-5

Typeset by MC Typeset, Rochester, Kent
Printed in Great Britain by Nene Litho,
and bound by Woolnough Bookbinders,
both of Wellingborough, Northants

Contents

Acknowledgements   vii

1 Beyond Industrialism   1

PART I THE CULT OF THE COUNTRYSIDE

2 Love of the Country   27
3 Reclaiming the Commons   39
4 The Countryman   60
5 Folk Song Restored   72

PART II TILLING THE EARTH

6 Agrarian Communes   93
7 Cottage Farmers   112
8 Farm Colonies   123

PART III RUSTIC ARTS AND CRAFTS

9 Handwork and Husbandry   139
10 Peasant Arts   158
11 Halcyon Cottage and Wild Garden   171

PART IV PIONEERS OF THE NEW LIFE

12 Rational Dress and Diet   187
13 New Schools   204
14 The Garden City   220
15 Pastoralism Rules   245

References   249
Index   261

Illustrations

Black and white plates (between pages 120 and 121)

William Morris, bas-relief portrait (*Jan Marsh*)
Red House (*Jan Marsh*)
Kelmscott Manor (*Jan Marsh*)
John Ruskin, cartoon published in *Punch*, 1876
Edward Carpenter (*Carpenter Collection, Sheffield City Libraries*)
Kate Greenaway illustration for Pied Piper of Hamelin, 1888
'At the Cottage Door', from *Birket Foster's Pictures of English Landscape*, 1863
'On Ide Hill', water-colour by Helen Allingham
Lopping Hall (*Jan Marsh*)
Mary Neal's Esperance Girls' Folk Dance team (*English Folk Dance and Song Society*)
A country couple at Hampton Lucy, 1890 (*Local Studies Department, Birmingham Public Reference Library*)
Nellie Shaw (*British Library*)
Arnold Eiloart (*British Library*)
Fels Fruit Farm (*British Library*)
Unemployed on the land (*Salvation Army International Archives*)
Starnthwaite Mill (*Jan Marsh*)
Farmhouse at Whiteway Colony (*Jan Marsh*)
Hand-spinning (*Museum of Rural Life, University of Reading*)
Sidney Barnsley (*Crafts Study Centre, Bath*)
Sidney Barnsley's house (*Jan Marsh*)
Munstead Wood
Terracotta panel (*Jan Marsh*)
Port Sunlight (*UML Ltd Unilever*)
Cultivation, Letchworth (*North Hertfordshire Museums*)

Line drawings

p.25   Garland for May Day
p.38   New Crusade
p.91   Design by Godfrey Blount, 1898
p.137   The Old Silk Mill
p.183   The Wild Garden
p.185   Letchworth's Reputation (*Letchworth First Garden City Museum*)
p.203   Rational Dress Society Gazette, 1888

Acknowledgements

The author would like to thank the following for their assistance in preparing this book:
Joan Abse; Maj. and Mrs Biddulph, Rodmarton Manor; Ruth Brandon; Hester Bury, Warner & Sons; Mrs D. Cadwallader, First Garden City Museum, Letchworth; Commons, Footpaths and Open Spaces Society; Margaret Dickinson; English Folk Dance and Song Society; Directorate of Ancient Monuments, Department of the Environment; Mary Greensted, Cheltenham Art Gallery; Haslemere Educational Museum; David Hart, Chipping Campden; Reference Division, Home Office; Reference Library, Ilford Central Libraries; Richard Jefferies, Watts Memorial Gallery, Compton; London Library; Alan Lupton; Harry Marsh; Fiona MacCarthy; R. Murry, Art Workers' Guild; National Trust; Nell Penny; David Postles, Sheffield City Libraries; Salvation Army archive department; Pat Thane; Local History Collection, Tower Hamlets Library Services; David Verey, Arlington Mill Museum; Victoria and Albert Museum; Lynne Walker, Newcastle Polytechnic.

The author and publishers would like to thank the following for permission to reproduce material quoted in this book:

Edward Arnold (Publishers) Limited for *Howards End* by E.M. Forster

Acknowledgements

All quotations from the Ashbee Memoirs (London Library copy)
    courtesy Felicity Ashbee 1982
Cambridge University Press for *Journals of George Sturt* edited by
    E.D. Mackerness
Faber and Faber Limited for *Where Beards Wag All* by G.E. Evans
Peter Kennedy, Folktracks for *Cecil Sharp* by Maud Karpeles
Methuen London for *The Wind in the Willows* by Kenneth Grahame

1

Beyond Industrialism

Towards the middle of E.M. Forster's novel *Howards End*, the sisters Margaret and Helen Schlegel are visited by a nondescript clerk with the drooping moustache of the period, who works in an insurance office and has aspirations above his status. He is characterized as third-generation urban, grandson to the 'shepherd or ploughboy whom civilization had sucked into the town', one who has lost the life of the body and failed to reach that of the intellect.

Leonard Bast relates a sort of 'adventure' to his attentive listeners, telling them of the desire to 'get back to the earth' which prompted him to spend a whole night walking in the country beyond Wimbledon, tramping up hills and through woods and stumbling among gorse and bramble until the dawn rose when, hungry, he took the first train back to London.

This is a curious episode, on the face of it. The Misses Schlegel are very impressed by Leonard's exploit – as is the author, who claims that his character has reached 'the destination'. Helen admires it so much that later, when Leonard's life has been ruined, she seeks, ineptly, to rescue him by taking him into her bed. Why, we wonder, was the Wimbledon walk so significant?

Howards End was published in 1912. By this date England had been transformed from an economy based on agriculture to one based on industry and commerce; the occupational structure was now overwhelmingly urban. Industrial development over the past century had brought coal mines, ironworks, foundries, textile mills, railways, gasworks, chemical works, heavy engineering, docks, printing works, factories and small workshops of all descriptions, together with the financial superstructure of banking and broking and the commercial network of warehouses, shops, offices, transport and trading firms to distribute the products of the expanding capitalist economy.

Even as it grew and expanded, belief in untrammelled progress was being questioned. Between 1801 and 1911 the proportion of the population living in urban areas rose from twenty per cent to eighty per cent, and regulations for health, safety and human exploitation were only gradually established through factory and public health legislation. Levels of pollution were appallingly high, urban sanitation an urgent necessity. Housing for the swelling city population always trailed behind demand, for as fast as cramped terraces were thrown up over fields and meadows on the outskirts of each town more people arrived to fill them. 'The March of Bricks and Mortar' as London spread outwards was caricatured by Cruikshank as early as 1829; by the end of the century the great conurbations were irremovably in existence, with no prospect of further accretion being arrested. Within the cities, trade fluctuations led to recurrent unemployment and periods when the workhouses were crowded with destitute families. In many manufacturing centres work was otherwise steady and overall income levels rose during the second half of the century, with a corresponding increase in consumption, but in the larger centres and particularly in London, which contained a multitude of small 'sweated' trades and a huge reserve army of seasonal and casual labour, the extent of poverty and distress was often desperate.[1]

Among the middle classes, who also grew in numbers as a result of economic expansion, concern for the problems of the urban poor became more vocal after the mid–century, as the demands on public and charitable relief increased, and as the first social surveys revealed the scale of the suffering.[2] In art and literature, the city came to be depicted as seething with a kind of verminous activity beneath the high Victorian prosperity, the poor preying on their fellows and the rich waxing complacent. The infernal nature of this new urban order, wealthy but dehumanized, is evident for example in both the Coketown of *Hard Times* (1851) and the Limehouse of *Our Mutual Friend* (1865). Gustave Doré's etchings of London are pure images of hell.

Social reform thus became one of the main preoccupations of the late nineteenth century. Orthodox political economy stated that market forces, working through a process of evolution to balance supply and demand, required no intervention. Liberal reformists nevertheless succeeded in introducing many measures, beginning with Chadwick's public health legislation in 1848 and moving through the introduction of compulsory education and the reform of local government to culminate in the social security programme of the 1906 Liberal government. For their part, the workers, through the organized labour movement that grew together with industrial capitalism, pressed for reform through their own struggles for higher wages, better conditions and self-help insurance schemes; a fairer share in the wealth they helped create would, they felt, enable them to live without charity. Late in the century some sections of the working class, together with some members of the intelligentsia, espoused a revolutionary position following Marx and Engels, believing that justice could only be achieved through expropriation. The bourgeoisie's fear of the mob intensified.

All sections of society assumed the continuation of Britain's industrial and urban condition. It was a different response to look at the misery, squalor and brutality of the Victorian city and identify the cause not as lack of compassion nor the effects of advanced capitalism, but as the urban industrial system itself, and to demand its removal. From this analysis, the solution was clear: the city must go, industry must be dismantled, the people must be resettled in villages and the economy return to craft workshops and guilds.

This notion acquired further validation following the collapse of agriculture in the 1870s and the grave decline in rural population which resulted. Competition from cheap food from overseas, transported by railroad and steamship and preserved in cans or refrigerated vessels ruined many English farmers and decimated agricultural jobs. Earlier in the century industrial expansion had drawn people off the land; now they were driven into the cities by poverty, hunger and lack of hope. The rural population fell between 1861 and 1901, a period when the total population of Britain was still rising, and the effect on those who remained was disastrous. Many village communities became depressed and stagnant, dependent on struggling farmers or landowners who were rapidly transferring their interests to more profitable areas. Much land went out of cultivation and large tracts were given over to game – the pheasant ousting the peasant, in the phrase of the time – as the well-to-do adopted new forms of conspicuous consumption for their wealth, which now came not from the land but from profitable business in manufacturing or finance.[3]

This rural decline was caused as much by the extension of economic imperialism to new arable lands overseas and by the Victorian attachment to free trade as by industrial development in Britain, but since it followed chronologically the connection was often assumed. Seeing the overcrowded conditions in the cities, with the hordes of unemployed workers, and at the same time aware of the emptying countryside, it was a simple equation to make. How far was it possible to resettle the workers on the land? Such a solution would do much to solve the city's problems.

At the same time, the visible decline of the countryside prompted a sudden rush of nostalgia for rural life. Traditionally, the country held an ambivalent position in English cultural attitudes, sometimes seen as the abode of joy and tranquillity, more often regarded as dull. Now, with the traditional countryside of England apparently disappearing for ever, pastoral attitudes were reasserted with intensity. The city was seen as physically and morally corrupting, damaged by 'the inner darkness in high places which comes with a commercial age', in Forster's words. Health and happiness were only to be found in the country, in rural life and agricultural occupations. The countryside carried forward the temporarily dimmed torch of the sun, 'until such time as the nation sees fit to take it up'.[4] So, love of the country became an article of faith, as essential to respectability as the belief in manners or morality. The 'lost' values of the English yeoman were resurrected by those living in cities and suburbs, and as the new century approached there grew a steady procession of urban emigrants to the countryside – 'Resident Trippers', as George Sturt rudely called them.

The attraction was partly personal, partly political and partly based on a pantheistic substitute for religion. Science and

Darwinism had undermined conventional Christianity, and Nature offered a viable alternative – the earth as the source of all goodness in place of God, a mystical deity without the archaic mythology. Politically, the misery of the urban poor aroused the consciences of the professional and rentier classes, who felt half guilty and yet could see no amelioration coming through the existing structures of church or state. Back-to-the-land was radical without being revolutionary.

Such an approach was supported, it appeared, by the ideas in the 'single tax' campaign of Henry George and his supporters, who grew in numbers as *Progress and Poverty* was published and re-published in the United States and Britain during the 1870s and '80s. George's analysis was compellingly simple: 'the wide-spreading social evils which everywhere oppress men amid advancing civilization spring from a great primary wrong – the appropriation by a few of the land on which and from which all must live'.[5] 'No power on earth,' he asserted, 'can rightfully make a grant of exclusive ownership in land.' Once this was sorted out, all ills – 'vice and misery, poverty and pauperism' – would dwindle away. The remedy was not expropriation, but the abolition of all taxation except that on land values. This had a powerful appeal in Britain, where land ownership was entrenched, and for many people *Progress and Poverty* made land into a live, polemical issue, leading easily into demands for 'the land for the people' and the right to cultivate it.

The return to nature also attracted those for whom the elaborate social system of conventions and proprieties seemed suffocatingly restrictive, preventing the expression of natural feelings and simple pleasures. Clothing, in the late Victorian period, was heavy and formal, furnishings heavy and ornate, food heavy and over-lavish. Social conduct was constrained by codes of behaviour. Respectability ruled, natural emotions were repressed, and the result was unhappiness. The solution, evidently, lay in a voluntary return to a plainer, simpler style of life, based on natural relations and the free expression of emotion. This, too, was more possible in the country than the city.

It was the children of the suburbs who took up these ideas most enthusiastically – the sons and especially the daughters of those who worked in the professions, the finance houses or the upper reaches of the civil service, but who had no pressing need for employment themselves. There were adherents, too, among the upper classes, who already lived 'on the land', at least for part of the year. Some hoped for the revitalization of rural life but found, like Lord Carrington when he tried to provide his estate workers with allotments, that the social and legal obstacles to change were very solid. Some, like Lord and Lady Bathurst, offered their patronage to artist–craftsmen attempting to escape from the city.

Among the working classes, who were all too familiar with a low level of consumption, there was little enthusiasm for a simpler lifestyle and less for a return to the country, where poverty prevailed. In general, the urban worker looked on his rural counterpart with contempt and pity, as a bumpkin fellow with mud on his boots and straw in his brain, but within the labour movement there also existed a continuing nostalgia for country life, expressed in pastoral imagery with no sense of incongruity. Nonconformist chapels and sunday schools sang out in favour of Blake's 'green and pleasant land', willing the destruction of 'those dark Satanic mills'. The popular journalist Robert Blatchford of the *Clarion*, whose book *Merrie England* – a title redolent of return rather than advance – sold over a million copies, described his programme for socialism as follows:

> First of all, I would restrict our mines, furnaces, chemical works and factories to the number actually needed for the supply of our own people. Then I would stop the smoke nuisance by developing water power and electricity. Then I would set men to work to grow wheat and fruit and to rear cattle and poultry for our own use.[6]

Committed to the same cause the artist Walter Crane designed cartoons and posters displaying similarly rustic iconography. In 'A Garland for May Day' (1893) socialism is a country maiden in flowing garments and bare feet with a halo of flowers. The usual slogans demanding shorter working hours, the end of child labour and 'Cooperation not Competition' are augmented with others sprinkled over the meadow reading 'The Land for the People', 'England Should Feed her Own People' and 'The Plough is a better Backbone than the Factory'.

Similarities between this anti-industrial impulse and that of the 1960s and '70s will already be evident. Even more striking is the clutch of associated ideas which in both periods attach themselves to the central core. There are three basic elements: the return to the land, the revival of handicrafts and the simplification of daily life. Subsidiary strands in the earlier as in the later period favoured vegetarianism, the wearing of loose robes and sandals, and varieties of eastern religion. Attempts were made to set up agrarian communes, craft workshops and 'new' schools. It was in the late Victorian era that cycling, walking and camping first became popular – taking to the open road and sleeping under the stars; at a certain point houses were designed with special bedroom balconies, for healthy open-air slumber. Exactly how this cluster of notions came together is not clear, but a large part of the appeal of this 'alternative' movement was its openness and flexibility. Although there were leaders or gurus, there was no formal creed, no dogmatic ideology; supporters were free to develop their own perceptions and tastes; everyone was encouraged to do their own thing; parts of the new lifestyle could be adopted or rejected, yet all shared in the exhilaration of the unorthodox.

Perhaps because of the very variety, this late Victorian movement has been almost totally forgotten and invisible, except when glimpsed, as it were, from another angle, like Bernard Shaw's often quoted Jaeger suit. Its virtual eclipse in the historical record is curious, although the unsuccessful are often submerged. This book represents a first attempt to rescue the men and women of that age and the ideas they lived by. In doing so it brings together much diverse material linked by a common thread of opposition to the urban, industrial, contemporary world. There is a problem of terminology, as well as one of termination. Several deserving topics failed to get in, for reasons of space, and just as it is difficult to find one phrase to cover today's 'ecological', 'alternative' or 'whole earth' manifestations, so in the late nineteenth century the terms 'Back to the Land', 'Back to Nature' and 'The Simple Life' were variously employed although none is fully representative; they stand as signposts to a region, not to a narrow path.

Certain guidebooks are available, illustrating the wide range of ideas and activities to be discovered. Key individuals and texts act as the inspiration for diverse experiments and revealing initiatives and without their example the movement would never have flourished as it did, although they were perhaps as much caused by it as they were begetters. Without inflating their importance, then, this chapter will now look at three men who helped to shape the back-to-the-land movement – John Ruskin, William Morris and Edward Carpenter.

Intended by his mother for the church, John Ruskin became a preacher of another kind. Having made his reputation in art criticism by demanding attention for the painters he admired, he moved by the 1870s to social and economic questions, challenging political economy by attacking the primacy of the 'laws' of supply and demand and commanding assent. He had a prolific and ultimately manic pen, owing to mental collapse, and many of his writings are rambling and self-indulgent, but the mood of his contemporary audience chimed with the fervour of his message, which many had felt without being able to articulate. His vision of an alternative, happier world was the same whether he spoke to the newly founded Working Men's College or as a Professor of Art at Oxford University, and thousands were inspired by his words, even when they disagreed with his arguments. He had led his followers from aesthetic issues to confront the 'advances' of industrial production with these precepts:

1. Never encourage the manufacture of any article not absolutely necessary, in the production of which invention has no share.
2. Never demand an exact finish for its own sake, but only for some practical or noble end.
3. Never encourage imitation or copying of any kind, except for the sake of preserving records of great works.[7]

Ruskin had a particular dislike of steam-driven machinery, which symbolized the industrial take-over, and hated railway locomotives most of all. 'I should like,' he once wrote, 'to destroy most of the railroads in England and all of the railroads in Wales.'[8] He always travelled by carriage and post-chaise, however slow and incon- venient. Like today's motorways, railways in the Victorian age were often under attack, and often triumphant.

By contrast, Ruskin considered trees and fields and flowers and all the greenness of the landscape to be 'essential to the healthy, spiritual life of man'. Physical labour on the land was dignifying not degrading, and the working man was unjustly and unnaturally coerced into industrial employment. In 1871 Ruskin began a series of monthly letters addressed to 'the Workmen and Labourers of Great Britain', under the title *Fors Clavigera*. Here were discussed, among numerous other matters, forms of action against economic inequity. There were three necessities, he argued: pure air, water and earth, and in order to give people access to these he proposed to set up a fund, based on the tithe, to buy land for cultivation. He wrote:

> We will try to take some small piece of English ground, beautiful, peaceful and fruitful. We will have no steam engines upon it and no railroads; we will have no untended or unthought-of creatures upon it; none wretched, but the sick; none idle, but the dead . . . we will have plenty of flowers and vegetables in our gardens, plenty of corn and grass in our fields – and few bricks. We will have some music and poetry; the children shall learn to dance to it and sing it – perhaps some of the old people, in time, may also . . .[9]

As it emerged, Ruskin's vision was of a quasi-feudal agrarian society with lords and labourers living in mutual service, and the girls dressed like Alpine peasants. Manual work would be combined with education and culture to produce refinement in all. Boys would learn cabinet-making, girls how to bake fine Yorkshire pies. There would be model schools, museums, libraries, art galleries – all the things Ruskin liked and none that he didn't. This fantasy Ruskin hoped to make real through his fund, to which he gave the Chaucerian name St George's Guild. Sympathizers were asked to donate a tenth of their income or property to buy land for the Guild. Only a few responded; Mrs Fanny Talbot (of whom we shall hear again) presented a row of cottages with sitting tenants at Barmouth in Wales, and George Baker, mayor of Birmingham, donated a stretch of woodland near Bewdley in Worcestershire, which Ruskin decided to leave in its natural state. It took a long time to set up the Guild, there being legal problems in vesting money in a non–commercial concern, but it was eventually established with Ruskin as master, and a tenth of his wealth, amounting to £7,000 capital and £1,000 per annum, at its disposal. There were a few other contributors and some Guild members, known as Companions.

The Guild's aims were primarily agrarian; as Ruskin wrote in 1882, it 'was originally founded with the intention of showing how much food–producing land might be recovered by well-applied labour from the barren or neglected districts of nominally cultivated countries'. The two subsidiary aims were to demonstrate that some degree of refined education could be given even to persons maintaining themselves by agricultural labour, and to persuade the upper classes that such labour was more honourable and pleasurable 'than their at present favourite occupation of war'.[10]

The acquisition of land proved difficult, however, and it is fair to say that the most successful of St George's undertakings was non-agricultural – the establishment of a small museum at Walkley near Sheffield for the use of working men, with a collection of minerals, coins, casts and copies of paintings, selected by the master himself. This was, in 1880, one of the Guild's five pieces of property, the most ambitious being St George's Farm at Totley, also near Sheffield, where land was purchased for a group of local people who wished to form a self-supporting commune. The history of this venture is described in Chapter 6; in the words of Ruskin's editors, 'St George's farms, it is to be feared, produced very little except a plentiful crop of disappointments',[11] but, as we shall see, that is not the full story.

There was also a smallholding near Scarborough, which Ruskin bought for John Guy, a subscriber to *Fors Clavigera* who had applied to the Guild asking to be given the opportunity of putting Ruskin's ideas into practice. Three-quarters of an acre of 'barren or neglected ground' was bought at Cloughton Moor and the Guy family installed. In an early letter to Ruskin, Guy describes the work as hard but cheerful. The difficulty of making ends meet, however, drove the Guys from the smallholding within four years, and they later emigrated.

Another aspect of Ruskin's vision which, as we shall see, was taken up by others in all parts of the country, was the revival of handspinning and weaving. He believed that all English girls should once again spin and weave cloth for their own households, as in medieval times, and he was therefore favourably disposed towards the proposal made to him by Egbert Rydings, who wrote from the Isle of Man to say that the skill of home-spinning there was likely to die out because the farmers' wives could find no one to buy their Manx-wool yarn. This was, political economists asserted, the inevitable result of technological progress and economies of scale, but Ruskin disagreed, and St George's Guild put up interest-free money for Rydings to establish the Manx Woollen Industry at Laxey, to make 'honest cloth from honest thread'.

St George's Mill, according to a visitor in 1886, was

> both a factory and a store. It contains, in the first place, the machinery for carding and spinning the wool and washing the cloth. The word machinery may very probably grate on the ear of the more devout Ruskinian, and I hasten to explain that the motive-power is a water-wheel. (It may here be noted, for the consolation of weaker brethren, that the prohibition on machinery by 'St George' is not absolute; it is only steam that is absolutely refused) . . .
>
> Mr Ruskin's mill is a store as well, and in this capacity it enables him to revive another piece of olden time . . . the good, old institution of barter. The farmers bring their wool which is stored in the mill, and are paid for it either by finished cloth or by yarn for home-knitting, or occasionally by wool prepared for home-spinning. One does not like to think what the rigid economists would say to this calculated interference with the division of labour; but then, as the lives of the peasants are the healthier, perhaps the other kind of wealth may be left to look after itself.[12]

The Laxey mill produced tweeds, home-spun serges, flannels, blankets, knitting wool and stockings. Several of the schemes it inspired feature in Chapter 10, and it also played a part in the passion for 'dress-reform' and 'all-wool clothing' described in Chapter 12. In 1906 the mill was still in operation, although production was by then wholly mechanized.

A final example of Ruskin's influence may be seen in the reintroduction of the May Queen into English schools and villages.

One of the master's followers was the reverend principal of Whitelands Training College for women teachers in Chelsea, who ingratiatingly asked if Ruskin would present his college with a prize, although it was well-known that Ruskin opposed all forms of competition and reward in education. He took the opportunity, however, to launch another of his pet ideas which, like hand-spinning, was associated with an earlier, happier age. A May Day festival was thus established at Whitelands, the students electing a May Queen whose main task was to distribute forty volumes of Ruskin's works among her fellow pupils, her own prize being a gold cross, differently designed each year. On May Day, for the coronation, the college was decorated with wild flowers from the countryside.

Devising this sentimental ritual no doubt gave Ruskin much pleasure – his vision of female beauty was always the innocently virginal – and inspired many imitations. As Whitelands-trained teachers spread through the English school system so did the May Day influence; in 1890 the principal remarked that not a year passed without his hearing of a new festival. This reconstruction of an old custom coincided with the rediscovery of English folk song and dance described in Chapter 5, much of which is associated with May Day, and their subsequent reintroduction into country villages, often in conjunction with May Day festivities. At these, the local schoolteacher or vicar's wife, and sometimes the lady from the big house, would organize the children to choose a queen and dance round the maypole in imagined imitation of their forebears, so that what had been a popular tradition maintained in defiance of parson and squire became an event promoted by these same authorities.

The influence of William Morris was one of example rather than exhortation. A great deal has, deservedly, been written about Morris and his influence on design and on the development of socialist thought, less on his views on the urban and rural environment, or about the way his actions affected others, and there is space here only to trace a selection of his multifaceted work.

Like his Pre-Raphaelite heroes and friends, Morris's initial response to contemporary industrial society was to turn his back on it, espouse the values of Malory and Chaucer and attempt as far as possible to live in the fourteenth rather than the nineteenth century. This escapist impulse was originally aesthetic, provoked by the horror of the Great Exhibition, and after his marriage in 1860 Morris created his home, the Red House in Bexleyheath, as a model of what might be done as an alternative to prevailing industrial design. Built by his friend Philip Webb as a kind of refuge of beauty and harmony, the Red House was an emblem of artistic sanctuary, modern in design but traditional in atmosphere. It is an L-shaped dwelling around an enclosed garden, with a cone-roofed well in the centre. Inside, the house was originally rich and dark, the walls covered with embroidered hangings of flowers, birds and trees, and portraits of legendary women. There were a number of pieces of massive, built-in furniture reminiscent in design of the Jacobean age and beyond.

Domestic life failed to live up to the expectations of the Red House, which Morris left in 1865, but he kept the image for life and searched for a replacement. In 1871 he found Kelmscott Manor in Oxfordshire, which he described to a friend as 'a heaven on earth; an old stone Elizabethan house like Water Eaton, and such a garden! close down on the river, a boat house and all things handy . . .' It was the embodiment of an ideal, built in warm Cotswold stone; even 'the roofs are covered with the beautiful stone slates of the district, the most lovely covering a roof can have, especially when, as here and in all the traditional old houses of the countryside, they are "sized down", the smaller ones to the top and the bigger ones towards the eaves'.[13] This delight in country craftsmanship was one of Morris's main legacies.

At Kelmscott, the ugly modern world might never have existed. Not for nothing had Morris opened his poetic romance *The Earthly Paradise* with the lines:

> Forget six counties overhung with smoke,
> Forget the snorting steam and piston stroke,
> Forget the spreading of the hideous town. . . .

and made his Fortunate Isles resemble the English countryside on a summer's day:

shaded lay
The sweet-breathed kine; across the sunny vale,
From hill to hill, the wandering rook did sail,
Lazily croaking . . . .

This endless poem, with its strong soap–opera element, was very popular for Victorian family readings and helped establish Morris in the public mind as a poet of Arcadia, his images reinforcing the escapist mood. In the visual arts, he had an equal reputation, based on his work as designer and craftsman.

Established by Morris and his friends in 1861 in order to produce the kind of furnishings they preferred, the firm which was later known as Morris and Company began with commissions from ecclesiastical and public clients such as that for the tea room at the South Kensington (now Victoria and Albert) Museum. But it also produced homely furniture – solid tables designed by Webb, green-painted chest, table and chair suitable for servants' rooms, and rush-bottomed chairs based on a 'Sussex' farmhouse pattern. Morris's main contribution as a designer was with wallpaper and printed fabric, where the patterns, of entwining flowers, fruit, leaves and sometimes birds, have an intensity that exerts fascination: although flat, they seem to have the depth of a thick hedge, presenting nature at once tamed and rampant. In the houses of aesthetic customers, set off by plain walls and woodwork, these designs suggest a burgeoning natural world outside, curbed by bricks and mortar, yet a source of vitality to those immured in the city.

It was Morris's practice to understand and if possible master the craft techniques involved before designing. He thus wove a tapestry unaided, and paid a working visit to the dye works which supplied yarn to Morris and Company, where he covered himself in indigo from the vats. He believed, like Ruskin, in the virtue and value of hand work, with the irregularities giving character to the product, and felt, too, that the introduction of chemical anilines had destroyed the subtle harmony of the older vegetable dyes (acid green had been developed in 1835 and bright purple in 1856). In his work Morris used softer greens and blues, stimulating the demand for the colours associated with the aesthetic movement ('greenery-yallery Grosvenor Gallery') based on the natural tones of field and hedgerow. The artistic generation that succeeded him took his example seriously, immersing themselves in the crafts, as Chapter 9 illustrates.

Equally influential was Morris's agitation for conservation, a new and at first largely derided idea. In his youth Morris had been a keen disciple of Gothic revivalism in architecture, but later he came to regard medieval-style building in a non-medieval age as a mistake, at the same time as popular enthusiasm for it spread, causing many authentic medieval churches to be rebuilt or repaired in the old style with new materials. In 1877 the planned remaking of Tewkesbury Abbey roused Morris to action, deploring 'all "restoration" that means more than keeping out wind and weather' in a letter which led to the founding of the Society for the Protection of Ancient Buildings, one of the original conservation bodies discussed in Chapter 3.

Through the S.P.A.B. Morris was led further into public life. He began to lecture and write about the environment and in particular the problems of the city. 'Think of the spreading sore of London,' he wrote, 'swallowing up with its loathesomeness field and wood and heath without mercy and without hope, mocking our feeble efforts to deal even with its minor evils of smoke-laden sky and befouled river; the black horror and reckless squalor of our manufacturing districts, so dreadful to the senses.'[14] What could be done? 'The first and most necessary step,' he declared, was 'the cleansing of England.' Industrialism had despoiled the country: 'We must turn this land,' he wrote urgently, 'from the grimy backyard of a workshop into a garden.'[15]

He outlined housing schemes with generous open space, so that 'every child should be able to play in a garden close to the place where his parents live'.[16] These were tall, spacious dwellings, with communal kitchens and laundries, for sociable living. He insisted that builders and contractors preserve the trees growing on sites acquired for building, asking if they understood what treasures full grown trees were in towns and suburbs[17] and he protested most vigorously against pollution, slating the wealthy classes for buying landscape paintings when their factory chimneys and power stations poured out poison onto the real countryside.

For inside the home he coined the maxim 'Have nothing in your houses that you do not know to be useful or believe to be beautiful', and his ideal was 'simplicity of life, begetting simplicity of taste . . . simplicity in the palace as well as in the cottage'.[18] His furniture list for a drawing room was: bookcase, table, chairs, bench, cupboard, set off by a bunch of flowers and some paintings. Nothing more was necessary. 'What tons and tons of unutterable rubbish' would have to be cleared out of London's houses if this precept were acted upon, he exclaimed – yet his advice was heeded, and the fashion swung towards plainness, just as it followed his ideas in architecture, as will be seen in Chapter 11.

Simplicity and socialism went together for Morris; then at least some of the uglier products of capitalism would not be needed.'Nothing should be made by man's labour which is not worth making,' he argued, 'or which must be made by labour degrading to others.'[19] Although he had struggled with and mastered Marx's theory, his approach was passionate rather than scientific, and touched always with pastoral imagery. Wealth, he said,

> is what Nature gives us and what a reasonable man can make out of the gifts of Nature for his reasonable use. The sunlight, the fresh air, the unspoiled face of the earth, food, raiment and housing necessary and decent; the storing up of knowledge of all kinds and the power of disseminating it; means of free communi- cation between man and man; works of art, the beauty which man creates when he is most a man, most aspiring and thoughtful – all things which serve the pleasure of people, free, manly and uncorrupted.[20]

Those employed in manufacturing should, he argued, 'by no means be compelled to pig together in close city quarters. There is no reason why they should not follow their occupations in quiet country homes.'[21] 'A Factory As It Might Be' is portrayed as well-built and spacious, surrounded by gardens, with school-rooms, canteens and recreation rooms – an ideal that found realization in the Garden City.

There are no factories in *News From Nowhere*, the political-pastoral romance which played a formative role in the careers of many in the labour movement. The picture it gives of the country after the revolution is, quite simply, the country. There are salmon in the Thames, woods in Kensington, apricot trees in Trafalgar Square. London is a small town; east of the City all is pasture. Elsewhere the great manufacturing centres have been cleared away:

> The town invaded the country; but the invaders, like the warlike invaders of early days, yielded to the influence of their surroundings and became country people; and in their turn, as they became more numerous than the townsmen, influenced them also; so that the difference between town and country grew less and less; and it was indeed this world of the country vivified by the thought and briskness of town-bred folk which has produced that happy and leisurely but eager life . . .

The dreamer of this dream is conveyed up the Thames towards Kelmscott, where haymaking is due to start. The New World begins in the country, and the old grey house in the meadows is its emblem.

Edward Carpenter was a member of the Society of Sheffield Socialists, an affiliate of Morris's Socialist League, and a leading apostle of the simple life movement. He lived in a cottage in the hills south of Sheffield, growing his own food and pursuing plain living and personal freedom. He was regarded as something of a sage or prophet, and pilgrimages were made to his door, though Carpenter himself disclaimed all desire to be a leader, which was perhaps prudent in view of his avowed homosexuality.

He was born in 1844 into a comfortable bourgeois family which lived on its investments and resided in Brighton, and as a boy he was, he said, 'pursued by the dread of appearances', and emotionally suppressed. As a mathematician at Trinity Hall he was offered a fellowship and being already disposed towards good works he took orders and became a local curate as well as a college tutor. It was an easy and lucrative life, but in 1874 he suddenly resigned both posts in protest against the empty university intellectualism. Seeking a lifestyle more in touch with the 'real' world, he went to work as a peripatetic lecturer with the University Extension Movement in the north of England, where for seven years he travelled the circuit before settling in Sheffield. Here the strong radical tradition was able to absorb him into its ranks, and he began to develop his own ideas, on egalitarianism, the open air and close contact with Nature. He adopted vegetarianism, took up swimming and sunbathing and started to feel 'the absolute necessity' of a more outdoor life. The idea of manual work seemed powerfully attractive.

In 1879 Carpenter became acquainted with Albert Fearnehough, a labouring man of about his own age, and with a local farmer, Charles Fox. These friendships proved momentous; as he related, it was the 'way out of that dingy wilderness, that *selva oscura*, in which I had wandered lost'. The two men 'represented . . . a life close to Nature and actual materials, shrewd, strong, manly, independent, not the least polite or proper, thoroughly human and kindly, and spent for the most part in the fields and under the open sky'.[22] Lodging in Fearnehough's cottage on Fox's farm, Carpenter began a series of Whitmanic poems later given the title *Towards Democracy*, an interminable and immensely popular hymn to working people, life, love and the future, which became an inspiration to the growing socialist movement. It is suitable only for declaiming aloud:

> To feel downwards and downwards through this wretched maze of shame for the solid ground – to come close to the Earth itself and those that live in direct contact with it;
> To identify, to saturate yourself with these, their laws of being, their modes of life, their needs (the Earth's also), thoughts, temptations and aspirations;
> This – is it not the eternal precept? – is the first thing: to dig downwards. Afterwards, the young shoot will ascend – and ascending easily part aside the overlying rubbish.

Literal digging was soon associated with the name of Edward Carpenter. In 1882 he used his inheritance to buy some land big enough for a market garden or smallholding, with the aim 'just to try and keep at least one little spot of earth clean', free from bricks and soot.[23] The motive, he maintained, was purely personal: 'I felt the need of physical work, of open-air life and labour – something primitive to restore my overworn constitution';[24] he had no political intentions. Yet his desire chimed with that of others, who credited him with making his move onto the land in pursuit of a wholesale scheme of social reform.

Carpenter's smallholding at Millthorpe, some miles to the south of Sheffield, was a true Arcadia: three fields running down to a brook, a wooded valley below and the moors above. Here a house was built for Carpenter and the Fearnehoughs, for Albert's wife and daughter were to look after the domestic side. Albert was allocated to the garden, with supervision and assistance from Carpenter who later described the early days:

> I worked for hours and for whole days together out in the open field or garden, or digging drains with pick and shovel, or carting along the roads; going into Chesterfield and loading and fetching manure, or to the coalpit for coal, grooming and bedding down the horse, or getting off to market at 6 a.m. with vegetables and fruit, and standing in the market behind a stall till 1 or 2 p.m.[25]

When not digging, he was writing, in a special study he constructed, like a summerhouse or garden hut, believing that for any creative work it was necessary to have 'the quietude and strength of nature at hand, like a great reservoir on which to draw'.[26] He saw the land as a sort of salvation: 'the vitality and amplitude of the earth . . . are real things from which one can only cut oneself off at serious peril and risk to one's immortal soul'.[27] With this example and that of Meredith's writing chalet on Box Hill, writing huts became a minor literary fashion desired by every aspiring author. Edward Thomas shared a purpose-built study with his landlord's beehives on the ridge above Steep, while today's visitors to Bernard Shaw's house at Ayot St Lawrence may see at the bottom of the garden his wooden writing hut, furnished with camp bed and electric fire, and built on a swivel base to turn with the sun.

In 1887 a collection of Carpenter's writings was published as *England's Ideal*, with thoughts on the condition of the classes and some tempting details of possible alternatives. The book described how on at least one occasion Millthorpe ground flour and baked bread from home-grown wheat, and it also discussed a cottage economy in detail for the benefit of would-be drop-outs who, Carpenter suggested, could easily adjust to living on £100 a year if they tried. A large garden was essential: a quarter acre would feed a family while seven acres, as at Millthorpe, would soon pay its way.

Outgoings for a year were calculated at just £60, with food and household expenses amounting to about 8d per person per day. Beyond this was ostentation.

This philosophy was clearly modelled on Carpenter's reading of Henry Thoreau's *Walden*, which was only published in Britain in 1886, some twenty-five years after the author's death and forty since he had lived self-sufficiently in the woods in New England, 'in a house which I had built myself, on the shores of Walden Pond, in Concord, Massachusetts, and earned my living by the labour of my hands only'. In Britain such a notion was novel. Following in Thoreau's footsteps, Carpenter delighted in informing audiences how far they could simplify their lives if they really wished. Any object which required dusting must be thrown out, he said, to cut down domestic work; unusually for a Victorian male, Carpenter helped with the housework. Another thing was to eliminate meat from the diet, to reduce costs and promote health. To those used to the multiple courses of a Victorian meal, Carpenter's menu was minimal: 'less than a pennyworth of oatmeal will make one person a large dish of porridge, and this with an egg, or some cheese and a little fruit, will form a first-class dinner'.[28]

Clothing received similar treatment. Counting the layers of garments customarily worn, Carpenter found eight unnecessary items, and devised for himself a simple yet practical outfit consisting of 'a good woollen shirt and coat and pants of similar material . . . just three garments, all simply made, easily washable and often washed'. He regarded the stiff formal dress of conventional society as a kind of shroud, 'only the head and hands out, all the rest of the body clearly sickly with want of light and air, atrophied, stiff in the joints, straight-waistcoated and partially mummified'. He ceremoniously threw away his dress clothes, the badge of gentility without which, he was assured, he could never enter the homes of the respectable again. 'As to the feet,' he observed, 'there seems to be no reason except mere habit why, for a large part of the year at least, we should not go barefoot, as the Irish do, or at least with sandals,'[29] which when George Adams and his family replaced the Fearnehoughs at Millthorpe Carpenter took to making. Based on an Indian pattern, these sandals were sold to admirers, who were happy to wait months for a pair made with the master's own hands. When Adams left, he took the sandal-making with him, ultimately to Letchworth, the first garden city, where a pair survives, black and curled.

In 1889 Carpenter published *Civilisation: Its Cause and Cure*, in which he further developed his ideas on the return to Nature and simplicity, arguing that 'primitive' peoples often showed a higher level of freedom and happiness than so-called civilized nations. Seen as a kind of text for the back-to-the-land movement, this book claimed that the way forward 'is the way back to the lost Eden, or rather forward to the new Eden'. Mankind, it was argued, must escape from civilization: 'Nature must once more be his home.' To those who remarked that the British climate made outdoor life impractical, Carpenter retorted that this was society's own fault, for 'it is we who have covered the lands with a pall of smoke and are walking to our funerals under it'.[30]

To catch this philosophy from the man himself, admirers and sympathizers came to Millthorpe in great numbers, often hoping to be given courage for their own modest experiments in natural living. Among the visitors were many who feature in other sections of this book: E.M. Forster, G. Lowes Dickinson, Cecil Reddie, C.R. Ashbee, Raymond Unwin. Other friends included Henry Salt, Olive Schreiner and Havelock Ellis. Less famous callers included earnest young couples who wished to discuss simplified household arrangements, and a host of what Carpenter disingenuously labelled 'faddists of all sorts and kinds': 'vegetarians, dress reformers, temperance orators, spiritualists, secularists, anti-vivisectionists, socialist, anarchists . . . all would call and insist in the most determined way on my joining their crusades'.[31]

The largest group of visitors, however, were young homosexuals, seeking the author of *Love's Coming of Age* (1896) and *The Intermediate Sex* (1908) in which tolerance and understanding of sexual varieties and needs were shown and requested. In casting off his class background, Carpenter had also shed conventional approaches to sex and arrived at a sane and frank expression of his own orientation. In 1898 he set up what would today be described as a gay household with George Merrill, a young working man who loved him until death. He had other friends too and from the gathering of like-minded men at Millthorpe sprang the ideas that later grew into the Guild of Handicraft which features in Chapter 9, and the new school movement, discussed in Chapter 13.

From his outside position Carpenter also criticized the marriage laws of the time and suggested that personal relationships should be free and joyful, healthy and creative, long-lasting or short and always unconstrained by external laws or expectations. He was thus one of the pioneers of the 'free love' movement, which, in his view, was closely connected with 'back to nature': 'sexual embraces,' he wrote, 'themselves seldom receive the benison of Dame Nature, in whose presence alone, under the burning sun or the high canopy of the stars and surrounded by the fragrant atmosphere, their meaning can be fully understood: but take place in stuffy dens of dirty upholstery and are associated with all unbeautiful things'.[32]

It cannot be guessed how this advice on alfresco sex was received by Carpenter's readers – but in the same year as his book was published, the young Helen Noble and Edward Thomas became lovers in a secret glade on Wimbledon Common, crowning their love with leaves and flowers; Millthorpe had no monopoly on open-air embraces.

Thus, to more timid souls, Carpenter was the prophet of the new life, one who had escaped from the city and all it stood for, and who offered a glimpse of what life might be like, returned to its free, natural, outdoor state. How he inspired a generation may be felt from the tribute paid him by E.M. Forster:

> The two things he admired most on earth were manual labour and fresh air and he dreamed like William Morris that civilisation would be cured by their union. The Labour movement took another course and advanced by committee meetings and statistics towards a state-owned factory attached to state-supervised recreation-grounds. Edward's heart beat no warmer at such joys. He felt no enthusiasm over municipal baths and municipally provided bathing-drawers. What he wanted was *News From Nowhere* and the place that is still nowhere, wildness, the rapture of unpolluted streams, sunrise and sunset over the moors, and in the midst of these the working people whom he loved, passionately in touch with one another and with the natural glories around them.[33]

In *Howards End*, Leonard Bast, one of the working people whom Carpenter might have loved, is killed by a combination of capitalist callousness and a heap of books – destroyed by civilization. But his and Helen's child lives to grow up in the country, where poppies bloom in the garden and hay is cut with a long-handled scythe. The 'red rust' of the creeping city is visible in the distance, but those who live at Howards End are sure that this 'new craze' will not last – urbanism is on the way out. It will be succeeded, they are certain, by a new civilization that will 'rest on the earth', and although all the present is against it, they say with a conviction that mirrors Leonard's Wimbledon walk, that the country 'is the future as well as the past'.

Part I

The Cult of the Countryside

· A · GARLAND · FOR · MAY · DAY · 1895 ·

Garland for May Day, design by Walter Crane, originally
published in the *Clarion*, 1895

2

Love of the Country

Since the city was so foul, it was desirable to live in the country, and, from around 1870, the rediscovery of the rustic world by the middle classes stimulated a modest reversal of the century's dominant trend of urban migration.

Those who moved away from the cities were a small minority, of course, compared to the numbers still leaving the land until at least 1900, and as the tendency was most popular among writers and artists, for reasons that will be explored presently, it is therefore over-represented in the literature and biographical records of the time. For each of those who achieved a house in the country (not to be confused with a country house) there were thousands who remained in the cities and suburbs. Yet the outward movement was observable: by the end of the century in some rural districts the population had at last begun to stabilize after three decades of steady and sometimes drastic decline, and while this levelling-out was uneven and may have been due largely to adjustments in agricultural employment, a contributory factor, remarked on at the time, was the growing number of non-agricultural residents in certain rural districts, particularly in the southern counties.[1]

The feeling for the countryside which led many people to dream of living there combined the residual Romantic impulse that had first made the wild places of Europe alluring but was now petering out in a vague love of rusticity, with growing anti-industrialism. Emotional value accrued to the farmland that was no longer England's economic base and the countryside became a symbol of escape from the dominant values of capitalism – bigger, better, faster. Ironically, it was only possible to move to the country if cushioned financially by the proceeds of the hated industrial system; those who deserted the city came largely from the bourgeoisie.

They were enabled to do so by another product of the age, the railway; for as the network grew, bringing virtually everywhere in England within a day's reach of London, it became possible to live and work in different places. 'In the older days,' remarked Gertrude Jekyll in her book *Old West Surrey,* 'London might have been at a distance of two hundred miles. Now one can never forget that it is at little more than an hour's journey.'² So commuting came into being, not so much for office workers as for higher-income business and professional persons, who were able to move their families out of the metropolis, away from the unhealthy smogs and distressing poverty, while continuing to attend to their affairs in the City on a daily basis, and to enjoy the benefits of fresh air at weekends. A similar pattern was admirably suited to those in the artistic professions, who did not have to travel to town every day but needed to keep in touch with editors, patrons and friends. Several well-known authors in this period lived in the country and went to London once a week, to see publishers, dine with fellow-writers, listen to the latest gossip and learn of possible commissions. Edward Garnett, living at Limpsfield in Surrey, was a typical figure.

The most desirable areas to live were those of unspoiled country within easy reach of London – above all the Surrey hills. In 1860 this district had been a quiet rural area much like any other, but within thirty years it had been 'overrun' by new residents. Miss Jekyll voiced the familiar dilemma: 'It is impossible to grudge others the enjoyment of its delights, and yet one cannot but regret, that the fact of its now being thickly populated and much built-over, has necessarily robbed it of its older charms of peace and retirement.'³

The south-west corner of Surrey, where Miss Jekyll lived, was popularized in the first place by the watercolourist Birket Foster, whose rustic scenes fixed an image of English village life that is still current. Foster rented himself a summer cottage at Witley near Godalming, and afterwards built himself a famous house, called The Hill.[4] It was the decayed picturesqueness of the region which appealed, and he collected weather-worn tiles from old cottages and farm buildings in the neighbourhood to use on his own new roof. The attractiveness of Foster's water-colours of local spots like Hambledon Common and Chiddingfold village is well expressed in the text accompanying a collection of his scenes, 'with their picturesque cottages roofed with thatch or red tiles, now fast disappearing, and their leafy lanes with happy children gathering wild flowers'.[5]

Other artists followed Foster to Surrey, among them Helen Allingham, who began her career as an admired illustrator of *Far From the Madding Crowd* before marrying the poet William Allingham and taking to water-colour. She too settled in Witley and the first exhibition of her work, in 1886, consisted of paintings of Surrey cottages. The catalogue[6] noted with regret that the charming old buildings were falling into ruin as a result of modern sanitary requirements (not to mention the loss of their roofing tiles to incoming residents) so that within a few years Helen Allingham's scenes would be the record of a vanished way of life. As the city folk came out to find country beauty, the genuine article was disappearing. . .

Thomas Hardy understood the problem well, observing that the village poor could hardly be expected to remain content in their shabby, ignorant picturesqueness for the sake of wealthier and better-educated onlookers.[7] His own early novels, however, had encouraged that very 'love of the country' that responded to picturesqueness and backwardness. Hardy's career, incidentally, illustrates in compressed form the social movements of the nineteenth century that we have been detailing. Born the son of a Dorset mason whose family had seldom moved far afield, Hardy was apprenticed to a local architect before joining a London office at the age of twenty-two – a not untypical move for an ambitious young man. Ten years later his first successful novel, *Under the Greenwood Tree* (1872) was published. It drew on his country background and was already nostalgic when issued, for it was based on the village people Hardy had known as a child in the 1840s and '50s, but it was seized upon by readers as the authentic face of country life.

Although they did not portray such a bucolic world, Hardy's subsequent country novels were also well-received and admired for containing comedy and tragedy and a sense of abiding values, based on the land.

With his growing literary success, Hardy left architecture and returned to Dorset, encompassing the rural–urban–rural migration within one lifetime. He designed himself a comfortable, non-picturesque house, from where he watched the rural scene, and when he began, in his later novels, to show the social decay and personal suffering then being caused by agricultural decline and economic struggle, he found his work far less popular. The presentation of insecurity in *Jude the Obscure*, particularly, made Hardy's readers uncomfortable. The Wessex novels, in contrast, offered a vicarious memory of an older, stabler world.

The creation of 'Wessex' is an apt illustration of the process that was happening on the ground, as certain regions were 'taken up'. The cult of the Cotswolds – a hitherto little-regarded area – dates from this period. Its popularity began in the 1880s when a group of artists, among them William Sargent and Guy Dawber, began to spend their summers at Broadway, where the houses 'are quaint and picturesque, being built of local stone . . . and all weathered'.[8] The place was made truly fashionable by the arrival in 1895 of the famous actress Mary Anderson, now married to a wealthy aristocrat. She lovingly restored the seventeenth-century Court Farm for her permanent home, and invited many distinguished guests to the neighbourhood. With the coming of the railway in 1904, Broadway became one of the most popular places in England among literary and artistic circles. Local nobility, such as Lords Elcho, Bathurst and Gainsborough, who appreciated the sporting rather than the aesthetic qualities of the local landscape, found themselves invaded by well-known visitors seeking natural beauty, amongst them being J.M. Barrie, Arthur Somerville, Edward Elgar, Axel Munthe, Sir George Lewis, Edmund Gosse, Henry James and Augustine Birrell.[9] The publication of four guide books by 1904 indicates the transformation of Broadway from a sleepy straggling village into one of the showpieces of rural England – which it still is for many tourists.

The cluster of public figures who settled at Limpsfield on the Surrey-Kent border were more careful in their choice of rural seclusion, keeping their distance from the railway and other buildings. David Garnett has described how his parents Edward and Constance bought half a field set in the middle of woodland, where they built a stone and timber house they named The Cearne.[10] Not far away lived Sydney Olivier, of the Colonial Office, Edward Pease of the Fabian Society, economist J.A. Hobson and writers E.V. Lucas and Ford Madox Ford. When around 1900 there were proposals from the local landowner to alter certain footpaths and rights of way, this gathering of influential persons proved useful.

With the desire to settle in the country went a wish to claim or adopt an ancestral connection with one particular region or county, in a way denying that very mobility which now enabled people to choose where to live. Such genealogical geography could be modified to take account of where one wished to live: long lines of forebears from, say, the Thames marshes might have to be transmuted into generations of Kentish yeoman, and the selection of regional identity was often revealing. Edward Thomas, son of a Welsh migrant to London, fantasized in his childhood about his true home in Wales, until he discovered Richard Jefferies' writing and switched his allegiance to Wiltshire, where luckily several of the Thomas family had moved to work in the Swindon railway yards.[11] Lady Ottoline Morrell, sister to the Duke of Portland of Welbeck in the East Midlands, claimed kinship with D.H. Lawrence, Nottinghamshire miner's son, by saying: 'Ah, then we come from the same part of the country!' In the absence of ancestors of the right kind, it might be difficult to find a piece of the country to claim. Rupert Brooke was born and brought up in Rugby School and when he moved to Cambridge he adopted Grantchester as 'my village' on the strength of lodging there for a few months. Visiting Canada in 1913 he told his hosts that 'his' village had been founded before the Roman conquest,[12] and his poem 'Grantchester' is of course a mock-heroic celebration of this local patriotism.

It was the sense of belonging to a place or region which made A.E. Housman's verse so popular, in its nostalgic evocation of lost lands and vanished friends. Housman's Shropshire, for all its use of actual place-names, is a location of feeling rather than landscape; lines like:

> In my own shire, if I was sad

> Homely comforters I had:
> The earth, because my heart was sore,
> Sorrowed for the son she bore

suggested to all those who found themselves unwilling, rootless inhabitants of suburbia that there was value in attachment to a particular rural place.

For those who could not move out of the city, holidays and weekends in the country became a desirable substitute, and the country cottage as a second home came into existence. The well-to-do had no difficulty in purchasing a little place for the weekend with roses round the door and damp in all the rooms, for the depopulation of the countryside meant many empty dwellings. These could also be hired for the summer season. Intellectual couples like Sidney and Beatrice Webb used their country holidays to finish serious pieces of writing, but the more usual purpose was active leisure – walking, swimming, fishing, sketching. The young took to cycling and camping, two newly-created activities that made the countryside accessible in novel ways to those with less money. Bicycles were truly liberating, making it possible for the city-bound clerk or artisan to explore virtually all parts of England. From the 1880s a network of cycling clubs grew up – one of the best-known being that associated with the *Clarion* newspaper – which drew their membership from the industrial areas. For the rather better-off, caravanning with a gypsy-style horse and van was a popular holiday and fully-equipped vans could be hired by the week for a slow perambulation around the New Forest, for example. [13]

It is not clear when holidays under canvas first became popular. Perhaps they were inspired by Stevenson's travels with Modestine together with the practical recognition that the British climate made rain-proof shelter essential. Certainly camping holidays pre-date the foundation of the Boy Scouts, and Baden Powell may have been influenced by this very English pastime as well as by his experiences on the veld. Because of its exiguous nature, camping was easily associated with the Simple Life and the freedoms that went with it. Inhibitions were soon shed amid the 'elemental' conditions, and the normal proprieties need not apply among a group of friends. Every summer from 1886 to 1914 Herbert and Agnes Valentine, of Workington in Cumbria, took a mixed party to camp beside

Derwentwater. One year they compiled a diary illustrated with their own photographs, which they called *Tales of a Tent*. It begins: 'Camping out is one of the most enjoyable and healthy holidays one can have. Living the Simple Life with a company of congenial spirits, practically in the open air the whole time, what could be more delightful?'[14] More than this, many believed that only Nature could provide the spiritual recuperation they required from time to time. Regular visits to the country were therefore essential, and to stay in the town for too long, it was thought, led to emotional atrophy and spiritual decline.

This need could be met, in part, by literature and in response to the demand 'country books' appeared by the thousand, as the shelves of second-hand bookshops today bear witness. As the years passed a veritable flood of country writing was published, in books, articles, illustrated guides. Country notes, nature lore and local tales were all equally popular and for every writer whose work is remembered (Edward Thomas is one, although his country books are perhaps best forgotten) there were dozens producing for the same market. Nor was the activity confined to professionals. Country notebooks became an amateur passion, particularly with women who had learnt to draw and were able to spend some of their abundant leisure time in sketching from nature. Edith Holden's *Country Diary of an Edwardian Lady* (1977) is representative rather than exceptional.

The type of country writing most popular in this period may be said to have begun with Richard Jefferies. Born on a small Wiltshire farm in 1848, Jefferies – ironically for one who contributed so much to others' 'love of the country' – refused to work on the land, preferring to read or ramble through the woods; his family thought him idle. He dreamt of culture and aspired to be a novelist, but he proved better at journalism and essays, which from the mid-1870s he began to sell to local and national newspapers. In 1876 he moved to London, like Hardy, to consolidate his career, and became a writer of country books, using his rural knowledge. In three years he published five such books: *The Gamekeeper at Home* (1878), *Wild Life in a Southern County* (1879), *The Amateur Poacher* (1879), *Hodge and his Masters* (1880) and *Round About a Great Estate* (1880). Jefferies' subjects and style were very much to the taste of his largely urban readership, and the last paragraphs of *The Amateur Poacher* sum up his message to them:

> Let us always be out of doors among trees and grass, and rain and
> wind and sun. There the breeze comes and strikes the cheek and
> sets it aglow: the gale increases and the trees creak and roar . . .
>
> Let us get out of these indoor narrow modern days, whose
> twelve hours have somehow become shortened, into the sunlight
> and pure wind. A something the ancients called divine can be
> found and felt there still.

Edward Thomas cannot have been the only reader who copied
these lines into his own notebook and dreamt of living by them. His
first independent act on leaving school was a long walk from
London to Swindon, notebook in hand. On 23 April he was at
Coate Reservoir, once the lake where Jefferies had fished. During
subsequent visits, Thomas made the acquaintance of an old country
couple who might have stepped straight from Jefferies' pages and in
a sense did so, for the cottage where Dad and Granny Uzell lived
was previously the home of Jefferies' gamekeeper. Deep-thatched
and hidden in the woods, the stone dwelling represented something
'divine' about the countryside to the younger writer.

Long country walks were a favourite recreation in the late
Victorian period, gaining in popularity as the necessity for walking
diminished through the advent of the railway and the tram. George
Meredith, who settled at Box Hill in 1868, was renowned for his
thirty-mile hikes over the hills of Surrey and Hampshire; from him
aspiring writers took the idea that fresh air and natural beauty were
necessary complements to the creative process.

On one recorded walk in May 1862, Meredith and his companion
Sir William Hardman tramped in high holiday humour from
Copsham to Burford Bridge singing snatches of old songs and
addressing each other as Robin Hood and Friar Tuck. Later came
the celebrated walking group known as the Sunday Tramps, who
included the distinguished Victorians Frederick Pollock, lawyer
and editor of the *Saturday Review,* and Croom Robertson, professor
of philosophy at University College London. Their leader was
Leslie Stephen, who combined his literary labours with walking
and mountaineering, and the Tramps met on alternate Sundays
from October to June to attack Box Hill, Leith Hill or the Hog's

Back and survey the condition of the world as well as the countryside as they walked.

For some, country walks became almost a substitute for religious observance, and not only because they usually took place on Sundays. Faith in a conventional creator was on the wane, and social and geographical mobility loosened the links between church and community so that many sensed a spiritual void in their lives. Drawing on Romanticism and classical ideas of pantheism, love of Nature helped to fill the gap, enabling many late Victorians to dispense with God gradually, as it were, without losing their sense of immanent divinity. Others, who continued to believe, found in Nature and Nature poetry an expression of quasi-religious feeling that fed their spiritual needs. All tended to find that transcendental terms were appropriate to this new form of worship.

Most of the major poets of the time – Tennyson, Arnold, Meredith, Swinburne – may be described as Nature-worshippers, and the many poetic anthologies published in this period reflected the belief in the spiritual qualities of natural beauty. But it was Richard Jefferies who above all filled the role of Nature-priest for a generation of readers, who regarded themselves as his disciples. Following the success of his country books, Jefferies began to express more elevated emotions in his writing, describing his own response to the beauties of Nature and developing ideas about the relationship between man and Nature in terms of the 'voice' of Nature speaking directly to the 'soul' of man. This was first presented through the device of childhood imagination, in *Wood Magic* (1881) and *Bevis* (1882) where Nature speaks to the child. Thus speaks the Wind:

> Bevis, my love, if you want to know all about the sun, and the stars, and everything, make haste and come to me, and I will tell you, dear. In the morning, dear, get up as quick as you can, and drink me as I come down from the hill. In the day go up on the hill, dear, and drink me again.
>
> Do not listen, dear, not for one moment, to the stuff and rubbish they tell you down there in the houses where they will not let me come. If they say the Earth is not beautiful, tell them they do not speak the truth.

In 1883 Jefferies came out of disguise with a straightforward account of his communings with Nature in *The Story of My Heart,* which became a key text of the age. At the age of seventeen, Jefferies recalled, whenever his 'heart was dusty' and his mind arid, he went up to a hill, where:

> I was utterly alone with the sun and the earth. Lying down on the grass, I spoke in my soul to the earth, the sun, the air and the distant sea far beyond sight. . . through the grassy couch there came an influence as if I could feel the great earth speaking to me.

Thus prostrated, Jefferies prayed 'that I might touch to the unutterable existence infinitely higher than deity'.[15] This, repeated in various ways, is the substance of the book, which today seems repetitive and over-wrought yet which at the time clearly chimed with the feelings of many readers. Jefferies' message to them was simple – and poignant, for by the time of *The Story of My Heart* Jefferies was immobilized by the disease which killed him in 1887 and was unable to get out of doors into the air and sunlight. But, as he exhorted his readers in *The Dewy Morn* (1884):

> All of you with little children, and who have no need to count expense, or even if you have such need, take them somehow into the country among green grass and yellow wheat, among trees, by hills and streams, if you wish their highest education, that of the heart and the soul, to be accomplished.
>
> Therein they shall find a secret – a knowledge not to be written, not to be found in books. They shall know the sun and the wind, the running water and the breast of the broad earth. Under the green spray, among the hazel boughs where the nightingale sings, they shall find a Secret, a feeling, a sense that fills the heart with an emotion never to be forgotten. They will forget the books – they will never forget the grassy fields.

Helen Thomas, as a young mother living in south London, took her baby son to lie on the grass of Wimbledon Common, so fervently did she believe in Jefferies' words.

As the countryside became the source of all that was divine, so the city was seen as infernal, with all the potent imagery associated with

hell. James Thompson's *The City of Dreadful Night,* written in the
early 1870s, is a depiction of despair – and of nineteenth-century
London, where

> The open spaces yawn with gloom abysmal,
> The sombre mansions loom immense and dismal,
> The lanes are black as subterranean lairs. . .

and where the atmosphere is 'dark and dense With many a potent
evil influence, Each adding poison to the poisoned air'. In the
iconography of the age, the city stood for misery and ugliness, the
countryside for bliss and beauty. For many of those who sought
happiness, the first step was a move to the country.

Not all were caught up in the prevailing pastoralism, however.
For all his liking for country walks, Leslie Stephen was sceptical of
the wider claims, remarking in an essay:

> a love of the county is taken, I know not why, to indicate the
> presence of all the cardinal virtues. It is one of those outlying
> qualities which are not exactly meritorious but which, for that
> very reason, are more provocative of a pleasing self-
> complacency. People pride themselves upon it as upon early
> rising, or upon answering letters by return of post. . .
>
> I too love the country – if such a statement can be received
> after such an exordium; but I confess – to be duly modest – that I
> love it best in books. In real life I have remarked that it is
> frequently damp and rheumatic and most hated by those who
> know it best.[16]

Contemporary readers may have smiled at the palpable hits against
enthusiastic country-lovers, but their feelings were not altered. Far
more representative than the sardonic Mr Stephen was the genial
Mr Grahame, who brought Rat and Mole up the moonlit river one
night to an island where they landed and found a grassy clearing set
around with 'Nature's own orchard-trees – crab-apple, wild
cherry, and sloe'. *The Wind in the Willows*(1908) is a book for
country-lovers as well as a children's story and contains in the
central seventh chapter, entitled 'The Piper at the Gates of Dawn', a
sustained passage of Nature-worship. On the island, the two

anthropomorphic animals come face to face with Pan, the spirit of Nature, before whom, 'crouching to the earth, (they) bowed their heads and did worship'. Then,

> sudden and magnificent, the sun's broad golden disc showed itself over the horizon facing them; and the first rays, shooting across the level water-meadows, took the animals full in the eyes and dazzled them. When they were able to look once more, the Vision had vanished, and the air was full of the carol of birds that hailed the dawn.

Such a vision, intense and perfect, was the promise of Nature and the country and the potential reward of love. But although characters in E.M. Forster's short stories also saw, or thought they saw, Pan in the woods, for Leonard Bast, 'the dawn was only grey, it was nothing to mention'.

For Our Country's Sake

AN ESSAY SETTING FORTH THE TRUE CONDITIONS
UNDER WHICH A RETURN TO THE LAND AND THE
REVIVAL OF COUNTRY LIFE AND CRAFTS ARE
POSSIBLE, AND NEW PROPOSALS FOR
CARRYING OUT THE SAME

By Godfrey Blount

Simplicitas Ars Ardor

Published by
ARTHUR C. FIFIELD
The Simple Life Press, 44 Fleet Street, E.C.
and
THE NEW CRUSADE
St. Cross, Haslemere, Surrey, and 8 Queen's Road, Bayswater, W.
LONDON
1905

Title page of New Crusade pamphlet by Godfrey Blount

3
Reclaiming the Commons

From a general or intense love of the countryside it was a short step to conservation – keeping the country from harm, decay or destruction. The late nineteenth century saw a sudden and sustained flowering of societies and committees for protecting and preserving pieces of old England from urban and industrial depredations only matched by the efforts of the conservationists in the 1970s. Had the original activists not been so successful, many of today's famous landmarks as well as countless less well-known open spaces would have vanished; the pioneer preservationists fought for posterity as well as immediate rescue and their own benefit. Largely practical persons, who enjoyed battling with the law and the landowners, they also worshipped the earth; keeping the countryside clear of bricks and mortar was their form of good works.

The first and foremost conservation body was the Commons Preservation Society (C.P.S.) founded in 1865 with the object of securing 'for the use and enjoyment of the public open spaces, situate in the neighbourhood of towns, and especially of London, still remaining unbuilt upon'. In 1878 Octavia Hill, who had failed in the fight to save Swiss Cottage Fields from the developer (of the subsequent Fitzjohns Avenue) launched the Kyrle Society, dedicated to placing objects of beauty within reach of the poor and to restoring old burial grounds and other small urban spaces for

recreational use in slum areas. We have already noted the foundation, in 1877, of the Society for the Protection of Ancient Buildings
(S.P.A.B.) with its aim of bringing public attention 'to the intrinsic
value of our ancient buildings, and the grievous loss we incur by
their destruction, and of teaching how much value, both artistic and
historical, depends on their being preserved in genuine condition'.[1]
In 1884 the National Footpaths Preservation Society (N.F.P.S.) was
formed, merging with the C.P.S. in 1899. A year or so earlier the
National Trust was inaugurated, as a fund to acquire and preserve
places of special interest or natural beauty. In addition to these
national bodies, there were countless smaller local preservation
groups formed in reponse to particular need, and also a number of
clubs and societies with the objective of enjoying the places so
saved, including the Cyclists' Touring Club and various walking
groups. In 1905 a number of the latter combined to form the
Fede:ation of Rambling Clubs, the forerunner of the Ramblers'
Association.

The activities of all the conservation groups were aimed, in
practice if not always in intent, at halting the unchecked progress of
industrial and urban advance across the land. Slowly, legislative
moves were taken in recognition of this aim. The first such statute
was the Ancient Monuments Protection Act of 1882, which gave
the state responsibility for surveying and listing sites of exceptional
historical interest, lest they be obliterated by building development
or greedy owners, and in the hundred years since then numerous
pieces of legislation have extended the protection of natural or
ancient features in the landscape and curtailed the rights of those
who wish to change them – as witness recent struggles against
those who wish to build motorways or airports.

The experience of current conservation efforts prompts particular
admiration for the work of the Commons Preservation Society,
acting without benefit of protective legislation. The C.P.S. was
founded on 19 July 1865 at a meeting in the chambers of G.A.
Shaw-Lefevre (later Lord Eversley) a leading Liberal lawyer,
attended by a phalanx of supporters from the haute bourgeoisie,
including John Stuart Mill, Lord Mount Temple (Ruskin's
admirer), Thomas Huxley and Thomas Hughes. At this meeting,

an immediate sum of £1,400 was raised to set up the Society, whose members were described by its historian as 'dedicated, eminent and influential, and imbued with vision, wisdom and liberal principles'.[2] Shaw–Lefevre himself was a member of all the Liberal administrations between 1868 and 1895, resuming his chairmanship of the C.P.S. when out of office. As Commissioner of Works in 1881–4 and 1892–4 he accomplished the public opening of Hampton Court Park, Kew Gardens and the remainder of Regents Park. For many years the C.P.S. solicitor was Robert Hunter (later Sir) who became better known for his role in launching the National Trust, and who undertook much of the legal work involved in reclaiming the commons through the courts. Over the years Hunter and his colleagues built up such experience in dealing with commons cases as to diminish seriously their adversaries' chances, but they did not win them all. Nor were the gentlemen of the C.P.S. as conventionally behaved as their age and occupations might suggest.

The battle for the commons began in London because here there was most pressure on land, and the amount of open space was rapidly shrinking. As the century progressed and London expanded, more and more areas were required for housebuilding; to the owners of such prime potential development sites as Hampstead Heath, Wimbledon Common, Wandsworth Common, Clapham Common, Blackheath, Hackney Marshes and Wormwood Scrubs, it appeared too good an opportunity to miss. Apart from the sale of sand or gravel (common lands being generally those unusable for cultivation) these areas brought in no other income. In addition, as the ancient commoners' rights to graze animals and gather firewood were no longer used, many of the open spaces were used as rubbish dumps and gathering places for 'bad characters' or the muggers of the day, so that far from being an amenity, the London commons were regarded as a nuisance and a problem. Building land was badly needed, for the poor as much as for the wealthy. Those who defended the commons 'on the ground that they are of infinitely greater value to the public as open spaces for health and recreation than as cultivated land or for building sites' were the far-sighted few.[3]

In 1864 Earl Spencer – who was Lord of the Manor of Wimbledon and hence owner of the common – proposed, with a proper sense of his patrician duty, to clean up the area, then 'dis-

figured' by gypsy camps and refuse tips. He planned to sell off
Putney Heath for residential building, buy out the remaining
commoners' rights and fence in the rest of the common as a park
containing a fine new house for himself surrounded by pasture and
gravel pits on lease. Unfortunately for him, the commoners of
Wimbledon were men of status and means, themselves owners of
some fine properties, and they did not like what was proposed.
Residents in Putney and Roehampton were particularly anxious
that there should be no more building in their areas. They at once
formed a committee to oppose the plan, demanding that the land be
left unfenced and uncultivated but under proper management, in
which they themselves could have a share. Lord Spencer was eventually persuaded to abandon his emparking.

A committee of the House of Commons recommended the following year that no open space within fifteen miles of London
should be reduced or enclosed. But this was not law; legally, lords
of the manor, as landowners, had the right to dispose of their land,
provided only that the commoners were compensated for their by
now largely nominal rights. Many landowners, alarmed by what
had happened to Lord Spencer, began unofficial fencing in the hope
that any objections would be too late; in this way Plumstead and
Tooting Commons were lost, as well as many acres of Epping
Forest.

The C.P.S. aimed to resist and prevent such action, and to urge
changes in the law. It was itself not able to initiate legal action, but
aided and advised those who could, i.e. those with commoners'
rights. The very first case in which the C.P.S. was involved was one
of the most important – the attempted enclosure of Hampstead
Heath. Here the lord of the manor was Sir Thomas Maryon Wilson
who, as land values rose, became increasingly eager to sell off
desirable plots which were otherwise of little benefit to him. All his
early efforts were blocked by his neighbour Lord Mansfield, owner
of adjoining Kenwood, but in 1865, thwarted by this opposition
and deprived, on his reckoning, of some £50,000 a year, he began
building houses on some of the most conspicuous parts of the heath,
as if to defy his opponents. Attempts by the local authority, the
Metropolitan Board of Works, to buy the land as open space were
frustrated by the high price Maryon Wilson demanded. The
Hampstead commoners, led by Mr Gurney Hoare, then raised a

committee, advised by the C.P.S., to defend their rights. The matter went to court but before it was resolved Sir Thomas died and his heir, not being litigious, agreed to sell the heath to the Metropolitan Board for £45,000, a tenth of the price previously asked. The C.P.S., characteristically, took the view that it would have been better had the matter come to issue, for an out-of-court agreement established no legal precedent.

Nor was the area wholly secure. Twenty years later it was again in the news, when the Earl of Mansfield's heir announced his intention of realizing the land values of his estates at Kenwood and Parliament Hill. At the same time it was found that there was no means of stopping a brickworks from being built on a piece of privately owned land adjoining the open heath. Although no common rights were now involved, the C.P.S., with confidence and public support was able to push through a parliamentary measure to facilitate public purchase. As a result the 260 acres of Parliament Hill were bought for £300,000 in 1889 and added to the heath. Kenwood itself was also preserved from development, but not opened to the public until 1925.

Through such efforts, the C.P.S. was able to rescue many important open spaces in London and to ensure, as time went on, that full responsibilities and powers be vested in public authorities, which thus became custodians of the ancient rights of the people. This was how it was perceived, with Shaw-Lefevre describing the process as one that restored to common land 'something of the attributes of the ancient Saxon Folk-Land'.[4] Securing public access to land was connected with the old systems of collective rights and responsibilities believed to have existed in England before the Conquest, or the Reformation, or the Industrial Revolution, or whenever the unpleasing present was deemed to have begun. Reclaiming the commons was a protest against the modern world of encroaching urbanism.

It soon became clear that efforts were needed on behalf of many rural commons as well. The second case taken up involved Berkamsted Common, twenty-five miles from London in the Chiltern Hills. This was a true common, covered with turf, gorse and bracken. It lies next to the great deer park at Ashridge, and for many years was leased as part of that estate, though remaining unenclosed. In 1862 however, the owners, the Trustees of Lord

Brownlow's estate, bought the manorial rights to Berkamsted with
the idea of adding it to the park. First the grass drives across the
common were closed, then the individual copyholders were bought
out with lump sums, and finally a new forty-three-acre recreation
ground was offered to the town in compensation for the inhabitants' right to cut turf and bracken. This last was offered as a
goodwill gesture, it being believed that such rights were
unenforceable.

By general agreement, the owners' next action was quite unlawful: the erection of a five-foot-high iron fence across two miles of
the common, closing all rights of way. Letters of protest were sent
to *The Times*; the Brownlow solicitor replied that 'the public has no
more right to pass over the Common than a stranger has to pass
through a private garden', and asserted that all who did so would be
regarded as trespassers.[5]

The inhabitants of Berkamsted were aroused and sought help
from the C.P.S. whose historian summed up the problem. 'The
only difficulty,' he wrote 'was to find a person possessed of rights
over the Common with a sufficiently long purse and with independence and courage, to try conclusions at law with Lord
Brownlow, who was so deeply interested in maintaining his
inclosures and in carrying them to the point of extinguishing the
common.'[6] Such a man was, happily, found in the wealthy Mr
Augustus Smith, benevolent dictator and Lord of the Scilly Isles,
and with him the C.P.S. hatched a plot, to demolish the fences 'in a
manner which would be . . . not less conspicuous than their
erection'. It was therefore

> arranged with a contractor in London to send down at night to
> Berkamsted a force of 120 navvies, for the purpose of pulling
> down the iron fences in as short a time as possible. On March 6th
> 1866, a special train left Euston, shortly after midnight, with the
> requisite number of labourers, skilled workmen and gangers,
> armed with proper implements and crowbars. The train reached
> Tring at 1.30 a.m. At this point the operation nearly miscarried.
> The contractor, it appeared, had sub-let his contract to another
> person. The two met together at a public house near Euston
> Station the evening before the intended raid, and drank so freely
> that neither of them was in a condition to lead the force into

action, and the navvies arrived at Tring without a leader and with no instructions.[7]

Luckily, the clerk sent along by the C.P.S. as an observer was able to step into the breach and he led the gang on the three-mile march to Berkamsted. 'Before six a.m. the whole of the fences, two miles in length, were levelled to the ground and laid in a heap, with as little damage as possible. It was seven o'clock before the alarm was given and when Lord Brownlow's agent appeared on the scene he found that Berkamsted Common was no longer inclosed.'[8]

As the word got round, local people flocked to see for themselves that 'the land was their own again'. In the resulting lawsuits judgment was given in favour of the commoners and Berkamsted Common remained unenclosed.

Epping Forest was a more difficult and lengthy rescue operation involving the revocation of existing enclosures and being entangled with ancient Crown rights under forest law. It became one of the C.P.S.'s most celebrated cases and, ultimately, one of its greatest victories.

The movement to save Epping followed hard on the loss of Hainault Forest – 4,000 acres of fine woodland in the same area, which was enclosed in 1851, the trees being felled and the land divided into farms. This raised the income from the estate from £500 to £4,000 p.a. but, as the C.P.S. commented, 'there was lost for ever one of the most beautiful natural Forests within easy reach of London'.[9] Epping itself had been steadily eroded by various manorial landowners without much protest from local residents because of the damage caused by the free-ranging deer and cattle. In 1866 however an issue arose which brought Epping to the attention of the C.P.S.

The lord of the manor in this case was the rector of Loughton, the Rev. Mr Maitland, who came to an arrangement with the local copyholders and then proceeded to fence off some 1,300 acres of forest. Nine acres were allocated as a village recreation ground and felling of the trees commenced. At this point the poor inhabitants of Loughton objected: from time immemorial they had enjoyed the right to lop branches for firewood between St Martin's and St George's Days (11 November – 23 April). Tradition held that this right was only maintained if the tree-lopping began on the stroke of midnight on St Martin's Eve, a ceremony usually accompanied by beer and a bonfire. In the year of the Rev. Maitland's enclosure, this custom was deliberately kept by a labouring man named Thomas Willingale and his two sons, who for some years had made a living by selling firewood. At midnight the Willingales broke down Maitland's fence and cut a quantity of branches. They were accordingly summoned before the justices and sentenced to two months' hard labour for malicious trespass. In prison one of the sons died of pneumonia.

Public indignation was aroused and the C.P.S. called in. A fund of £1,000 was quickly raised and a suit commenced in the name of Willingale on behalf of the Loughton parishioners, claiming the right to firewood and appealing for an injunction to stop Maitland felling any more trees. The C.P.S. had to give Willingale an allowance of £1 a week, as he was now unable to find employment in the neighbourhood, most of the wealthier residents being on Maitland's side. Accommodation was a great problem too, for to retain his right to press the suit it was essential for Willingale to remain a resident of Loughton. He was offered £500 by the opposition to abandon the case but, bitter at the rector's behaviour and the death of his son, the old man stood his ground until his own death in 1870. This was unfortunately before the case came to court, and meant that the C.P.S. had to find a new plaintiff to prevent the enclosure going ahead.

A delegation then approached the Corporation of the City of London, which held undisputed commoners' rights in Epping Forest by virtue of its ownership of 200 acres at Little Ilford in the Manor of Wanstead. It is a measure of the general support which the battle for the commons now enjoyed that the City, 'perceiving that great popularity might be achieved by fighting for the interest of the public in a case of such importance and magnitude',[10] agreed to take on the defence of Epping. The City's ample finances were a great asset, enabling the C.P.S. lawyers to dig deeply into medieval records and to discover that all commoners had rights over the whole forest. Thus a Wanstead commoner could challenge an enclosure in Loughton – and also every one of the piecemeal enclosures made in previous years.

Concern for Epping persuaded the government of the day to appoint a royal commission to inquire into the forest's condition and make recommendations. While it was sitting, judgment in the City's civil case was given on 24 July 1874, wholly in favour of the commoners and ordering that all fences erected since 1851 be removed. Dismissing the defendants' claim for costs, the Master of the Rolls declared that their case had rested on a 'vast bulk of false evidence', for which he rebuked their legal advisers, and stated, 'The Lords of the Manors have taken other persons' property without their consent and have appropriated it to their own use . . . It does not appear to me that [they] are entitled to any consideration as to costs.'[11]

The Royal Commission on Epping Forest reported in March 1875 to much the same effect, affirming that the inhabitants of Loughton had an immemorial right to firewood. It added that while the general public had for generations used the forest for recreation, this probably did not constitute a right in law. The C.P.S. pressed ahead, to ensure that the land deemed unlawfully enclosed was in fact released and added to the 3,000 acres which remained and were now free from threat. A further struggle led to success in 1878; Shaw-Lefevre wrote triumphantly:

> It may confidently be affirmed that never in the past experience of the law courts was there a decision by which upwards of 400 persons were compelled to disgorge 3,000 acres of land wrongfully enclosed, and by which there was secured for ever an area of double the size for the enjoyment for all time to come of the people of London.[12]

The language and arguments of the C.P.S. indicate how this was seen: as a step towards the restoration to the people of the land which had been seized in times past by kings and barons, whose modern equivalents were equally rapacious. In winning the right to return to the land at least at weekends and holidays, the people were reversing the process of dispossession. In the same spirit, the ancient offices of Ranger and Verderers – those appointed to manage the forest – were revived at Epping. But there was one last hiccup. The City of London, which now took control of the whole forest, declined to recognize the Loughton villagers' lopping rights.

On Martinmas Eve, 10 November 1879, the C.P.S. sent two members to Loughton to join in the midnight demonstration in a final attempt to preserve the medieval custom. Over 5,000 local people gathered, who 'perambulated the Manor by torchlight and then held a meeting previous to commencing the lopping', as Shaw-Lefevre recalled. 'I addressed this midnight meeting in the Forest and informed the people that it would be the last occasion on which such lopping would be permissible by law.'[13]

A settlement was eventually reached whereby the City Corporation paid the villagers £7,000 in compensation for their firewood rights. Cottagers who had actually exercised their rights received £1,000 each, and the remainder went to build a village hall in Loughton, known as Lopping Hall. But events turned a little sour when the foundation stone came to be laid, for 'with singular infelicity the local managers responsible for it invited the Lord Mayor of London to perform this ceremony, unmindful of the fact that the Corporation of London had done their very utmost to defeat the claim of the inhabitants to any compensation for their rights'. To add to the insult the original villain, the Rev. Maitland, as rector, was asked to open the proceedings with a prayer – he who had attempted to enclose the whole manor and caused the imprisonment of the Willingales. 'There were those,' commented Shaw-Lefevre, 'who were of the opinion that a white sheet would have been the most appropriate garment for the rector on this occasion!'[14] Later the City was with difficulty persuaded to award old Mrs Willingale a pension of five shillings a week to keep her from the workhouse.

On 6 May 1882, after nearly twenty years, Epping Forest was finally and irrevocably opened to the public by Queen Victoria, in a ceremony at High Beech whose symbolism pleased the C.P.S.: 'Restitution was thus in a sense made by the sovereign of land which in very ancient times had probably been taken from the folk-land for the purpose of a Royal Forest, and the Forest was dedicated for ever to the use and enjoyment of the people.'[15]

With commons and open spaces so stoutly defended, attention turned to smaller but equally vital matters – country footpaths. 'For a long time there has been felt the need,' said the *Birmingham Daily Post* in 1884, 'of some organisation which should make it its duty to see that no encroachments are made upon the field paths which for so long have been the source of health, comfort and recreation not only for persons living in their immediate vicinity but to lovers of the picturesque who have happened to be in their neighbourhood.' These unconsidered country paths and tracks, the paper continued, were fast disappearing through the actions of 'rapacious landlords and careless trustees'. The establishment of the National Footpaths Preservation Society (N.F.P.S.) was therefore most welcome. Without such a pressure group, it was certain that many of the finest field paths 'would be sacrificed to private ends, it being impossible for the villagers who suffer most by the removal to effectually protest against the practice and the local authorities being too closely welded to the squirearchy to permit them to move'. Several paths were at that moment threatened with extinction, and the N.F.P.S. had not started a day too soon.[16]

The N.F.P.S. was launched by Henry Allnutt, an energetic figure who was previously editor of the *Estates Gazette,* and author of books on disparate topics. What made him take up the cause of footpaths is not known, but the Society was founded in July 1884 and held its first meeting on 30 September with Allnutt as organizing secretary. There was an executive committee that included Frederick Pollock, editor of the *Saturday Review* and one of Leslie Stephen's Sunday Tramps, and an annual subscription of 5s (or 10s 6d to include free legal advice). By the end of its first year the N.F.P.S. had 178 members and five affiliated groups. The scale of the problem with which it sought to deal is indicated by the figures given by Allnutt: 124 cases of footpath interference notified to the N.F.P.S. between August 1884 and July 1885, of which the Society intervened in only fifteen.

Although largely a middle-class action group, with the newfound enthusiasm for country walks fuelling the concern over closed footpaths, the N.F.P.S. had supporters and informants in all ranks. Villagers probably benefited more than ramblers from the paths, which provided them with valued short cuts to work or when going visiting, and they were often very perturbed at closures. In his first Annual Report Allnutt printed a letter from a correspondent in the Lake District, complaining of Mrs W.S. Rawlinson's action in closing a footpath at Duddon Bridge which the writer claimed was an old Roman Road. He himself had used it 'for the last 35 years without any interruption':

but now the Road is taken out & carted away some portions of it
is Completely Blocked up with Small timber and other Rubbish
that it is almost imposeable for foot People to Climbe over it . . .
at one Place there is a brest of Earth about 5 feet high ware the
road as been taken out for her own Convenances Since she as
Builded a new Villow or house.

The writer expressed his hope that the new Society would take the
case up and protect the interests of those 'who may have the need of
travelling by such footpath & Bridal Roades'.[17]

The footpath protectors did not follow the commons preservationists in marshalling heavyweight legal guns and taking cases to
the highest court. They preferred to seek redress at a lower level,
using local groups, direct action and, where appropriate, the sym-
pathies of new residents of independence and professional standing.
In many cases the members of the vestry or parish council which
had to approve closures were tenants or tradesmen in a position of
dependence on the landowner, who was in any case long used to
making arrangements to suit himself rather than his neighbours,
but as organized opposition grew it became increasingly common
for an encroaching squire to discuss the matter with the local
footpath society first and to try to reach amicable agreement. In
later years a majority of the cases in which the N.F.P.S. was
involved were resolved in this manner.

Where no such settlement was possible, the footpath protectors
took to direct action, it being generally believed that English
common law allowed for such intervention in the face of unlawful
behaviour. One early case illustrates this. A correspondent wrote to
the N.F.P.S. from Heckington near Sleaford in Lincolnshire concerning a path across William Little's farm. Farmer Little had nailed
up the stile, obliging the villagers to go the long way round, and
when some continued to use the path he threatened prosecution.
The local highways surveyor Matthew Partridge then intervened,
encouraging people to use the right of way. A local labourer named
Asher Trollope forcibly opened the path and Partridge was
subsequently called before the magistrates to be charged with
incitement and aid to wilful damage. The court dismissed the case,
but denied that the path was a public right of way. Asher Trollope
'again ventured to walk where his forefathers had gone generations

before him' and he was duly summoned, convicted and fined. Partridge paid the fine, determined that the path should not be lost. He again encouraged Trollope and another villager John Nash to trespass again; this time they were legally defended by counsel who called aged witnesses to testify to rights of way in common use, despite whom both men were convicted, at a total cost to Partridge of £10 2s 6d. Undeterred he took the case to appeal and won, with costs.

In triumph Partridge replaced the stile and opened the path again. But this was not the end of the matter. As Allnutt's informant related, William Little's widow promptly

> pulled up the stile and bridge, nailed it up again and put a large stack of thorns which completely obstructs the path. The poor labourers whose work lies that way scramble through the hedge at the end of the stack, but females cannot go, thus we poor people are treated when the magistrates are personal friends of the owners of a large portion of the village.

The letter ended: 'Can you help us – I cannot do any more myself being nothing more than a working man.'[18] A few days later Allnutt was informed that Mrs Little was having a deep trench dug to stop the path being used altogether. At this stage the N.F.P.S. stepped in with a formal protest. Such attention seems to have done the trick, for the next communication informed the Society that the trench was being filled in again and the path being re-opened.

Not every path was successfully saved. The pages of the N.F.P.S. reports contain dozens of case histories, some of which end in defeat for the protesters, who were occasionally too keen even for the Society. In 1897 some open land at One Tree Hill, Honor Oak, south London, was enclosed for a golf course, despite public protests. 'Very riotous proceedings have taken place,' commented the N.F.P.S., 'and fences have been broken down. Three gentlemen have called at our office to explain the case . . .' The N.F.P.S. secretary investigated the matter, but found 'no indication whatever of a right of way'. The protesters were advised that they could not claim the right to roam over land at will.[19]

Many cases however were lost for lack of protest or because the evidence, derived from elderly residents recalling a path used thirty or forty years before, was not sufficient to persuade the courts. The law was only partly on the side of footpath preservation, and at one stage in the struggle it was deemed that to be a right of way a path had to lead from one settlement to another. In 1900 however the case of Richmond Hill, Surrey, established – to the relief of all keen ramblers – that there could be a public right of way to a single spot, such as a summit or viewpoint.

In 1899 the Commons and Footpaths Preservation Societies merged. At once the legal style of Shaw-Lefevre and Hunter is evident. One celebrated case was fought over Limpsfield, Surrey, where the Leveson-Gower estate proposed to stop up and divert two paths across Tidy's Green. The collected legal documents from this case number some 200 and fill a box in the House of Lords Record Office. The Limpsfield villagers, who opposed the closure, were reinforced by the cluster of middle-class residents who had chosen the district for their new homes in the country and who included the redoubtable Octavia Hill. These new-style villagers were somewhat dismayed to discover that in parish matters, votes were weighted according to the value of the property owned; so, although the vestry voted 75 to 46 against closure, the rateable value turned this into a majority of 103 to 76 for closure. Other methods had to be tried. Sydney Olivier and Horace Seymour got up a petition and the local footpaths society supported a number of villagers with commoners' rights – the tenant of the Carpenters' Arms, and two labourers living in old cottages – in their attempt to assert these rights by taking firewood from the disputed area; prosecutions for theft followed. Represented by C.P.S., the men were discharged, although other cases followed and Leveson-Gower did not lose them all. Despite the preservationists' proposal that Tidy's Green be put under parish council management allowing residents 'free access for games and recreation at all times', the issue dragged on for many years. It was not until 1951 that the Green finally passed into public ownership.[20]

In their campaigns for public access, the pressure group leaders sometimes tended to ignore the dangers. As it happened, the only major case the C.P.S. failed to win involved this issue.

During a storm on the last night of the nineteenth century, two of the massive stones from Stonehenge's outer circles came crashing to the ground. Others had either fallen or were in danger of doing so.

The Times's rather fatalistic comment was, 'Little we fear can be done to keep the remaining uprights standing. They will fall when their time comes.'[21] This aroused great indignation, and advice on how the stones might be secured. Thanks to a generation of persuasion by the S.P.A.B. and its followers, there was little support for full restoration or rebuilding (as there had been in the eighteenth century, when it was proposed to reconstruct the original circle); the aim was now to prevent further deterioration. There was added anxiety because of the recent establishment of a military camp on Salisbury Plain and the concomitant arrival of a railway branch line; both were likely to increase the number of Stonehenge's visitors. Already names were being chiselled and picnic fires lighted on the fallen stones, while beer bottles and other litter accumulated. There was thus a very real risk of permanent damage.

The owner of Stonehenge, Sir Edmund Antrobus, shared these worries and after the New Year's Eve collapse he invited the Society for the Protection of Ancient Buildings, the Society of Antiquaries and the Wiltshire Archaeological Society for advice. Their view, as he announced on 3 April, was that the newly fallen stones should be put back, that the others be shored up by modern engineering techniques, that the whole site be fenced off, and that the ancient ridgeway track through the centre of the circle be diverted. Antrobus added that in order to deal with the increase in visitors, he intended to instal a custodian and a turnstile. The new system opened on 24 May 1901 and the admission charge was one shilling.

There was an immediate outcry from the members of the countryside lobby. Canon Rawnsley of the National Trust wrote to the *Manchester Guardian*, reminding his readers that 'Stonehenge has stood for ages on a wild barrow-haunted down' where 'men's feet all up the ages have been as free as air to come and go . . .' Now, the harm done to the landscape was immeasurable: 'Go where you will, this barbed wire fencing, with all its association of suburban privacy and petty ownership, insults the eye and offends the heart.'[22]

There developed a struggle between pressure groups, each equally convinced. On one side there were the S.P.A.B. and the Society of Antiquaries, primarily concerned with the preservation of the fabric of Stonehenge; on the other were the Commons and Footpaths preservers, intent on people's enjoyment. Privately, the C.P.S. conceded that there should be restrictions on visitors; what perturbed them was Antrobus's action in charging for entry to what they saw as part of Britain's heritage, and the implications should his action pass unchallenged. What, they asked, was to prevent him, or owners of other historic sites, from raising the admission charge to £1, or from dismantling the whole monument and selling it to the United States? The C.P.S. wanted Antrobus to transfer Stonehenge to the nation; if he declined to do this, it would fight him over the issue of public access, for while a site remained in private hands, the only means of preventing the owner from doing as he liked with it was to invoke the public rights of way across the land. These Antrobus sought to divert, which required permission from the local authority. If the diversion took place, stated *The Times*, 'the people of this country will be completely deprived of all the right of access to a monument of absolutely unique interest and singular impressiveness – a monument to which they have freely resorted from time immemorial'. By what means such a heroic site had become private property in the first place was not known, the newspaper added, suggesting misappropriation, and concluding: 'the nation should now recover its property'.[23]

The C.P.S. opened its campaign with a public letter urging that the rights of way be protected on the grounds that access to the ancient site 'must be deemed to have been dedicated to open use in very early times', and ending on a populist note by asking, 'Why should access to the monument be restricted to those who can afford to pay 1s and refused to the far greater number who cannot afford to pay this sum?'[24]

A public inquiry opened in March 1902, with objections from the parish council and local residents strongly supported by the C.P.S. One witness was a driver accustomed to taking sightseers along the old track through the Stonehenge circle; quoted in broadest Mummerset by Canon Rawnsley, he told the inquiry:

> these roads to that theer circle was used long afore the Squire wur born, and he never put them stones theer, and we just said that if we woz to be summoned, why we woz, and that was all about it, and we dro' right on . . . None of us had any thought, no more nor a child, as he wur agoin to put up barbed wire and shut up the Stones, and he wouldn't adone it, not he, zur, if them great gentlemen from London hadn't acome down here and advised

him, you know, zur; leastways that's wat we thinks hereabout, not he, zur.[25]

The inquiry decided that public rights of way to Stonehenge were not proved, a rather surprising judgment which the C.P.S. felt ought to be tested in Chancery, where their experience suggested a good hope of success. In April 1905, however, despite further testimony from aged villagers, judgment was given against public access. The C.P.S. had failed and Sir Edmund Antrobus was vindicated. Negotiations had in fact been proceeding between him and Wiltshire County Council for the purchase of Stonehenge, for Antrobus was not inclined to make the nation a free gift. The original asking price of £125,000 for 1,300 acres plus the stones was later reduced to £50,000 for the stones and eight acres, but even this was too much for the county and the site remained private until 1915 when the venerable megaliths were finally acquired by the Ministry of Works. The number of visitors, now prevented by high fencing from entering the circle at all except on special occasions, still causes anxiety and argument.

The question of ownership was one of the reasons behind the launching of the National Trust in the years 1893–4, for there were undoubted difficulties in owning special sites. As early as the mid-1880s Robert Hunter had perceived the need for a corporate body to hold property in trust for others. This the C.P.S. could not legally do, so that it was saving stretches of countryside and common land without being able to ensure their future preservation. Protection and careful management were essential for many ancient sites and historic buildings; stone circles, monastic ruins and great tithe barns were as much features of the English countryside as its woods and hills. Manor houses, timbered cottages and country churches were, as walkers and watercolourists knew, integral aspects of the natural landscape.

Hunter and Shaw-Lefevre hoped that the government would come to acknowledge a national duty to protect and conserve places of beauty and historic interest, and a beginning had been made with the Ancient Monuments Protection Act. As the case of Stonehenge showed, however, the provision for placing sites under the

guardianship of the Commissioner of Works was not sufficient
encouragement to owners, and during the Act's lifetime only about
forty sites in the whole of England, Scotland and Wales were listed
and thus protected from further damage. In any case, most of them
were of prehistoric date, and even when the law was amended in
1913 with the Ancient Monuments Consolidation Act, enabling the
state to acquire ancient structures through purchase or gift,
churches and houses currently in use were excluded from its pro-
visions, as were stretches of open countryside. As these were
precisely the places which the C.P.S. and its friends most cared
about, it was not surprising that they should look to ways and
means. By 1894 it had become clear to Hunter that further statutory
conservation measures were unlikely. His concern was shared by
Octavia Hill, and by Rev. Hardwicke Rawnsley, Canon of Carlisle,
who devoted his very considerable energies to the cause, the founding of the National Trust for Places of Historic Interest or Natural
Beauty. Proposed as a non-profit-making company at a meeting on
16 July 1894 hosted by the Duke of Westminster at Grosvenor
House and attended by up to a hundred eminent Victorians, the
National Trust was dedicated to 'the permanent preservation for
the benefit of the nation of lands and tenements (including buildings) of beauty or historic interest; and as regards lands, to preserve
(as far as practicable) their natural aspect, features and animal and
plant life'. To this end, the N.T. was registered on 12 January 1895
as a body which could acquire such properties by purchase or gift.

The first acquisition by the N.T. provided a symbolic link with
the man who had inspired so many – John Ruskin. In 1895 Mrs
Fanny Talbot of Barmouth in Wales had given eight cottages to The
Guild of St George. Twenty years later she presented four acres
lying behind the cottages of 'picturesque and rugged cliff, known as
Dinas Oleu, overlooking the estuary at Barmouth', to the N.T. 'for
the enjoyment of the people of Barmouth for ever'.[26]

The Trust's first building reflected the medievalism which had
originally directed both Ruskin and Morris towards their love of
old English architecture. Alfriston Old Clergy House in Sussex was
recognized as probably the only surviving fourteenth-century
vicarage in southern England. Timber-framed and thatched, the
house was in a sad state when brought to the N.T.'s attention by the
Alfriston incumbent. Negotiations were opened with the Eccle-

siastical Commissioners, who agreed to sell it for a nominal £10, and with the S.P.A.B., which undertook to supervise the renovation work. The cost of this was estimated at £350, which took several years to raise.

The public were more willing, it appeared, to subscribe towards open spaces: when Barras Head at Tintagel was sold in 1895 and it became known that the new owners had notions of disposing of it for a hotel site, the Trust stepped in, asking for first refusal on a re-sale. In a spirit of generosity the owner agreed to let the Trust have the headland for the price he had paid, and the whole £505 was raised from the public within five months. The N.T. was very proud of this acquisition, describing it as 'one of the most impressive spots upon a coast of singular charm' and claiming that its preservation 'in its wild natural condition is, we are convinced, a service for which the nation will hereafter be grateful'.[27]

The scope of the Trust's activities in its first few years is illustrated by the following list of places under inquiry 1895–9:

Bute House Estate, Petersham
Carmelite Crypt, Fleet St
Cheddar Gorge, Somerset
Coleridge's Cottage, Nether
   Stowey
Cowper's House, Olney
Croft an Righ, Edinburgh
Croxted Abbey
Devil's Dyke, Newmarket
Ebbsfleet Cross, Kent
Falls of Clyde
Falls of Lodore, Lake District
Glastonbury Abbey
Ivy Cottage, Tonbridge
Antonine Wall, Scotland
Churchyard Bottom Wood,
   Highgate
Wicken Fen, Cambridgeshire

Millbank, London
Joiners' Hall, Salisbury
Johnson's Birthplace, Lichfield
Kenilworth Castle
Lord Leighton's House, London
Malvern Hills
Clergy House, Haughton
Roman Villa, Bignor, Sussex
Roman Villa, Darenth, Kent
Turner's House, Chelsea
Tyndale's House, Little
   Sodbury
West Hill, Hastings
White Horse, Berkshire
Shooters Hill, Pangbourne,
   Berks
Old Post Office, Tintagel

In addition, the N.T. successfully prevented the demolition of Trinity Almshouses, attributed to Wren, off the Mile End Road in

London, the most energetic protester here being C.R. Ashbee, whose Guild of Handicraft – of which more in Chapter 9 – was at nearby Essex House. By no means all the places investigated by the N.T. were acquired by it; in fact by 1898 it held only five possessions, by 1902 only twelve. But it had prevented the construction of at least two railway lines, at Henley and Lynmouth, and it was steadily and surely changing public attitudes.

The Trust's failures underlined the need for its activities, as when the British Aluminium Company applied for permission to begin operations at Foyers, on the banks of Loch Ness, with the effect, as the N.T. feared, of destroying the Falls of Foyers by harnessing the water power, and of polluting the neighbourhood with chemical fumes. There being no preventive legislation, the company went ahead, despite vociferous protests from the N.T. against 'the destruction of a British waterfall' by 'this piece of vandalism', although it is consoling to record that the industrial site at Foyers is long since derelict and the shores of Loch Ness have regained their wild uninhabited aspect.

The N.T.'s most energetic campaigns were for the preservation of large parts of Ruskin's beloved Lake District, for which the credit goes largely to Canon Rawnsley. In 1901–2 a total of £7,000 was raised to buy a stretch along Derwentwater, thus securing public access, and further efforts followed on behalf of Gowbarrow, Ullswater, when £12,000 was collected. Rawnsley and Octavia Hill proved superlative fundraisers, mobilizing support throughout the nation, stimulating committees in all the northern cities, persuading famous artists to donate their works for sale, and generally winning such publicity for the cause that money poured in. Although targeted on members of the aristocracy and the wealthy or landowning classes (whom the N.T. needed to win over and who therefore featured in its lists of life members and honorary officers) the N.T. was appreciative of the smallest donor; in acknowledging a gift towards the Gowbarrow appeal, the Trust reported:

To illustrate the way in which people in the great towns value the beauties of nature, it is sufficient to quote the case of a working woman in Sheffield. In sending a postal order for a small sum, she said that after 30 years' work in a Sheffield factory, it was her greatest joy to spend her holidays on the moors, for she found refreshment there. She hoped some day to go as far as Ullswater and Derwentwater.[28]

It would be intriguing to learn whether this anonymous donor, twenty or thirty years earlier, had heard and heeded the arguments for a return to the land made by the members of St George's Farm commune in Sheffield and by Edward Carpenter.

Steadily, N.T. acquisitions in the Lake District increased. In 1909 the side of Borrowdale from Grange to Rosthwaite came on to the market; it was an area outlined by the Trust as full of natural beauty, and its cost was £2,400, or seven guineas an acre which, in the Trust's opinion, was 'a very small price for securing the preservation of the famous Borrowdale Birches and public access to the 310 acres which form the heights and steep slope of Grange Fell'.[29]

It was some time before the Trust's hope of attracting benevolent donations was realized to any great extent, but in 1908 it was delighted to report a gift of fifty acres at Morte Point, on the coast between Ilfracombe and Barnstaple, which was being presented by the owner, Miss Chichester, in memory of her parents, with the stipulation that it be left in its wild natural state. It was a place 'full of wild charm', rhapsodized the Trust, '. . . surrounded on three sides by the sea . . . a bleak spot in winter . . . but with a dread beauty of its own'. It added that nearby Woolacombe Sands was in the course of development as a holiday centre and Miss Chichester was to be congratulated for not turning her property to profit by building hotels.[30]

The National Trust is today one of the largest landowners in Britain with an enviable reputation for rescuing and preserving fine sites, which it cares for in the manner of the most benevolent patrician. In addition, virtually every area now has a local conservation group, dedicated to the fight against commercial and municipal vandalism. Despite the many advances, National Parks and preservation orders, public protest – and in many cases direct action – is still necessary to protect the environment.

4

The Countryman

Love of the countryside extended easily into love of country life and country people. For centuries rural folk had been regarded and portrayed in literature as dull-witted bumpkins, honest perhaps but entirely lacking in intellect and the higher virtues. In pastoral, of course, country characters might appear as idealized inhabitants of Arcadia, but were all the time courtiers and other members of the upper classes dressed as shepherds and shepherdesses. Rarely were country people presented both positively and in their own clothes. Wordsworth's figures were among the first to whom different criteria were applied, but although drawn from life, these figures tended to have little in common with the typical English farm worker in the lowland counties, whose poorly-educated, poorly-paid and poorly-housed agricultural labourers were known by the collective name of Hodge. This is a diminutive of Roger, but sounds like a patronizing compound of hedge (where the labourer spent much of his time, particularly in bad weather) and clod (the substance on his boots and in his brain). Richard Jefferies, farmer's son, wrote both critically and movingly about Hodge, but did not attribute to the lowly labourer any of the country wisdom that he ascribed to his gamekeeper or small farmer. Nor, for all his sympathy, did Hardy: Tess Durbeyfield, he keeps telling us, is an exceptional farm servant.

It was some time before the virtues and values being revealed in the countryside were discovered in the inhabitants too, for in the 1880s and '90s farm workers were, in Robert Frost's phrase, 'the genuinely submerged classes'[1] – an oppressed and ignorant social group dependent on the farmer for work and the workhouse for welfare. As such they were taciturn to the point of muteness.

Owing to the agricultural depression that began in the 1870s, the condition of the English countryman was at a very low point during the last years of the nineteenth century. Large numbers of agricultural workers had left the land – forty per cent of farm labourers vanished into other occupations or emigrated during the last quarter of the century – and for those who stayed life was monotonous, narrow and hard. In winter women and children worked picking stones from the fields at sixpence per bushel, while the men took to migrant labour in the hope of earning something in the urban areas. Farm workers in Suffolk, for example, spent half the year working in the maltings at Burton-on-Trent. 'The hours on the farm were six-thirty to five-thirty in the summer,' recalled one man, 'but you'd do a haysel and a harvest and perhaps they didn't want you after that. So I signed on for Burton at the Ipswich Railway Hotel.'[2]

Industrial employment offered not only a more regular wage but an impersonal one, whereas in the village quasi-feudal attitudes persisted and the farm worker was frequently obliged to acknowledge his inferior status, whether demonstrated through contempt or charity. Game laws prevented villagers from supplementing their families' meagre diet with rabbits and pigeons, and some landowners prohibited even the gathering of blackberries and nuts. Labourers had to trudge many miles by road, being forbidden to set foot in fields and woods except when working there; even today the sign 'Trespassers will be Prosecuted' has power to intimidate, although it has no force in law.

George Sturt, who inherited a wheelwright's business in Farnham, Surrey, was critical of the general attitude towards the labouring poor in his district. When a footpath was closed, he wrote of 'that servility to wealth which is so conventional as to be almost unconscious in England'. He described the rich as 'openly unscrupulous and oppressive as a class', who 'threaten and browbeat and bully those who cannot afford to offend them'.[3] The absolute social gulf was illustrated for him when two ladies called while Sturt was supervising the laying of a garden path. The visitors sat down unceremoniously on the stone step with Sturt and 'were very cordial to me, but took no notice of the men at work – who immediately became subdued, distant, submissive, and soon were putting their things together'.[4]

In 1889 Sturt had been a reader of William Morris's paper *The Commonweal* and sufficiently convinced of the value of agrarian life to request further information on Ruskin's St George's Farm at Totley. His interest in progressive ideas made him an acute observer of character and change, and his literary aspirations enabled him to record these aspects of the local scene in books which have been regarded as touchstones of rural authenticity – *Change in the Village* (1912) and *The Wheelwright's Shop* (1923). Sturt's close acquaintance – friendship in his words – with the men who worked for him allowed him to present a relatively direct account of their way of life and thought.

His first book – written under the name of George Bourne – was about a countryman; it was entitled *The Bettesworth Book: Talks with a Surrey Peasant* (1901) and was based on acquaintance with Frederick Bettesworth – then an old man but still supporting himself and his wife through casual and strenuous local jobs. Bettesworth had worked for others all his life, in different parts of Surrey and Hampshire, as a landless labourer rather than a peasant and, as Sturt recorded, his manner was remarkable for its 'unconscious oddity' and old-fashionedness. In fact, as Sturt admitted, when he first began to make notes of his conversations with Bettesworth, he regarded him as 'something of a comic character', full of 'garrulous and good-tempered quaintness', a veritable Hodge.

Gradually the comic picture was displaced by one of stoicism and good nature, with so much 'silent suffering as to make me wonder and admire where before I might have laughed' and by respect for the breadth of Bettesworth's practical knowledge as well as for his 'racy phrases and words fat with meaning' in a language which, 'although defective in much besides aspirates . . . is a form of English, and deserves to be written as nearly as may be in the normal manner'. Sturt had no tape-recorder and in any case Bettesworth rarely spoke at length or with any direction. But, as Sturt learned, 'whoever would hear Bettesworth must let him have his own way in talk, or nothing will be got from him'. The result is episodic, discursive:

> Most quiet was the old man's talk: and though he said merely what the moment suggested to him, yet its very quietness sounded full of experience, as though it belonged to remote time. He was kneeling to fit the turfs into their places – an uncomfortable attitude, I was thinking – when he said, 'Pleasant work, this. I could very well spend my time at it, with good turfs.' Our turfs were anything but good; but 'No, we mawn't waste none,' said Bettesworth. 'Feels like cuttin' beef steaks,' he murmured, trimming one with his knife. 'But 'twon't do to waste none, now we bought 'em. Same as ol' Bob Jenkinson over his dinner one day. "Your dinner stinks, Bob," I says to 'n. "I can't help that," he says. "I bought it an' I got to eat it." I used to laugh when I was at work for he. One day, when he was buildin' they houses down 'long the Hatches, the Middlesham Pa'son came along. What a shame 'twas, he says, to build right in front of other people an' shut out their view. "How high by'ye gwin?" he says. "Up to the top," Bob says. The pa'son he didn't know what to say, and I had to walk away for fear he should see me laughin'. Bob never cared nothin' about views. 'Twas a shame, the pa'son said. "They should look upwards," Bob says.'
>
> Meanwhile the turfs were being laid slowly, and with great care, because they had been so badly cut.[5]

This way of rendering rustic speech is too discredited to be used successfully today, but Sturt's aim was to present Bettesworth in his own words, without mediation. Few others listened so carefully, and Sturt was aware that the unlettered labouring class to which his old employee belonged was a disappearing one, soon to vanish with the advent of universal education, urban growth and changing employment. He lamented the fact that 'destiny has decreed that this class of men, by centuries of incalculable struggle and valiant endurance, should prepare England's soil not for themselves but for the reaping machine and jerry builder'.[6] The images betray Sturt's pastoral bias.

The Bettesworth Book was well received. Following Jefferies and Hardy, it helped to raise the position of the country labourer in reputation if not reality, for as the majority of the population ceased to have any direct link with the land, so popular mythology created, at least among the educated classes, a kind of rustic hero, possessed of qualities hitherto unrecognized. Bettesworth became an archetypal countryman. Some readers were particularly touched by the stoicism with which he endured poverty in old age; others complained that for all his life amid Nature, the old Surrey peasant did not seem to have much poetry in his soul. In a note to a subsequent edition (the book was reprinted four times between 1901 and 1920, an index of its popularity) Sturt angrily denied that Bettesworth's life had been tragic or narrow. Quoting a few of the old man's simpler remarks – 'That sunshine's what we wants!' for example – he asserted: '. . . old Bettesworth and his kind are not without poetry because they lack verse. Out of their wind-blown, sun-burned toil they suck more than we who live within doors may understand.'[7] Arcadia is not far off.

Sturt wrote several other books based on life in village and small country town, as well as recording his own acts and views in a long-kept journal. He regarded himself as a progressive, socialist thinker with ideas drawn from Morris and Ruskin and a particular interest in rural questions. His later books devote a good deal of space to analysing the issues and developing his theme that the old country way of life held its own valuable form of culture, largely based on work. Countrymen, he wrote,

> are connoisseurs of local handiwork; they know from the inside the meaning and attractiveness of simple outdoor crafts; in the texture of materials – timber, stone, lime, brick-earth, thatching-straw – there is something that goes familiarly home to their senses; and so there is in the shape of tools, such as they themselves have handled.[8]

Ironically, for one who saw himself as lamenting the ultimate loss of the old English 'country' tradition of rural work and leisure, Sturt was later discovered and promoted as the authentic representative of that tradition by the *Scrutiny* group of critics in the 1930s and '40s – so that images from a Farnham wagon-builders in the 1870s and '80s became for a generation of industrial and urban-educated readers fixed points of moral and literary value, which could never be regained. No present-day employees learned 'secrets' from the grain of the wood; making motor cars and wireless sets, their work was mechanical and soul-destroying. This approach survives remarkably intact: as recently as 1980 Denys Thompson, who together with F.R. Leavis helped to instal Sturt as a major figure in the 'English tradition', published a collection of 'country' pieces (mainly by Sturt) to support his view that the time has come to abandon automation and mass production and return to the scale of pre-industrial operations. 'There will be no need to start a back-to-the-land movement,' writes Thompson; 'it has never stopped since the peasants were dispossessed.' 'The country,' he says without qualification or fear of contradiction from a readership which has adopted these values implicitly, 'is so much needed for our physical and psychic health', and 'there is no doubt that many people grope after a more sustaining way of life than they find in our present towns'. Soon, 'the inadequacy of industry-directed civilisation' will be clear to all and a new relationship between men and the land will be created.[9]

To establish his choice of values, Thompson also uses W.H. Hudson's *A Shepherd's Life* (1905), which was coincidentally dramatized on television early in 1981 as a record of English rural life in the mid nineteenth century. Hudson, brought up in Argentina and primarily a naturalist, was in 1901 awarded a Civil List pension which he used to travel the southern counties of England, observing human and bird life. Indeed, his approach to the two species was similar: of talking to one elderly informant he remarked that direct questioning was useless. Patient attentiveness was the approach – 'not unlike the one we practise with regard to wild nature. We are not in a hurry, but are always watchful, with eyes and ears and mind open to what may come; it is a mental habit and when nothing comes we are not disappointed – the act of watching has been sufficient pleasure; and when something does come we take it joyfully as if it were a gift – a valuable object picked up by chance in our walks.'[10]

One such joyful gift was his meeting with Caleb Bawcombe, a Wiltshire shepherd then aged ninety-two, infirm but tenacious, to whom Hudson returned again and again for reminiscences. These form the basis of *A Shepherd's Life,* which aimed to give a picture of country life 'in the olden time'. It is thus a backward-looking book – many of Bawcombe's memories were in fact stories told to him by his father, dating from around 1800 – which presents the shepherd's life as hard but happy. Caleb's words displayed a fortitude that approached true contentment:

> 'Fifty years,' he said, 'I've been on the downs and fields, day and night, seven days a week and I've been told that it's a poor way to spend a life, working seven days for ten or twelve or at most thirteen shillings. But I've never seen it like that; I liked it, and I always did my best. You see, sir, I took a pride in it. I never left a place but I was asked to stay. When I left it was because of something I didn't like. I couldn't never abide cruelty to a dog or any beast. And I couldn't abide bad language. If my master swore at the sheep or the dog I wouldn't bide with he – no, not for a pound a week. I liked my work and I liked knowing things about sheep. Not things in books, for I never had no books, but what I found out with my own sense, if you can understand me.'[11]

Hudson re-created for his readers a momentary glimpse into a lost world, where the changes remarked by Sturt had not yet happened – but he claimed it for the present, not the past:

> For the labourer on the land goes on from boyhood to the end of life in the same everlasting round, the changes from task to task, according to the seasons, being no greater than in the case of animals that alter their actions and habits to suit the varying conditions of the year. . . It is a life of the extremest simplicity, without all those interests outside the home and the daily task, the innumerable distractions, common to all persons in other classes and to the workmen in towns as well.

'Incidentally,' Hudson concluded, 'it may be said that. . .speaking generally, the agricultural labourer is the healthiest and sanest man in the land, if not also the happiest, as some believe. . .'[12] Thus was the pastoral myth realized in the person of an English shepherd.

From Old Bettesworth and Caleb Bawcombe it was a short step to the presentation of country figures in imaginative literature. According to the definitions of art then current, this was deemed difficult if not impossible, except in terms of traditional pastoral – to which Arnold's *The Scholar Gypsy* must be assigned. The typical countryman was too ignorant, too inarticulate, too brutalized, to have any place in poetry. The generation of writers who emerged in the new century challenged the prevailing view of verse which held that the only object of poetry was beauty, and attempted with varying degrees of success to portray country people, having assimilated the cult of the countryman. A small stream of 'peasant plays' accordingly appeared. Synge, who in the preface to his *Poems* (1908) declared 'there is no timber that has not strong roots among the clay and worms' and that 'before verse can be human again it must be learn to be brutal', brought present-day people from the country districts of Ireland into his plays. John Masefield, who had some claim to a country background himself, having been brought up in the market town of Ledbury, set his *Tragedy of Nan* in a country community at Broad Oak on the Severn. The play was cautiously received by the London literati when it was performed in May 1908, for the coarse and mercenary manners of its characters offended their sense of how country people ought to behave, just as Synge's *Playboy* upset those accustomed to the fairer versions of Irish peasantry presented by Yeats and Lady Gregory. Masefield's fellow-Georgian, Lascelles Abercrombie, moved in 1910 from Liverpool to a cottage near Ledbury and in 1913 attempted a poetic drama based on the rustic characters in the village inn. *The End of the World* was a comedy, based on the recent visit of Halley's comet, and although eagerly awaited, it proved disappointing. D.H. Lawrence angrily complained of its 'ridiculous imitation yokels' exuding meanness and 'rancid hate',[13] despite Abercrombie's protest that he himself thought his characters were very nice people.[14]

At about the same date, Edward Thomas was including country figures in his poems. The casual labourer in 'Man and Dog' is someone Hudson might have met, a character with his own history and qualities which obliquely depict the rural condition:

> Then he went on against the north-east wind –
> Straight but lame, leaning on a staff new-skinned,
> Carrying a brolly, flag-basket and old coat –

In 'Lob', his longest and best-known poem, Thomas used the device of a country character to express what he saw as the quintessence of English rural life, found in, for example, vivid village sayings:

> He first of all told someone else's wife
> For a farthing she'd skin a flint and spoil a knife
> Worth sixpence skinning it. She heard him speak:
> 'She had a face as long as a wet week'.

Also included is what may be called the country tradition of folk history and local names – which the town-born country-lovers of Thomas's generation took particular delight in:

> . .Lob-lie-by-the-fire, Jack Cade,
> Jack Smith, Jack Moon, poor Jack of every trade,
> Young Jack or old Jack, or Jack What What-d'ye-call,
> Jack-in-the-hedge, or Robin-run-by-the-wall,
> Robin Hood, Ragged Robin, lazy Bob,
> One of the lords of No Man's Land, good Lob. . .

This tradition, in the poem, is still alive but elusive, hard to find; just as some villages are virtually invisible except from the air, so the countryside holds a secret which hides in the lives of its inhabitants. Earlier, in one of his prose books, Thomas had sarcastically remarked that as the old-style country people were fast vanishing from rural England, a pair ought to be put in a zoo for endangered species, alongside a couple of gypsies, for the sake of posterity.

Impelled by the same concern, Gertrude Jekyll was already doing what she could to preserve and record the countryman's habitat and possessions. Her own corner of the countryside in south-west Surrey was, as we have seen, among the first to be discovered and 'developed' by the new breed of country-loving residents. Easier communications and economic changes meant the disappearance of the old way of life. She became perturbed by the way in which the furniture, tools and utensils 'of pure materials and excellent design' which had been owned and used in every farmhouse and cottage were being replaced with 'cheap pretentious articles got up with veneer and varnish and shoddy materials'. Instead of scrubbed flagstones, country homes now had floors covered with lino, she complained, while 'the walls have a paper of shocking design and are hung with cheap oleographs and tradesmen's illustrated almanacs'.[15] To every generation its own nostalgia: these cheap and nasty artefacts – tin boxes, old advertisements, tinted pictures – are now eagerly bought and sold in antique shops and markets by those for whom they hold intimations of an older, stabler age – just as rush-lights and toby jugs did for Miss Jekyll.

Gertrude Jekyll made a collection of the old items, and compiled two books – *Old West Surrey* (1904) containing 330 photographs taken by herself, and *Old English Country Life* (1925) a more systematic and wider-ranging account with illustrations from many sources, indicative of the expansion of interest in the subject. In the preface to the first book, the author commented that 'since the desirability of this, however fragmentary, record of the ways and things of the older days occurred to me, I have regretted that I did not think of it thirty years ago'.

Her record of cottage life began with the fabric itself – the timber-framed, tile-hung cottages particularly characteristic of West Surrey. Her eye for detail was combined with decided taste and fluent, persuasive expression, as when discussing roofing tiles:

> Not unfrequently plain weather-tiling was repaired with tiles of a scale or diamond pattern, or they may possibly have been originally hung together, just as they came. This happy-go-lucky way of using local material often has a good effect, as may be seen in the cottage at Kirdford and the one at Tiltham's Green. It is a matter for regret when, as is so often done now in repairing old cottage roofs or even building new ones, ridge tiles are used in place of the proper hip-tile. There is a special charm about the fine old saddle-shaped, locally-made hip-tiles, with their saw-edged profile telling well against the sky, just as there is a charm, and the satisfying conviction of a thing being exactly right, about all the building details that are of local tradition and form the local style.[16]

As we shall see in Chapter 11, Miss Jeykll's own house at Munstead Wood was built exactly to these principles.

From buildings the book went on to describe, with copious

illustration, the cottage fireside, deep and wide, with ingle-seat, pot hangers and bellows; cottage and farmhouse furniture, of the kind that Morris and company had admired, and not forgetting smaller items such as knife-boxes and warming-pans. All this furniture, commented Miss Jekyll in true Arts and Crafts style, was 'sufficient, strong, well-made and beautiful of its kind', while the new factory-made products were wretched, rubbishy and pretentious. If it occurred to her that this decline of quality inside country people's homes was due to their impoverishment and social decay rather than their lack of taste, she did not record it. In her chapter on home industries, dealing with spinning, straw-plaiting, bee-keeping and broom-making, she gave her opinion of past and present:

> How much fuller and more interesting was the rural home life of the older days, when nearly everything for daily use was produced on the farm or in the immediate district; when people found their joy in life at home, instead of frittering away half their time in looking for it somewhere else; when they honoured their own state of life by making the best of it within its own good limits, instead of tormenting themselves with a restless striving to be, or at any rate to appear to be, something that they are not. Surely that older life was better and happier and more fruitful and even, I venture to assume, much fuller of sane and wholesome daily interests.[17]

Here the social attitudes which lay behind much pastoral nostalgia are clearly visible. But it should not therefore be dismissed: country people were often the first to admit the deterioration in the quality of life and to stick with pride to time-honoured crafts and skills when these were demonstrably unable to compete in cost and time with industrial processes. The efforts made by groups such as the Peasant Arts Society, described in Chapter 10, were representative of wider efforts to preserve not just the countryman but his livelihood also.

The desire to maintain the old way of life was evident in Miss Jekyll's admiration of country people's dress – the old-fashioned caps and bonnets still worn in some districts, and the now-disappearing smock-frock, of which she remarked: 'no better thing has ever been devised for any kind of outdoor wear'. Around the turn of the century, when the smock-frock was all but extinct among farm workers, it was taken up in artistic circles as a suitable garment for everyday wear, not only in the studio but for other types of work, and there was a period when smocks and sandals were the favoured form of dress among progressive persons.

Like other observers, Miss Jekyll recorded with keen delight 'the terse old phrase and local saying' from her conversation with country people, noting dialect variations and expressive local accents:

> Yeast with the older people is still called 'barm' and faggots are 'bavins', pronounced 'bahv'n'. A thorn is a 'bush'. They say of a dog limping on three legs, 'He's got a bush in his foot'.
>
> The 'a' is always broad, sometimes very much lengthened or drawn out. Driving along one summer day I came upon the scene of an accident. The tail board of a farm-cart had come out and had let down a tub with a loose cover. The road was covered with a beery-smelling foaming pool.
>
> 'What's that?' I asked: 'beer?'
>
> One word alone the carter answered, but he made the most of it – 'BAA-A-A-A-RM'.[18]

So the countryman was raised, in a short period of perhaps thirty years, from a dumb boorish fellow to a loved and respected figure bearing the weight of all the wisdom and virtue ascribed to the English countryside. He might still be slow and unlettered, but these were now assets. Hodge's lowly status was transformed. When Maurice Hewlett, a successful popular poet and countryman by adoption, composed an epic celebration of the heroic role of the countryman over the ages, he wanted to call it *The Hodgiad,* in recognition of the farmworker's new cultural position. It appeared under the title of *Song of the Plow* in 1916, when men from the depressed districts of rural England were dying by the thousands in France.

5

Folk Song Restored

In 1961 a plaque was unveiled on the wall of a vicarage garden in Somerset, recording the fact that, 'In the garden of this Vicarage in September 1903 CECIL SHARP . . . heard JOHN ENGLAND sing "The Seeds of Love". This incident inspired the Folk Song revival in England.'

By the 1960s, of course, those who had launched the folk song revival over a decade before Sharp's momentous experience were long dead and half forgotten, and there was no protest against his version of history. For although the revival of folk music in England is largely Sharp's story, it is by no means exclusively his; many others, with less flair for publicity, were also involved. As we have seen, the cultural value of the countryside rose in proportion to its material decline and, like the carts and candlesticks which Miss Jekyll collected from cottage homes, so the rural culture of songs and music was rescued from oblivion just at the moment when it was about to vanish for ever.

In one sense folk music had not so much disappeared as been simply despised and disregarded. While the educated classes of Britain had from the eighteenth century admired the music of Scotland and Ireland for its picturesque and romantic elements, they regarded the cultural heritage of the English peasant as consisting of a few crude and comic songs. The Rev. Francis

Etherington, one of Sharp's collectors, confessed to thinking of the countryman as a bumpkin, his singing a matter of a glassy stare and 'curious mechanical jarrings of his vocal apparatus'.[1] The rural population at this date belonged to such a depressed class that it was not difficult to assume they possessed no musical traditions, and indeed – a measure of the class conditions then prevailing – by and large country people shared this view of themselves. They despised traditional songs to such an extent that early collectors were often offered and obliged to listen to music hall songs in place of the old tunes they had requested, the singers unable to believe that the latter were the more admired. As people became more urbanized and educated so the contempt for country songs increased; it is ironic that the sudden nostalgia for the old country ways which led to the folk song revival came as a direct result of social and economic processes which were steadily eroding rural culture. Gypsy singers tended to retain the old melodies better than settled villagers.

Up to the late 1880s, then, it was widely believed and lamented that England had no national music such as that which was forming the basis of cultural renaissance in other European countries. Some commentators believed that in very remote places it might be possible to find some lingering melodies, but the evidence was not hopeful. Forty years earlier the Rev. John Broadwood and G.A. Dusart had published a small collection of *Old English Songs as now Sung by the Peasantry of the Weald of Surrey and Sussex and collected by one who had learnt them by hearing them sung every Christmas from early childhood by The Country People, who go about the new Neighbouring Houses, singing or 'wassailing' as it is called, at that season.* But all such country customs were rapidly dying out and it was doubted if many songs now remained. Towards the end of the decade, however, interest began to grow. The Rev. John's niece Lucy Broadwood enlarged and reissued her uncle's collection under the title *Sussex Songs* (1889) and in the same year the remarkable Rev. Sabine Baring-Gould in Devon began to publish *Songs and Ballads of the West,* collected by himself, the Rev. H. Fleetwood Sheppard and the Rev. F.W. Bussell.

This collaboration perhaps marks the true beginning of the folk song revival. According to Baring-Gould, the idea was broached in 1888 when he was dining with a neighbour and the Devonshire songs they had heard in their youth in inns on Dartmoor and elsewhere came into the conversation. Baring-Gould was already a prolific novelist, hymn-writer, author of 'Onward Christian Soldiers' and a sixteen-volume *Lives of the Saints,* but as rector and squire of Lew Trenchard he was also interested in local antiquities and customs. His own musical skill was not great, so he enlisted the help of fellow clergymen who could take down the tunes while he transcribed the words, and the enterprise began. Fleetwood Sheppard could spare little time from his parochial duties, and most of the collecting appears to have been done by Baring-Gould and the Rev. Dr Bussell, Oxford don and dandy, who had a holiday cottage on the Lew Trenchard estate.[2]

The songs they gathered came mostly from semi-professional song-men, who in earlier days had entertained the quarrymen and labourers of the locality, or from their sons, who inherited the repertoire. One such was James Parsons, who would come to Lew House to sing for Baring-Gould. Other singers were old and bed-ridden and had to be visited, and when the clerical pair called on old Sally Satterly, one of their few women singers, they had to compete with her domestic tasks:

> she was busy, she had to do her washing. Mr Bussell seated himself, inconsiderately, on the copper for the boiling, till she lighted the fire under it and drove him off. I had to run after her as she went about her work, jotting down her words, while Bussell followed, pencil and music book in hand, transcribing her notes.[3]

Over 200 songs were collected in this way and issued in suitably amended form in several volumes as they were edited and arranged. The modal tunes were generally preserved, for it was in such archaic simplicity that their value was felt to reside, as well as in their rustic settings, 'under the greenwood tree' or 'down in a valley'. The country figures of ploughboy and milkmaid were retained, but their narratives were altered when they dealt too directly with sex (albeit in the metaphors used in folk song) or illegitimate offspring. The reason for this was partly delicacy on the part of the collectors (who could be highly embarrassed by the songs they were noting down) and partly because from the start they aimed not just to collect and record in the manner of an antiquary but also to publish and popularize the songs, in order to resuscitate the traditional music of the English people. To do this, the conventional pro-prieties of the age had to be observed, or the songs would be suppressed not because they were old-fashioned but because they were indecent.

Other enthusiasts were also at work. In 1890 W.A. Barratt, musician, vicar-choral of St Paul's and music critic of the *Morning Post,* issued his collection of fifty-four *English Folk Songs,* 'noted from the lips of singers in London streets, roadside inns, harvest-homes, festivals on the occasion of sheep-shearing, at Christmas-tide, at ploughing matches, rural entertainments of several kinds and at the "unbinding" after choir suppers in country districts'. In the same year Frank Kidson from Yorkshire published a volume of folk music, *Old English Country Dances,* followed by *Traditional Tunes* (1891). In 1894 the melodies from William Chappell's collection of broadside ballads, *Popular Music of the Olden Time,* drawn from printed sources and originally published in 1859, was revised and reissued.

Interest in the music of the people may thus be said to have quickened around 1890. It was almost without exception seen as country music; folk songs from industrial areas and occupations were seldom searched for and rarely found, despite the fact that cities and towns and non-agricultural settings – for example ale-house songs, sea-songs, and songs featuring London – were common in the repertoires of country singers. It was generally believed that folk song only existed in country districts, since the city was degenerate, febrile and committed to the latest fashion in commercial 'popular songs'. Certain country areas were culti-vated – picked or gathered would be better terms – by different collectors, in the belief that each county had its distinctive culture, rather like its landscape, until it was found that most songs turned up all over Britain.

Lucy Broadwood has as good a claim as Sharp to have launched the revival. After the republication of *Sussex Songs,* the publisher Andrew Tuer of the Leadenhall Press suggested an anthology of folk songs from all over the country; this was undertaken by Lucy Broadwood and J.A. Fuller Maitland, music critic of *The Times* who, in reaction against 'the tyranny of classical music' had already rescued and published a collection of early music in the *Fitzwilliam Virginal Book* and was involved in the contemporaneous efforts to revive madrigal and glee singing. 'With varying success' he and Miss Broadwood searched England for songs and then retired to the Broadwood home in Sussex to do the editing, whereupon 'it was discovered that songs to the number of 700' could be remembered by the family gamekeeper, and so a new store was added.[4]

Fuller Maitland claimed that the publication of *English County Songs* in 1894 marked the start of the revival and led to the founding of the Folk Song Society in 1898. In that year a public meeting was called for 16 June, to establish a society 'for the purpose of discovering, collecting and publishing Folk Songs, Ballads and Tunes'. At the first general meeting seven months later, the F.S.S. had 100 members and a financial balance of £24 18s 9½d. The inaugural address by Sir Hubert Parry placed the F.S.S. firmly within an anti-urban, anti-industrial perspective, invoking 'our terribly overgrown towns' of 'pawnshops and flaming gin palaces', where 'miserable piles of Covent Garden refuse which pass for vegetables are offered for food'. From this environment issued the debased modern song – the enemy of folk music, which 'grew in the hearts of the people before they devoted themselves so assiduously to the making of quick returns'.[5]

The driving spirit of the early F.S.S. was its honorary secretary, Mrs Kate Lee, who as well as organizing the meetings was herself an energetic collector. At the first meeting she described her early efforts at Wells-next-the-Sea in Norfolk in November 1897, giving a vivid picture of the amateur collector at work:

> I hadn't the faintest idea how or where to begin. First of all I asked the clergyman and the doctor, but they couldn't assist me at all. I did not know any of the people about, so the only thing to do was to be audacious. Accordingly I wandered down one morning to the quay, where I had noticed that four old fishermen always stood. . . I boldly went up to one of them, and said 'Do any of you sing?' 'Do any of us sing?' was the startled reply – as they were generally only asked about the weather and the boats – 'Sing! No, none of us sings.'[6]

With some persistance Mrs Lee got the names of some old men who were reputed singers, and although the first of these was too nervous to sing when summoned to a lady's house, others were able to oblige, providing her with her first bunch of country songs.

Back in London, Kate Lee was offered others by a Mrs Bodell of Clerkenwell, whom she thought 'might be a burglar in disguise' but who 'did not take anything, although she left, I think a good deal' – in the form of fine songs. Then the two Messrs Copper, farm foreman and landlord of The Plough respectively, were discovered at Rottingdean in Sussex. These brothers were 'so proud of their songs and sang them with an enthusiasm grand to hear, and when I questioned them as to how many they thought they could sing, they said they thought "about half a hundred".' Some of these songs were selected for performance at the F.S.S. meeting. Typically, they opened with a variant of the line 'As I walked out on one May morning', continuing with purely pastoral lines:

> As I rode out on Midsummer's morning
> For to view the fields and to take the air,
> Down by the banks of the sweet primroses
> There I beheld a most lovely fair.

The heroine in a Welsh song sung by Mr Edge of Wells however belongs to the real world:

> Her home and her parents are highly respectable,
> Her mother milks cows on a three-legged stool;
> Her father's a farmer, who grows the green turnip-tops,
> Her sister's a dairy maid, her brother's a fool.

In May 1900 W.P. Merrick presented to the F.S.S. his collection of fifty-two songs taken from Henry Hills, a sixty-eight-year-old Sussex farmer now living in Shepperton. Mr Hills's recollections may stand as representative of the vanished world briefly brought back to life by folk song:

> Just take up a stone and rattle it on the handle of the plough and sing to them, and the horses would go along as pretty and as well as possible. I almost feel as if I could go to plough and sing away now! We used to have a carter-chap living in the house, and he could sing scores of songs; sometimes of an evening we would sit up for ever so long – first one would get hold of a ballad, and

then another would get hold of a ballad, and so on. Sometimes a friend would come to stay with us from London or somewhere else, and if he could sing a song that I liked I would get him to sing it over until I learned it. I used to hear a lot of songs, too, at harvest-homes, tithe-feasts, rent-dinners, rabbit hunts and one place and another. Some of the farmers and men around there could sing out-and-out well – capital they could.[7]

Kate Lee became ill in 1900 and died four years later, and as a result the F.S.S. became virtually defunct, leaving the field open for an equally enthusiastic successor. Cecil Sharp was then principal of the Hampstead Conservatoire of Music, a good teacher and aspiring composer, and he had first encountered folk music at Christmas 1899 when staying at Headington outside Oxford. A group of village men strangely dressed in white, with ribbons and bells, came to the house and performed five morris dances in the hope of earning some money at a time when work was slack. The side had recently re-formed, perhaps with some awareness of growing interest on the part of the gentry. Watching the morris men, Cecil Sharp was enthralled and the next day noted down the tunes from William Kimber, the young accordionist. He later pointed to this incident at Headington as the start of the folk music revival, although it was clearly already under way. In any case, Sharp did little about his new interest apart from joining the F.S.S. in 1901 and browsing through earlier collections to make a selection of 'traditional' songs suitable for teaching purposes. He was already dissatisfied with conventional musical education, and pleased by folk tunes, but they were not his 'finds'.

Then late in the summer of 1903 Sharp went to the village of Hambridge in Somerset to stay with old friend the Rev. Charles Marson, where one afternoon the vicarage gardener John England (an emblematic name) was heard singing 'The Seeds of Love'. Sharp immediately noted it down and composed a harmony so that it could be performed and with typical dispatch took Father Marson on an urgent search for further treasures. Within a month forty songs had been noted, mostly coming from the sisters Louie Hooper and Lucy White. Sharp returned to Hambridge at Christmas and regularly thereafter, combing the villages of Somerset and North Devon for new and old songs; by 1905 he claimed to have collected 500 tunes, of which 125 were modal tunes. In commenting that he had got a high proportion of his songs from women, Sharp attributed this to the presence of cottage industries in the area, where until recently women gathered making shirts and gloves and singing together.[8] Mrs Hooper remembered Sharp with a rare affection considering the social gulf between them. She spoke of the many happy hours she and her sister spent at the vicarage singing for Sharp, who 'used to pay us very well', and recalled the kind gift of a new blouse from Mrs Sharp. The old men who sang for Sharp received tobacco.[9]

Included in Sharp's Somerset collection were many that we now recognize as 'classic' English folk songs: 'I'm Seventeen Come Sunday', 'Blow Away the Morning Dew', 'Hares on the Mountains', 'The Trees They Do Grow High'. Not all were new discoveries, but Sharp's versions with their careful piano accompaniments have become accepted, owing to his vigorous salesmanship. Other collectors regarded their songs as precious treasures – often too valuable to be exposed to the public. Sharp believed in maximum publicity, a task he undertook without payment and at some expense to his family. In his eagerness he also trod on a few corns, as when, fired with new enthusiasm, he proposed the establishment of a new folk song society. Instead, he was elected to the committee of the F.S.S. which thereupon revived.

Sharp believed fervently that the folk songs which were being rescued from ageing singers all over the country represented England's 'national music', which had been neglected in favour of foreign imports and which ought to be restored to the nation forthwith. He defined folk song[10] (a term only recently coined) as song created by the common people, by which he meant 'the remnants of the peasantry . . . who resided in the country and subsisted on the land' and were unlettered but not ignorant. Such music, evolving unconsciously over generations, Sharp believed, 'is transparently pure and truthful, simple and direct in its utterance', and wholly free from 'the taint of manufacture, the canker of artificiality' – therefore possessing a virtue and value not to be found in composed music of however high a quality. We may note that the words Sharp uses to commend folk music are ones like 'simple' and 'pure', while those to which it is opposed reflect the

Ruskinian disdain for the industrial world: why else should 'manufacture' be regarded as 'tainted'? Sharp's admiration was however reserved for the melodies, which were of 'utmost value' musically; he thought the words usually poor – jumbled and incomplete narratives, scraps of a dying traditional literature. To some modern ears the fragmentary nature of many folk lyrics gives them a poignancy that a full story cannot possess, but Sharp and most of his contemporaries favoured the complete narrative and tended to judge the lyrics accordingly.

Little hope was held out for reviving folk music naturally, that is through the oral tradition, which was regarded as having been in absolute decline since at least the youth of most of Sharp's singers, now in their sixties. Their sons and daughters, who ought to have inherited the tradition, had since the 1860s turned away from the old songs. In a few years the remaining singers would die and the quality of the music demanded that it be rescued from the same fate, for a number of reasons. First, it could provide the basis of a national school of music which would in time produce great English musicians and composers – sadly lacking in the past – for 'when every English child is, as a matter of course, made acquainted with the folk songs of his own country, then, from whatever class the musician of the future may spring, he will speak in the national musical idiom'. In addition, folk song could be made the basis of the musical education provided in school, both state and private; if this were done 'not only would the musical taste of the nation be materially raised, but a beneficent and enduring effect would be produced on the national character'. Aesthetic and patriotic uplift would go together, and the corrupting power of city civilization would be vanquished: 'the mind that has been fed on the pure melody of the folk will instinctively detect the poverty-stricken tunes of the music-hall, and refuse to be captivated and deluded by their superficial attractiveness'. 'Flood the streets with folk-tunes,' Sharp urged in full missionary style, 'and those who now vulgarize themselves and others by singing coarse music-hall songs will soon drop them in favour of the equally attractive but far better tunes of the folk.' This would not only make the streets pleasanter for those with 'sensitive ears', but also help to civilize the masses. Above all, it would 'purge the streets of towns and cities' and even those of country villages, of the contamination of manufactured music, and return England, musically at least, to its pre-industrial condition.[11]

In order to bring about this happy prospect it was necessary that the people should have access to the tunes of the folk, so Sharp set about arranging them, publishing them and performing them. Beginning in 1904 he issued his own *Folk Songs from Somerset* in five parts, containing a total of 133 songs, and he also re-arranged Baring-Gould's *Songs of the West* for a new edition published in 1905. The same year Sharp and Baring-Gould co-edited *English Folk Songs for Schools,* containing fifty-three songs arranged by Sharp. These were the basis of the 'folk song revival' which swept English primary schools and remained the basis of much music teaching until the 1950s, as certain generations can testify. In retrospect, there is something perverse in trying to maintain 'traditional' culture through the formal education system, but in the absence of radio or television it was in fact the only available oral medium. And it seemed the decision was correct, for the songs were immediately popular. Teachers claimed that children found modal songs easy and attractive to learn and – more importantly – took to singing them in the playground and in the street, thus leading Sharp to believe that in time the true oral tradition would re-establish itself. He noted that in the Somerset villages where he had been collecting, children were taking the old songs home from school and their parents were learning then anew. In time, of course, folk songs of the Sharp variety became themselves distinctly old and tired.

At the start the enthusiasm was almost overwhelming. It was to be expected that those members of the intelligentsia who had already espoused the 'country' cause should take up folk songs, but even they were surprised and delighted with the quality revealed in the songs and music. A whole generation of poets of whom Walter de la Mare and John Masefield are the most enduring forsook the style and language of late Victorian verse to write in a manner which approaches that of the folk lyric and ballad, and in music the impact was even greater. The greatest impression was however in education. In 1907 Sharp persuaded Novello, the music publisher, to issue a cheap series of folk song collections, together with single songs at 2d each, so they would be within the reach of all. He worked hard at providing suitable arrangements and accompaniments which would make the songs accessible without harming their musical simplicity, and he spread the word as far and wide as he could. Something of the success of this personal 'folk song crusade' can be gauged from the fact that from 1904 to 1907 he was employed to teach music to the royal grandchildren, the sons and daughters of the later George V and Queen Mary, who learned from him peasant songs from Somerset.

At the other end of the social scale, he encouraged Mary Neal to introduce folk songs to the Esperance Working Girls' Club she ran in the Cumberland Market area of London. The club members worked for the most part in the sweated garment trade in a since-redeveloped slum district not far from Euston station. To her surprise Miss Neal found that the songs were very popular with the girls, and as they were already enthusiastic about Scottish and Irish dancing, she asked Sharp if there were any English dances to teach them. He referred her to William Kimber of Headington (despite the fact that the morris is traditionally an exclusively male dance) who travelled to London to demonstrate the steps. By 3 April 1906 the Esperance girls were sufficiently skilled to give a public per-formance which aroused great interest, as it was the first oppor-tunity for most of the audience to see traditional morris dancing. There was an immediate demand for more performances, for tunes and for instruction in the steps. Most of these were supplied by Esperance girls, some of whom went on to become professional dance teachers. Sharp undertook to publish a series called *The Morris Book,* in collaboration with Herbert MacIlwaine, then musical director to the Esperance Club. *The Morris Book* and its companion *Morris Dance Tunes* contained the music and the notation for eleven dances, the majority from Headington, although others were beginning to be recovered from other places. In their introduction the editors pronounced themselves not interested in musical archaeology, but 'concerned with the morris as a lapsed yet living art', calling for revival 'as heralds to the sweetening of the town life of England and the repeopling of her forsaken countryside'. William Kimber's visit to Cumberland Market was described as a momentous event:

The first dance that was set before these Londoners – upon this occasion which we enthusiasts make bold to call historic – was Bean-Setting. It represents the setting of the seed in springtime. Of course the music, its lilt and the steps that their forefathers had footed it to in the olden times, were as little known to the London born as the tongue and ceremonial of old Peru. As little known yet not strange at all, it was a summons never heard until now, yet instantly obeyed; because although unfamiliar and unforeseen it was of England and came even though it was centuries upon the way to kinsfolk. . . Within half an hour of the coming of these Morris men we saw the Bean-Setting – its thumping and clashing of staves, its intricate figures and steps hitherto unknown – full swing upon a London floor. . . .

We had given back to these children of the city no less than a birthright long mislaid.[12]

The fifth morris book (1913) included processional dances such as the Helston Furry and Castleton Garland, described as spring or fertility dances:

To this end fresh green branches and flowers, the symbols and proofs of resuscitated nature were gathered and worn by the participants; while the cottages, farm buildings and sometimes even the animals were decked with them. May garlands were carried through the village usually containing within them the form of a human effigy, the anthropomorphic representation of the nature sprite. The tree being the largest and noblest product of the plant world was set up and worshipped by rings of dancers; while ceremonies were performed at the sacred shrines, groves and wells upon all of which flowers and blossoms were formally placed. By these means the villagers hoped that they together with their flocks and herds and the cultivated fields, might all share in the awakened spirit of nature, and prosper accordingly.[13]

Such a vision of the long-lost Merrie England in which these customs flourished was well established; as we have seen, Ruskin created his own version of the May Queen at Whitelands College in the 1880s. But with the folk song and dance revival the vision took on a new vitality, and as Margaret Dean-Smith remarked in her account of events, 'a species of Mankind, the Folk, came into being without nation or habitat but vaguely assumed to be country dwellers, unlettered but poetical, musical and graced with dignity. . .'[14]

Folk dancing was introduced in villages and schools throughout England by teachers, clergymen and benevolent ladies who had seen or heard of the enthusiastic performance of the Esperance Girls. Other surviving English dances, principally the northern sword dances but also the easier all-join-in country dances, were collected and published so that all who desired could learn the movements. In general a single instrument, piano or accordion or fiddle, was sufficient accompaniment for the revived dances, although the morris was traditionally accompanied by pipe and tabor (or whittle and dub as it was rustically known) as well as by the dancers' bells. All over the country morris 'sides' reappeared – no doubt distinguishable, as Hardy remarked, from the genuine article by the cheerfulness with which they performed – and if there was incongruity in the idea of members of Winchester public school performing English country dances in public it was certainly not felt by the participants. The aim was to restore to all the people the musical heritage which had been so nearly lost, and it was even argued that it was the highly educated, most sophisticated and urbanized classes of society who had most to gain from the vigour and simplicity of the old dances.

The revival served not only to bring the country traditions to deprived city dwellers but also to restore to country people musical property which had been temporarily mislaid, as it were; on many occasions revivalists took dances into villages where none had been performed in living memory. In some places old residents were stirred by the performance to remember the dances of their youth, and new variants were recorded. The most common form the revival took in rural districts was that organized by an enthusiastic local lady, such as May Morris at Kelmscott or Lady Constance Lytton at Knebworth. Thaxted in Essex became a famous centre of folk dancing and music under the direction of Conrad Noel and his wife. With the patronage of landowners and clergy, competitions were established at county shows for the best village dance team. Sharp was often an adjudicator at these occasions, as once at Reading where the sides were drawn from Women's Institutes. Most of the teams were young girls, but one was composed of older women, dancing in thick serge skirts and full blouses. Their teacher recorded Sharp's courteous words to her team, saying he hoped their husbands enjoyed watching them as much as they clearly enjoyed dancing, for

> one of the greatest charms of folk-dancing [is] that it was not
> intended only for the young, but for the recreation of the
> workers of the world, as it has the power like nothing else of
> taking their minds off the daily drudgery which must fall to their
> lot. The dancing of this team showed that in this respect it has
> completely fulfilled its purpose.[15]

Listening to this tribute, the village ladies were too surprised and
delighted to resent the patronizing account of their working lives.

The popularity of folk music led directly to organizational rival-
ries. In 1907 Mary Neal called an informal meeting, attended by
Sharp, to propose a society, which was founded the following year
with herself as secretary; the original title was the Association for
the Revival and Practice of Folk Music, but this was soon changed
to the Esperance Morris Guild, emphasizing its partisan status. On
his side Sharp established in 1909 a school of morris dancing at
Chelsea P.T. College, with himself as director, the main aim being
to instruct prospective teachers in folk dancing which they would
then transmit through their schools; evening classes were also held.
To widen the circle of appreciation students were used as display
teams, the first of which included the sisters Maud and Helen
Karpeles who formed the Folk Dance Club in April 1910 to give
private and public performances under Sharp's general guidance.

By 1911 there were thus a number of folk dance groups in
operation all over England. The Esperance Guild attracted large
numbers of recruits for classes and displays, while Sharp's own
classes were somewhat more select – particularly his Tuesday
evening class at Chelsea, where he tried out newly collected dances
and favoured students might have the joy of witnessing the first
performance of a new discovery. Most of the collecting was done
verbally, from the recollections and explanations of the informants,
rather than visually, for few dances were still performed in the
villages. Owing to his collecting experience, Sharp was concerned
with the 'truth' or authenticity of the dances when performed by
others, and he was especially critical of the Esperance style of morris
dancing. A dispute then arose over the 'correct' form, which led to
acrimony between Neal and Sharp, and resulted in a struggle

between their respective supporters over the proposed folk dancing summer school to be held at the Shakespeare Festival at Stratford in 1911. The Esperance Guild was first invited to direct the sessions, but doubts over the authenticity of the Neal style of dancing led in the end to Sharp's programme being substituted. For four weeks over sixty students attended daily dance classes, lectures and singing sessions, with weekly displays in the Memorial Theatre Gardens. Visiting dance groups also participated. Commitment and exhilaration were high, and for many the Stratford summer school was a time of enchantment. Sharp then proposed that a national body under his general direction be formed and in December 1911 the English Folk Dance Society was formed, with the object of 'preserving and promoting the practice of English folk dances in their traditional form'. Sharp, Maud Karpeles and Ralph Vaughan Williams were on the committee and Helen Karpeles was secretary. Again, training dance teachers to a recognized standard was one of the main functions, together with running the summer school and other regional programmes.

Subsequent attempts to bring Sharp and Miss Neal into the same association were unsuccessful, as neither would submit. Neal claimed to work within the tradition of direct transmission of dance forms, saying: 'I unhesitatingly say that they should be learnt in the first instance from the traditional dancer and passed on in the same way.' As William Kimber had taught the Esperance girls, they were now part of the traditional chain.[16] She did not like Sharp's practice of publishing the notation of dances and insisting on its exact reproduction in what she considered a form of petrifaction. To his 'pedantry', she opposed 'those in touch with life itself'; the teaching of old dances was a vital process concerned more with joy than with correctness. As folk music was communal in origin, so the transmission 'should also be left in the hands of the simple-minded and of those musically unlettered and ignorant of all technique'.[17] Finally, the results were good: 'Our boys and girls dance it much better than if they had been taught by a professional dancer with technical terms and a settled technique.'[18]

In Sharp's view this approach led to sloppy if enjoyable dancing and some very untraditional practices, such as that of bending the knee during the morris jump. He saw folk dancing not just as cheerful amusement but as a disciplined art form and insisted adamantly on a high level of proficiency and adherence to the recorded figures, instilling in his students a firm respect for the authenticity of the tradition they became responsible for handing on. Under his influence the English folk revival thus took a purist rather than a populist line, although he was often at pains to correct this assessment. He rejected the idea of folk music as a cult 'appropriated and patronised by a few choice spirits and protected from the common herd. Whereas it was the common herd to which they belonged and to whom it was my intention to restore their lost heritage,' he said later.[19]

In 1932 the English Folk Dance Society amalgamated with the Folk Song Society to become the English Folk Dance and Song Society, as which it remains and flourishes to this day. Its headquarters in Regents Park Road London were opened in 1929 when Maud Karpeles and William Kimber laid a foundation stone which reads: 'This building is erected in memory of Cecil Sharp who restored to the English people the songs and dances of their country.'

Other people certainly deserve some credit also – notably the composer Ralph Vaughan Williams, friend and colleague of Sharp who helped to realize Sharp's other ambition of restoring a national musical idiom to England. Vaughan Williams was an early admirer of folk song, as a neighbour and friend of Lucy Broadwood, and in 1902–3 lectured to adult education groups in Bournemouth and Gloucester on the subject of folk music. Later in 1903 he began his own collecting in the district around Ingrave in Essex, discovering a number of very fine songs. The influence of traditional music on his own compositions was extensive and varied; one aspect is to be seen in the conception of his comic opera *Hugh the Drover,* composed between 1910 and 1914 with libretto by Harold Child. Outlining his ideas, Vaughan Williams wrote of an opera of English country life, 'written to *real* English words, with a certain amount of *real* English music'. He felt that 'the whole thing might be folk song-y in character, with a certain amount of real ballad stuff thrown in'.[20] Through Vaughan Williams's own work and the contemporaneous music of Gustav Holst, Percy Grainger and John Ireland, on all of whom the rediscovery of English music made a considerable impact, Britain's musical reputation began to rise, in much the way Sharp had hoped.

Vaughan Williams projected that his next operatic work would be based on George Borrow's *Lavengro*. No such work was ever written, but it illustrates how the revival of folk music accompanied a resurgence of interest in gypsy lore and life. The 'simplicity' and 'freedom' of the travelling people was contrasted with the restricted conventional habits of the average citizen, and the gypsy tended to become a kind of icon of the 'alternative' way of living which awaited those courageous enough to cast off the shackles of house-dwelling civilization. Gypsies were also closer to the 'country' tradition. During his song collecting, Sharp made a point of contacting gypsies wherever possible for, owing to their relative isolation, they had preserved many of the old songs which had been submerged elsewhere. From a young gypsy woman called Betsy Holland and from her grandmother Rebecca Holland Sharp acquired some of his finest songs. Describing the occasion in a letter to his wife, Sharp recounted how he and his companion waited with Betsy's husband for her to return from hawking:

> It was a peaceful little scene and he showed us his stove and the contrivances for making a tent in which they camped out every night – only using his van during the winters. Presently out came the wife, Betsy Holland, aged 26, a bright, dark-eyed woman. The baby cooed with delight directly she appeared. We attacked her about the songs which she had learnt from her grandmother. A little persuasion and she sat down on a stone, gave her baby the breast, and then began a murder song that was just fascinating. Talk of folk-singing! It was the finest and most characteristic bit of singing I had ever heard. . . I cannot give you any idea what it was all like, but it was one of the most wonderful adventures I have ever had. . .[21]

The link between folk music and gypsies is central to Edward Thomas's poem *The Gypsy,* written in 1915. Earlier Thomas had prepared a study of Borrow, while his own long walks in the southern counties to gather material for his 'country' books had often taken him past gypsy encampments. Ascribing to the travellers his own feelings about urban areas, Thomas said gypsies belonged 'to the little roads that are dying out: they hate the sword-like shelterless road, the booming cars that go straight to the city'.[22]

His later poem brings together all the elements which the folk song collectors responded to and wished to preserve:

A fortnight before Christmas gypsies were everywhere:
Vans were drawn up on wastes, women trailed to the fair.
'My gentleman,' said one, 'you've got a lucky face.'
'And you've a luckier,' I thought, 'if such a grace
And impudence in rags are lucky.' 'Give a penny
For the poor baby's sake.' 'Indeed I have not any
Unless you can give change for a sovereign, my dear.'
'Then just half a pipeful of tobacco can you spare?'
I gave it. With that much victory she laughed content.
I should have given more, but off and away she went
With her baby and her pink sham flowers to rejoin
The rest before I could translate to its proper coin
Gratitude for her grace. And I paid nothing then,
As I pay nothing now with the dipping of my pen
For her brother's music when he drummed the tamborine
And stamped his feet, which made the workmen passing grin,
While his mouth-organ changed to a rascally Bacchanal dance
'Over the hills and far away'. This and his glance
Outlasted all the fair, farmer, and auctioneer,
Cheap-jack, balloon-man, drover with crooked stick, and
    steer,
Pig, turkey, goose, and duck, Christmas corpses to be.
Not even the kneeling ox had eyes like the Romany.
That night he peopled for me the hollow wooded land,
More dark and wild than stormiest heavens, that I searched
    and scanned
Like a ghost new-arrived. The gradations of the dark
Were like an underworld of death, but for the spark
In the Gypsy boy's black eyes as he played and stamped his
    tune,
'Over the hills and far away', and a crescent moon.

Part II
Tilling the Earth

The land as source of all goodness, design by
Godfrey Blount from *Our Daily Bread*, 1898

6

Agrarian Communes

Living in the country, protecting it from encroachment and preserving the culture of its inhabitants was not all that was inspired by Victorian anti-industrialism. For some, going back to the land meant more than just living there, it meant a deeper sense of returning to cultivation, to agrarian life and a closer, intimate relation with the earth. And this led to individuals and groups – motivated by the same desire as that which impelled similar young people in the 1960s and '70s to leave London for hill farms and rural communes – seeking out smallholdings and plots of land, where they endeavoured to grow their own food and live out the Simple Life. Characteristically idealist, they saw their experiments as models for the future, when the whole population would abandon the competitive, commercial world of the city and join the pioneers in a new life of peaceful co-operation and personal harmony.

One of the first such endeavours was at St George's Farm, established by Ruskin at Abbeydale, Totley, just outside Sheffield, which represented an early attempt by industrial workers to set up an agrarian commune as part of the escape from wage slavery and monopoly capitalism. Religious and millerarian communes of this kind have a long history in England,[1] and in the 1840s the Chartist movement built nearly 300 cottages in five settlements for supporters who wished to become independent smallholders, or radical

English peasants. Those who joined the agrarian communes of the latter years of the century, however, were inspired less by religious or political ideas than by reaction against the urban environment – or perhaps it would be truer to say that their political ideas took the form of a pastoral escape from the industrial world. This was the idea that took hold of a group of working-class socialists in Sheffield who in 1875–6 attended a Mutual Improvement class for political discussion and self-education. As their thinking progressed, they adopted the term communist – derived, it appears, from the concepts suggested by the word commune for collective living and owning – and formed a society whose aim was 'to propagate Communist views, our ultimate object being to live the lives of Communists. To do this we proposed buying or leasing some land on which to erect suitable buildings, both for dwelling and business purposes.'[2] The members of the group were largely practical persons, and they did not mean to abandon their manufacturing skills, but rather to create a self-supporting enterprise which would grow food, make tools, clothing and furniture, selling such items to buy whatever could not be produced. Cultivation and production were basic to the scheme's conception.

St George's Farm has in general received a bad press, owing to Ruskin's view, supported by his editors, of the whole enterprise as a disastrous failure, which it was not, or at least not in the way Ruskin presented it. Little is known about the members of the original group, apart from the fact that it included two women and a boot and shoe maker whose enthusiasm was later to bring the plan to grief. One member whose history is known is Joseph Sharpe, who ended his days working from time to time on Edward Carpenter's market garden at Millthorpe; his career illustrates what was happening to independent craftsmen in this period of industrial consolidation, and why the idea of a farm co-operative was such an attractive alternative. In his youth Sharpe had been a butcher's apprentice, policeman, factory hand and Chartist, but in the 1850s he bought a harp and taught himself to play and sing as an insurance against lay-offs, 'so that when the time came that I was thrown out I took to that entirely'.[3] Training his son to play the fiddle, Sharpe built a good living for himself, providing music for village feasts such as those associated with Derbyshire well-dressing, when 'dancings and drinkings went on all night long in farm parlours and public house upper chambers' as the rural community held its annual festivities.

With the decline in rural prosperity and population in the 1870s, Sharpe's livelihood faded. He opened a small retail shop in Sheffield which his wife minded when he was away playing, but its potential customers were not wealthy enough to support it. The small crafts and trades on which Sheffield was founded were losing their independence as the concentration of industrial capital favoured large enterprises and mass production; several of those involved in the early socialist activities in the city were threatened by the prospect of wage-labour in a machine shop, with its concomitant risk of unemployment in times of recession. From this sense of insecurity the idea of a commune developed.

Early in 1876 the little museum established by Ruskin at Walkley, near Sheffield, was opened. Knowing of the communists' dreams, the curator suggested they ask Ruskin for financial assistance. The communists were not too enthusiastic, as they had established their own savings fund and did not like Ruskin's views on authority. Nor did they wish to join St George's Guild. When Ruskin paid a visit to the museum, they raised and disputed the subject of authority versus collective responsibility with him, and were surprised some weeks later when he wrote offering to buy a piece of land in order to bring their project closer to realization. The offer was not purely altruistic: St George's Guild had been in existence for five years, without one notable achievement; it was high time, Ruskin felt, for a demonstration of its ideals. Almost before the agreement was reached, he was telling his readers that here, at last, was 'a little piece of England given into the English workman's hand, and heaven's'. With some disregard for the content of the debate at Walkley, he continued:

A few of the Sheffield working men who admit the possibility of St George's notions being just, have asked me to let them rent some ground from the Company, whereupon to spend what spare hours they have, of morning or evening, in useful labour. I have accordingly authorised the sale of £2,200 worth of our stock, to be reinvested on a little estate near Sheffield, of thirteen acres, with a good water supply.[4]

The impression given that Ruskin, on behalf of the Guild, was making land available to the workers was not quite accurate, for the members of the Sheffield group, having selected the farm at Totley, then signed a contract with the Guild agreeing to repay the purchase price within seven years. This was a quicker means than their painstaking weekly savings fund, but it meant a mortgage and heavier responsibilities. None of the would-be communards had any agricultural knowledge and, being relatively hard-nosed, they decided that for the time being they would defer their idea of living on the land in favour of continuing at their usual trades while employing a farm manager and assistant to run the agricultural operations. Later a third man was sent by Ruskin. The members of the commune went to Totley in their free time, to help with cultivation, and continued to plan for the day when they would all live there permanently, in equal partnership. The venture attracted much attention, as Mrs Maloy, one of the members, later recalled: 'We had parties to visit us during the summer, taking teas, for which we charged. Another woman member and myself found our hands very full at this time, for between us we prepared all the teas and sold eggs and fruit, doing all we could to add to the income.'[5] In addition, they took produce from the farm back to Sheffield and sold it to members of the commune, hoping thereby to increase the profits.

Trouble began when the impatient bootmaker, anxious to live at Totley now rather than in the future, received a £100 gift from Ruskin, which the rest of the committee wished to return, refusing to agree to his proposal that they look after his cobbling business while he and his family moved to the farm. The bootmaker then addressed himself to W. Harrison Riley, whom Ruskin, unwilling to allow the commune to be wholly self-governing, had appointed as his 'representative' in Sheffield. The two men then arranged to take possession of St George's Farm and evict the hired men. Considering, as Mrs Maloy noted, 'that the society had agreed to pay Ruskin back on his own terms, the thing seemed impossible and a chosen number of the committee went to the farm to seek an explanation'. They were met by Riley, 'who coolly informed them that he was master at Totley and they had no rights. He met their remonstrances with sneers and in one case with threats of personal violence.'[6] Two letters to Ruskin went unanswered, and the committee then formally renounced all connection with the farm, which reverted to the Guild.

For a year or so Riley attempted to run the farm. It cost Ruskin £24 for manure, hired help and fodder and £30 18s to keep the Riley family, against income totalling £7 8s 2½d from the sale of farm produce. Eventually Riley left for the United States (where a few years later Edward Carpenter met him on a farm in Massachusetts) leaving Ruskin with direct responsibility for the farm. Ruskin dispatched David Downs, his head gardener from London, to manage the little estate. Downs had been sent to the rescue before, when Ruskin had appointed him to supervise the undergraduate roadbuilding at Ferry Hinksey. Under him, the Totley farm was to be run as a 'vegetable and botanic garden', a living museum of plant types, as well as 'furnishing model types of vegetable produce to the Sheffield markets'. In order to fulfil St George's objects, it would also offer 'employment to any workmen or workmen's children who like to come so far – for an hour's exercise'.[7]

How many workmen or their children took advantage of this offer is unrecorded. Downs ran the farm for five years, at a loss of around £70 per year, and in 1884 new tenants were sought. At this point, Edward Carpenter entered the story. He had not been living in Sheffield at the time of the original commune, but he later knew both Riley and Joseph Sharpe and his own smallholding at Millthorpe was partly inspired by that at Totley. During the early 1880s he was involved in much of the vigorous socialist activity in and around Sheffield, as well as becoming known to a wider audience through his writing. When St George's Guild began to seek someone to take over the farm, Carpenter put forward the names of 'another body of Communists – John Furniss, George Pearson & Co.'[8] who would, he asserted, preserve the original aim of the property but be less voluble and more practical than the original group.

Furniss was a considerable figure among the Sheffield socialists, an old-style radical preacher and impressive speaker; he used Totley as a base for his political work. A quarryman by occupation, he is recorded as giving his support as a Christian Socialist to the Radical candidate in the 1885 general election.

The autumn of the following year St George's Farm was visited by G.L. Dickinson and C.R. Ashbee, two young Cambridge ideal-

ists then staying at Millthorpe with Carpenter. Ashbee recorded his
impressions of the new commune:

> There we have a community of early Christians pure and
> simple – some ten men and three women – no sectarianism, no
> selfishness – at least as far as one can see; and no private property
> except in wives . . . they have rented 180 acres of land, have
> opened three quarries and work hard all day for love of work not
> gain, placing all profits in the common stock. There was a
> brightness and clearness in the faces of most of them which
> bespoke 'enthusiasm for humanity'.[9]

And he concluded admiringly, 'They have taken a lease for 21 years
for they expect the land to be nationalised by that time!'[10]

Together with Furniss, the Pearson family appear to have been
the mainstay of the community. Their hopes in relation to land
nationalization were not realized and it was some forty-five years
later, in 1929, that George Pearson, then very elderly, purchased the
property from St George's Guild. It had reverted to the style of the
original settlers, being worked as a nursery and market garden
rather than a farm. When visited in 1979, St George's Nurseries
were still being worked by the Pearson family, albeit in a commercial rather than communal manner. Old Joseph Sharpe, who
was among the original idealists, died in 1889 at Millthorpe; his
obituary by Carpenter in *Commonweal*[11] inspired contributions
from Mrs Maloy and Harrison Riley recalling events at St George's
Farm. Another correspondent, incidentally, was George Sturt of
Farnham in Surrey, who asked for 'more light on these experiments
at Totley' and expressed his own belief in their importance.

Four miles from Farnham, at Tilford in Surrey, another farm
commune was being started by Harold Cox, a Cambridge graduate
'bitten by the creed of simplicity' in imitation of Carpenter. After
visiting Millthorpe to see how it was done, Cox in 1885 rented
Craig Farm, an uncultivated holding on the Surrey heath, with the
intention of reclaiming it. He employed an experienced farm
worker, George Gibbs, and his family, and invited his idealistic
friends to join the little community. Lowes Dickinson, being similarly full of Thoreau and Carpenter, accepted the invitation with the
conviction that this was the 'right kind of life – manual work on the

one hand and intellectual creation on the other'. The whole enterprise was 'desperate from the start', he acknowledged, adding 'but I knew and cared little about that'.[12] The work was hard, the company uncouth, and within a few months Harold Cox had gone off to India, Dickinson had returned to academic comfort, and the Gibbs family had gone back to Kent. Henry Salt, the apostle of simplicity, who lived near Tilford, was angry with these young university men for playing at going back to the land in this way; it detracted, he felt, from true value.[13]

By the end of the 1880s a good deal of the energy which had gone into socialist politics of one kind or another altered its course towards anarchism. For a while a fierce sectarianism reigned before the labour movement emerged, with as much pragmatism as idealism, leaving both the hard-line Marxists and the anarchists somewhat on the sidelines. The latter, however, kept alive the idea of 'true communism' as it had been understood by the Totley group, and continued to attempt the creation of free communities based on common ownership and personal liberty. These drew heavily on the writings of Kropotkin and Tolstoy, fundamental amongst them being the renunciation of the industrial system and the adoption of self-supportive manual labour on the land. As the anarchist journal *Freedom* expressed it: 'To the Anarchist, who places the happiness of men, women and children above all other aims, the freedom of the human race not merely from authority, but also from bad surroundings, bad conditions and hard and uncongenial work, there can be no cry more fascinating and so full of hope as "Back to the Land!" '[14]

Kropotkin, who settled in Britain in 1886, was a prolific author and propagandist against the prevailing economic view that the survival of the fittest applied to people as much as animals, believing that co-operation and mututal aid were more naturally human than cut-throat competition and inequalities of wealth. In 1888 he published a series of articles whose titles, 'The Breakdown of the Industrial System' and 'The Industrial Village of the Future', were indicative of his line of thought, and whose ideas were re-worked in *Fields, Factories and Workshops* (1898). This argued against the expansion of heavy industry and global trade, urging that each

nation and each community become self-sufficient by returning 'to
a state of affairs where corn is grown and manufactured goods are
fabricated for the use of those very people who grow and produce
them'.[15] It was the *Small is Beautiful* of its day. The vision, one
suspects, like the growing popularity of anarchism in the 1890s,
reflected the cycles of economic recession accompanied by the
growth of industrial monopolies, developments which prompted
some radicals to espouse decentralization as the cure for all ills.

One of Kropotkin's proposals involved the establishment of
intensive greenhouse cultivation in mining areas where coal (for
heating) was relatively cheap and where there was a ready market
for fresh vegetables. This idea was taken up by a group of communally minded anarchists in Newcastle; although Kropotkin
declined to become their patron, he kept in touch with their
endeavour.[16] The Clousden Hill Communist and Cooperative
Colony started in 1895 with two single and two married men,
according to Frank Kapper, a Czech refugee who was the commune's moving spirit (and who evidently regarded the two wives as
moveables rather than members). Each contributed to a common
fund, out of which, with some help from a well-off sympathizer,
the group leased twenty acres on the outskirts of Newcastle at a rent
of £60 a year, plus a down payment of £100 for existing stock, crops
and implements. Each member received pocket money if the farm's
account was in credit, meals were taken communally, and there was
no formal authority, the work being voluntarily undertaken. Early
in 1896 Kapper wrote that 'the number of applications which we
have received clearly shows the desire of workers to return to the
land, and demonstrates the necessity of agricultural colonies similar
to our own'.[17] The commune grew in numbers until it comprised
some two dozen members, nearly all single men and including
several from other parts of Europe. To begin with the main activities were milk and poultry production, some sixty-four geese and
eight turkeys being fattened for the first Christmas, but as the
glasshouses were built the emphasis moved to vegetables.

Because of the strong labour movement in the north-east, the
enterprise was well supported locally. As Ben Glover, one of the
original members of the commune, recalled over fifty years later:

Sunderland and Newcastle Cooperatives took a large quantity of tomatoes, cucumbers, and vegetables, flowers etc. Also Bradnums of Newcastle Green Market took a lot of vegetables, flowers etc., in fact they had good markets. Also local people used to come to the colony and purchase tomatoes etc. They got them about 2d per pound cheaper than they could buy them in the shops. And I had all the dances to supply them with their buttonholes which brought good prices, 1s 6d for ladies and 1s for gentlemen.[18]

It seems that Clousden Hill was an economic success owing to a fair degree of sense and skill in horticulture. Certainly the commune seems to have lived relatively well. For home consumption they kept hens, rabbits, hares, pigs and bees, with a horse and cart for transport. As Glover recalled: 'They used to grind their own wholemeal and I can tell you that their brown bread was a treat. I wish we could get the same quality today, it was as sweet as a nut. They fed well and as regards entertainment they used to have some jolly evenings, Rolf Wondestick with his mandolin, Charles Davis recitations and others singing a song or two.'[19] Within five years, however, the colony had disbanded, apparently through disagreements which there was no machinery to resolve.

Another short-lived commune was the Norton Colony, established in 1896 near Sheffield by Hugh Mapleton and some others with an anarchist perspective, encouraged by Edward Carpenter. There were no rules, according to Mapleton, as 'all business is discussed and work arranged over the communal breakfast table'.[20] The work was horticultural, using a large garden and five greenhouses, and it was soon clear that growing vegetables for the colony's own vegetarian consumption was easy compared with trying to sell them in order to cover other costs. It was decided to concentrate on crops fetching the highest prices – tomatoes, cucumbers, lettuce, mushrooms. Even so, taking produce to the wholesale market was scarcely profitable, so

We created a market for our tomatoes, cucumbers and mushrooms by selling them from door to door in the neighbouring villages, and although we all disliked the idea at first, yet it has been entirely successful, everything having been sold week by week, the people preferring to buy our fresh produce instead of

the often stale market goods. Early last spring we commenced
the sale of seeds, buying them in bulk, and this department
proved very helpful just then when there was very little other
income.[21]

By budgeting very carefully, the Norton Colony was able to
keep itself solvent, and even distribute a small amount of pocket-
money to its members. Following the example of Carpenter and
George Adams, both of whom lived nearby, they took up sandal-
making, hoping that 'our indoor sandals at 3s per pair will be a
means of introducing them to people who would otherwise not
venture to try them . . .' The colonists themselves wore sandals
indoors and out, causing the local people to regard them with
misgiving. They were the archetypal collection of 'cranks';
Mapleton's account ended: 'Included in our "Return to Nature"
principles is vegetarianism, teetotalism, non-smoking and
abstention from salt, chemicals, drugs and minerals and all
fermenting and decomposing foods.'[22] Despite their lack of salt and
minerals, the Norton commune lasted until 1900, when the lease
ran out and the colonists moved on. Hugh Mapleton later founded
the health food firm that still bears his name.

A colony which survived, despite enduring virtual starvation at
the outset, was the 'free' commune at Whiteway in the Cotswolds.
Its actual origins are somewhat intricate, but its inspiration is clear.
From Tolstoy came the basic principle of 'bread labour', whereby
the first duty of man was seen to be producing food, shelter and
clothing – the source of which was the land, which should therefore be made free for all to use. Other duties were also adopted:
comradeship, honesty, the abjuration of all forms of violence and
coercion, and the rejection of authority in terms of laws, taxes, legal
marriage and even money. Great importance was placed on internal
change, new relationships and a new consciousness, with the hope
that eventually society would be transformed through the individual. The anarchist idea of progress was a kind of moving back-
wards, shedding all forms of elaboration and structure, down to the
base points of community and production, eliminating both waste
and oppression and enabling individuals to regain the pure condition of man's supposed natural state. It appealed powerfully to
those who felt that socialism had turned out to be less about

brotherhood than bolshevism.

The story of Whiteway begins with the Fellowship of the New Life founded in 1883 by a group of idealists inspired by dreams of a community of superior souls. It was not without elements of humbug. After its foundation, two strands emerged, one emphasizing personal progress and the 'higher life', the other – later the Fabian Society – committed to reform through political pressure. The two groups split in 1884, 'one to sit among the dandelions, the other to organise the docks', as Bernard Shaw is alleged by Henry Salt to have put it.[23]

The Fellowship of the New Life continued to attract many with socialist and libertarian views, including Havelock Ellis, Olive Schreiner, Edith Lees, Edward Carpenter, Cecil Reddie and J. Ramsay Macdonald. Membership fluctuated over time and by 1889, when a quarterly magazine entitled *Seed-Time* was launched, the name of the group appears to have become the New Fellowship. Its main activities were fortnightly discussion meetings[24] and 'rustic gatherings' in the summer – at one of which the theme was 'The Return to Nature' which for the speaker included 'all return to truth, beauty and simplicity of life'.[25] The desire to leave the city grew stronger and by 1894 the idea of an agrarian commune was being frequently discussed in *Seed-Time*'s pages. In one article Henry Binns outlined the dream:

> We will begin – some few of us – fellows for fellowship and honest living – to put ground under these air castles we love. We will take land and we will live on it . . .
>
> I think, then, as I hoe the weeds and break up the soil anew among the growing plants – that we will lease a plot of land somewhere, with a big farmhouse on it, or better, several cottages and a great barn . . .[26]

He sketched out practical details of acreage, crops, cash outlay and commune membership, suggesting that some would contribute money and some skills; those without either would wait until the colony achieved self-sufficiency. Finally, he thought it important to include women on an equal basis, 'not a group of families, nor a free-lovers' paradise but an open, honourable, honest fellowship [with] women who want to work for their own living and all truer living' and knew how to use their hands for more than the usual feminine accomplishments. To this article the editor attached a note urging readers to respond to this appeal 'to join hands in some such simple and co-operative life . . . which has always been an aim of the New Fellowship'.

By this time the New Fellowship's base had shifted from central London to Croydon and was merging with the Brotherhood Church, through the efforts of Bruce Wallace, founder of the Brotherhood movement and John C. Kenworthy, who in 1895 was pastor of the Brotherhood congregation in West Croydon.[27] Both were charismatic figures who acquired followers on the fringes of the recognized churches. As well as Sunday services of a quasi-religious nature, Kenworthy's group took tea together 'in the true spirit and understanding of brotherhood' and ran a shop selling groceries, fruit, grains and 'all labour, socialist, vegetarian and other advanced periodicals'. In addition, Kenworthy wrote,

> some of our members are now seeking for a piece of land, five acres or thereabouts, in our neighbourhood, where we can pitch 'Brotherhood Camp' [and where] we may, during the summer, inaugurate our longed-for exodus to a life of honest labour in the country, by days and afternoons of holiday-making upon our own acres. Next year it is hoped serious cultivation may begin, for the supply of produce which our store will sell. In such ways, a new society, rid of old cruelties and dishonesties, *may* be built up; the point of doubt is, Have we sufficient faith and unselfish-ness to give ourselves up to the work?[28]

The answer was obviously yes, and the idea grew from an allotment into a full-time commune, to which members could dedicate their lives. In 1895–6 Kenworthy visited Tolstoy in Russia and returned re-inspired with the master's ideas. There were, not suprisingly, different views within the Brotherhood and at this point many were driven away by the Tolstoyan doctrines of 'no voting' and sexual chastity. But others were attracted, seeing in the ideas of 'brother-hood' and 'freedom' some of the principles that seemed to be ignored by both squabbling sectarian socialists and humdrum trade union and municipal organizers. An alternative route to the millennium was needed.

Kenworthy, an energetic if unstable character who later became insane, began to issue his own journal, *The New Order*, in January 1897, evidently poaching much of the readership of *Seed-Time*, which closed a year later. By this date the Brotherhood possessed a press, a meeting room, a shop and, presently, a small hostel for young male recruits. Activities and ideas mushroomed among the Brotherhood (which included some sisters) and a prospective land fund was set up, into which members pooled their resources. Some participants were relatively well off and able to put amounts of family money into such idealistic ventures; others were less well off, with little hope of ever achieving more than a precarious respectability. Founder member Nellie Shaw began, as she described it, 'in business as a draper' with her widowed mother, and found herself selling cheap goods produced by sweated labour. She longed to do something useful and with the only skill at her command, turned to advanced dressmaking, as advertised in the *New Order:*

CROYDON BROTHERHOOD DRESSMAKERS
Dress cut and fitted on scientific principles (artistic and rational costumes specially designed)[29]

Now, she found she was making clothes for those who were already well-clad, and she turned her attention to joining a free commune, 'where, at any rate, I could produce potatoes'.[30]

A site was sought for the commune and ten acres were eventually found in Essex, near Purleigh, south of Maldon. In the winter of 1896–7 the experiment began. Three young idealists from Croydon, William Sinclair, Sudbury Protheroe and Arnold Eiloart settled at Purleigh to prepare the ground. They were joined by William Hone, a skilled gardener brought in to see to the agricultural side, and his family, who were supported by £1 a week provided by Eiloart. One of the wealthier members of the commune, Eiloart gave up his career as a chemistry lecturer to return to the land; he was described by Shaw as 'the embodiment of free healthy abundant life, with a ruddy complexion . . . and luxurious nut brown curly mane' who tried 'many and extraordinary modes of living including camping in tents near the Thames' in his attempts to live without money.[31]

The New Order carried a monthly bulletin on progress at

Purleigh. In May 1897 it was recorded that the colony had acquired
a goat but that most of the eggs in the incubator had failed to hatch.
In June tomatoes and grapes were planted in the newly-built glasshouse, while brickmaking had proved hard work, especially 'tread-
ing' the clay with bare feet on cold mornings . . . In July there were
no notes owing to pressure of work; in August a fair crop of peas
and two Russian visitors were reported; in September over 100 local
people attended an 'open evening' with music and political discussion at the colony; in October the glasshouse recorded a splendid
crop but the outdoor plants failed; in November a total of fifteen
colonists were living at Purleigh, with many more sympathizers
round and about; and in December the notes recorded the planting
of apples, pears, plums, gooseberries and currants, together with
the sowing of 1¾ acres of winter wheat.

'Most of us have come here with the wish to live simpler and
more useful lives,' wrote Hubert Hammond, a former bank clerk,
in April 1898 in an open letter describing the Purleigh commune for
the many inquirers. Following the horticultural details, he outlined
the way 'the necessary business affairs of the colony and details of
work are discussed and arranged at a weekly committee meeting at
which all the colonists, who care to, attend. Nothing is undertaken
unless all the colonists are unanimous.' This, he claimed, had
worked very well. 'We have no rules,' he continued. 'Each one is
left to do as he or she likes, held in check only by one's good sense
and the general opinions of comrades.'[32]

Had the vegetable growing been more successful, it is possible
that the problems Purleigh encountered might have been over-
come, but by the end of 1898 the strains had become severe. No
conditions were imposed on new members, and in the absence of
rules there was no way of ensuring that all pulled their weight, or at
least did not consume more than they helped to produce. In
November William Hone complained that some members were not
really trying to make the commune self-sufficient; 'Much time
spent in meditation coupled with vague visionary ideas that
somehow things will come out right,' he wrote, 'will never accom-
plish much.'[33] A firmly practical man, with a family to support, he
did not agree with the Tolstoyan principle of 'never actively object-
ing to the action of others', or letting people get away with shirking.
There were further arguments about admitting new members,

some believing that the commune should be open to all, others urging the rejection of two new applicants – an attitude the former group felt was based on class prejudice, the two being manual workers, although it was later conceded that the original assessment had been correct when one of the men absconded with the communal funds.[34]

The arrival of Kenworthy and Vladimir Chertkoff, Tolstoy's agent in England, only served to exacerbate the conflicts at Purleigh. Kenworthy was eccentric and Chertkoff autocratic and, as one observer wrote: 'those of us who kept our sanity did not always keep our tempers'.[35] Not surprisingly, the commune disintegrated, but a number of the most idealistic members at once set out to found their own, truly free colony elsewhere. They included Eiloart, Sinclair, Protheroe and Nellie Shaw. In the late summer of 1898 Nellie Shaw and Arnold Eiloart cycled from London to the Cotswolds, attired in their distinctive progressive clothing. Nellie related:

> I was wearing what was then termed 'rational dress' consisting of knickers and a neat Norfolk jacket reaching to my knees. As the weather was very hot my companion gradually divested himself of various garments till all he wore was a short-sleeved vest, red braces, knickers and sandals. It is hard to say which of us attracted most attention.[36]

They found a smallholding named Whiteway, near the villages of Sheepscombe and Miserden, six miles from Stroud, with forty-two acres of hilly ground and a bare stone house of four rooms and an attic. It was purchased with money belonging to the colonists, and immediately a moral dilemma arose: none of the collective owners wished to put their names to a legal document, yet the deeds of the property had to be transferred to them. It was proposed that the name of the rightful owner – God – be entered, but eventually three volunteers were persuaded to sign, after which the document was solemnly burnt – 'this by way of emphasising the fact that the land was never again to be held as private property'.[37]

Eight members of the commune moved to Sheepscombe in October 1898, some living in rented accommodation as the house was not big enough for all. The group included the two 'rejects'

from Purleigh and two 'free union' couples who refused legal
marriage. Others, like Nellie and her rational dressmaker colleague
Lucy Andrews, were to join when their affairs were settled. In
accordance with their 'no money' beliefs, Eiloart and Sinclair travelled from Purleigh to Whiteway on foot, relying on charity and
goodwill. They looked forward to a society in which all necessities
would be freely available. From the start, however, money proved
a problem. One of the couples decided to leave and withdrew their
share of the funds earmarked for food and seeds during winter and
spring. When Nellie joined the commune in March 1899 she added
what little she had into the common fund, but it was quickly
depleted. A petty cash box was kept on the mantelpiece of the old
farmhouse, 'at the disposal of all . . . we had "all things in
common" ', but there was rarely enough. The last £20 went with
the absconding Purleigh reject.

At this stage the commune consisted of Sudbury Protheroe and
his companion Jeannie, Nellie and Lucy in a cottage at Climperwell,
seven single men and 'Madge' (whose free union had dissolved)
with her two children in a third cottage at Wishanger. All gathered
daily at Whiteway, the men working outdoors and the women in
the house – at least in theory, for they were committed to the open
air and when possible the washing was done out of doors and meals
were held under a tree by the roadside. Visitors were numerous the
first summer, and were welcomed and fed by the colonists, who
held 'a simple childlike belief in the inherent goodness of human
nature and imagined that given good conditions, equal and loving
treatment, people would respond and give us of their best'. Visitors
might stay for weeks or months, and the stock of food and money
rapidly diminished, as did the clothing, kept washed and mended in
an open cupboard for people to help themselves. One principle was
that 'a thing should belong to the person who needed it' and thus the
men's shirts, for example, were soon shared out among the visitors.
Such was the prodigality of the summer that the following winter
all money and food ran out; a benefactor provided coal for heating
but there was little food and the idealistic trust in human nature was
put to the test. Hay from Whiteway's fields had been given to a local
farmer, 'it being understood that he would help us with food in the
coming winter. But he never did.'[38]

These bleak months were later referred to by Nellie as 'those old days of stress and privation' during which the colonists nearly starved; nevertheless, she wrote:

> As the lowest ebb from a material point was reached the moral or spiritual condition improved in proportion. All the half-hearted had left, and our numbers got down to a mere dozen or two, who lived exclusively on potatoes and parsnips, which vegetables were the only kinds left after the depletion caused by our having to feed such a large number of visitors and casuals. Not even an onion or carrot remained. On this limited diet we remained healthy and happy, a really good spirit prevailed and the deprivations were less felt because borne in company.[39]

The commune was also affected by scandal, for the dress and behaviour of the colonists shocked the neighbourhood. The women wore short skirts and no hats while the men often went around bareheaded, barelegged and barefooted. They lived together in what must have seemed cheerful promiscuity and even bathed together in a pond, until the presence of 'prurient sightseers' led to the abandoning of mixed bathing. Worst of all, of course, were the free unions. When it was discovered that Madge and Eiloart had entered a new union, outside attempts were made to close the commune on the grounds of immorality; the burnt deeds prevented this but shortly afterwards Madge and Eiloart left Whiteway.

At the end of his life, Eiloart remarked to Nellie Shaw that 'idealism is, I fear, too often just a selfish egotism and, like patriotism, is not enough'.[40] This conclusion was reached at Whiteway early in 1901 when, with a good deal of agonizing, communal cultivation and cooking were abandoned: 'It was decided that each man should take up a portion of land, as much as he felt he could work, and become responsible for it. There he would grow whatever kind of vegetables he chose for his own consumption. Failing that, he would have nothing to eat.'[41] As a result of this decision, a new pattern emerged. On their chosen plots, the colonists built themselves wooden cottages and huts, until all the land was occupied, and settled down in comfortable but non-communal propinquity. For a while the community survived without using money, but eventually most members succumbed to some form of earning. Nellie Shaw's companion, a Czech refugee aristocrat by the name of Francis Sedlak, worked at intervals for local farmers, one of whom, observing that this was no ordinary labourer, ventured to remark: 'You have seen better days, my man,' only to be told: 'No, not at all, the best days are now!'[42] Sinclair took to cows, developing a dairy business that by the 1930s was supplying over 100 customers with milk, butter and cheese. Prothcroc took up baking, at first selling his loaves from a sack in Sheepscombe and later through the Food Reform Depot in Cheltenham. His bakery is still in business in Whiteway, producing delicious wholemeal bread.

Between 1901 and 1914 other settlers arrived at Whiteway, normally staying in the old house until they had built themselves a home. All the land was thus gradually allocated, the existing residents being secure in the knowledge that those who were not suited to the life would sooner or later leave, and that no one could claim ownership of the land otherwise than by occupation and use. Most of the new colonists had left industrial or commercial employment and shared the ideals and interests of the pioneers. Peter Mylles, a former analytic chemist, lived with his family at Whiteway for several years before moving to Letchworth to teach handloom weaving. Beatrice Adams established a colony workroom where weaving, dressmaking and other crafts were carried out in the inter-war years. In 1934 the *News Chronicle* discovered 'the last sandal-maker in England . . . Mr Stanley Randolph [who] lives in a shack at Whiteway Colony',[43] and had learned his craft at Letchworth from Edward Carpenter's former partner George Adams.

By this date Whiteway had ceased to be a commune and had become a settlement of independent cottagers with what would now be termed a residents' association and some social activities. Something of the old spirit remained. In her account of the colony published in 1935 when she was over sixty years old, Nellie Shaw described one contemporary, a wood craftsman named Fred Foster as:

> a true successor to the school of William Morris . . . He makes to order all kinds of furniture beautifully finished, pleasant and simple in design . . . He is also a builder and has erected several of the houses at Whiteway. He desires, as do some others, to

continue living here, cultivating a little land and growing sufficient for his own needs, at the same time making a living by his
craft. But it is difficult to do this, and sometimes it appears as if he
may be driven back to town on account of economic pressure.
This would indeed be a calamity, for undoubtedly there must be
a refinement and beauty in things created under such conditions
impossible in the ordinary workshop or factory in the towns.
This, moreover, is a concrete example of a determined but
hazardous attempt to live such a life as was originally intended by
the founders of the Colony.[44]

7

Cottage Farmers

Motivated by a similar idealistic desire to cultivate the land but less enthralled by the idea of communal living were many young men who dreamed of peasant proprietorship. The vision of contentment with 'three acres and a cow', invoked in the contemporary campaign to win security for the farm labourer, also inspired the artisan and clerk, who may have known less about the reality of rural life but found it immensely attractive in prospect. Unlike in France, where public policy encouraged small and often uneconomic agricultural holdings as a defence against the proletarian mob, land tenure in Britain had further consolidated during the nineteenth century; it was both very difficult to buy a smallholding where large farms and estates were the rule, and very hard to make a living on one, as all marketing arrangements were geared to large-scale production. Nevertheless, the thought of escaping from the city to become a 'cottage farmer' was very appealing and was attempted often enough to become a recognizable social phenomenon.

There is no way of telling how many city dwellers took up farming nor how long they lasted, for they were not distinguishable, in census terms, from the much larger number of smallholders who originated in the country districts. Those who reversed the normal country-to-city migration can, however, never have been numerous enough to affect either population distribution or agricultural output. They represent something less than a social process and yet more than just a nice idea. For if there are no statistical surveys, there are several first-hand accounts, available because back-to-the-land aspirations were felt by and exchanged between educated, urban persons who were used to finding their inform-ation in books.

Roughly speaking, the ex-urban cottage farmers fell into two types, settling on the land either alone or in small groups. Some aimed at commercial viability; others simply to break even and enjoy life. Most could rely on nothing beyond their own efforts. Like the communes, they attracted visitors, especially in the summer, who came to see how it was done and share, temporarily, in the rustic dream.

One of the earliest cottage farm settlements, the Methwold Fruit Farm Colony in Norfolk, was founded in 1889–90 by Mr R.K. Goodrich, who formerly ran a small business in London and who within ten years had fifty neighbours on two- and three-acre plots similar to his own. In 1893 he was visited by Herbert Rix of the New Fellowship and in 1899 by A.C. Sambrook, editor of the *Cable*, a magazine for the farming community founded by Lord Winchilsea. This account of the Methwold Fruit Farm Colony is taken from their words.[1]

Mr Goodrich had planned his escape carefully: 'For three or four years he spent his evenings studying books on the land and the various occupations, such as fruit farming, poultry and bee-keeping, connected with it . . . It looked so feasible that he began to think he would like to try it himself. His scheme was to colonise a small estate, to bring all possible skill and industry to bear on its cultivation and to sell the produce direct to the consumer.' Eventually he took the plunge: ' "I decided to leave London and put it to the test. Just at that time the lease of my place in the City expired . . .".' He bought a two–acre field at Methwold. ' "The first thing to be done was to build a house. I drew the plans of my villa at Hornsey, the arrangements of which suited us very well, and built it myself. That is to say, I did not employ a contractor but the villagers of Methwold built it under my supervision. Then I planted about half the ground with fruit trees, made poultry runs and laid the remainder for vegetables. I had a good connection of friends in the City and obtained orders from them to take all the produce I could spare. And so the Colony was started." '

Once established, Goodrich wrote to several newspapers describing what he had done, and ' "it was not long before shoals of letters came from people who were anxious to give up their life in the towns and settle on smallholdings in the country . . . Some of those who wrote to me paid a visit to Methwold and decided to come. Some have found that it was not exactly what they liked. A few have gone away. But the majority are still here." ' The thirteen new plots were carved out of an adjacent field, each colonist paying £70 for two acres. Later other fields were subdivided in this way for new groups of settlers. Each plot was individually owned; as Goodrich was at pains to point out, he was no capitalist, buying up land to lease to others. He had no private means and his family was thus wholly dependent on their produce. 'There is no margin for luxuries, you may be sure,' he told Sambrook. 'We live simply and work hard but we are well and happy.'

Each colonist needed, however, about £500 to get started; this covered purchase of land, building of houses, purchase of tools, seeds, fruit trees, etc., and survival for up to two years before the holding began to bring in money. Brick-built four-room cottages cost £80; stone-and-flint £150. A colonist known as the Hermit, whom Herbert Rix visited, lived in a two-room wooden hut, cheapest of all at £15. At the time of his visit in 1893, Rix inquired if anyone lived entirely upon the produce of his two acres and 'could not get any clear affirmative. I was told that one family did so, but I found reason to suspect some other small sources of income. Three other colonists, I was told, were "near the living point".' Goodrich himself was certain that money lay in soft fruit and jam.

Six years later there was indeed a small jam factory at Methwold, to use the surplus fruit, but the steady income came from boxes of vegetables, fruit in season and new-laid eggs (for which there was a constant demand) sent weekly to customers in London at a fixed charge of 5s or 10s 6d including carriage. By selling direct to the consumer in this way, Goodrich reckoned to earn £120 a year instead of the £40–50 offered for the same produce by a wholesaler. Even so, this was not a high income. But, as he told Sambrook: 'Ready money at Methwold goes a very long way. Everyone lives as far as possible on what he produces. There is no rent to pay. Rates and taxes are very low – £2 10s a year. You are not obliged to pay for any labour. There are clothes to be bought, of course, but under the circumstances they do not form a very serious item.' All in all, Mr Goodrich was very pleased with his venture. He drew attention to the many advantages – the sunshine, pure air, birds' song, beautiful views, the 'whole treasure-house of Nature . . . and nothing to pay for it', and succeeded in persuading his visitor that the very landscape of Methwold 'seemed to give a silent invitation to town-driven workers to come there and rest'.

In its editorial, the *Cable* drew the wider conclusions:

'Back to the land' is an old and familiar cry. In a general way, nobody responds to it. Perhaps one reason is that it is so often proclaimed by agricultural teachers who themselves take very good care to live in towns. At any rate, the villages become more depleted every year. City life, with its opportunities for money-making and for pleasure, seems to possess an ever-increasing attraction for the rural mind. But at Methwold, in Norfolk, a new order of things has been inaugurated. The land there is being taken possession of not by the country folk, but by clerks and tradesmen from London and other large centres of population . . .

[At Methwold] men, accustomed to an entirely different mode of life, with very few exceptions, have taken kindly to the cultivation of the soil and to such pursuits as poultry and bee-farming. It points to the fact that agriculture is man's natural occupation and that, in many cases, the love of it is inherent . . .

We see no reason why similar Colonies should not be started elsewhere. The idea would not commend itself, perhaps, to those who make haste to be rich; but to many men, to whom money-getting is not the whole aim and end of their existence, the free, healthy and not unprofitable life which is led by the Colonists at Methwold would be full of attractiveness.[2]

Back in Essex, not far from the commune at Purleigh, another settlement of smallholders was established at Mayland, near Althorne. The leading spirit here was Thomas Smith, who in 1895 left his employment as a printer in Manchester and, inspired by back-to-the-land ideas, invested his savings in eleven acres of Essex clay, on which he built himself a house and commenced cultivation.

More land was available locally and Smith advertised for fellow-cultivators in publications like the *Labour Annual*. The principle was 'individualist ownership, tempered by voluntary co-operation'; 'socialist settlers' were assured of 'skilled advice and like-minded comrades'.[3] A number of new settlers were recruited, mostly from urban occupations, and set to work on their small plots to raise vegetables for the London market.

The high hopes of providing an alternative to industrial employment were not immediately achieved. The smallholders had no knowledge of farming and no material base for co-operative effort. The *New Order* in January 1897 attributed the teething troubles at Mayland to the lack of a 'true bond of union' among the settlers but this was mere rivalry, as the Purleigh colony, some twenty miles away, had just begun. (One of the Mayland settlers, formerly a brickmaker, gave the Purleigh colonists help in home-made brick production during their first year.) Thomas Smith was in fact pragmatic and resourceful. Without feeling compromised, he took other occasional jobs to earn money, even returning to Manchester for a while. He also learned from his experience. The most profitable produce at Mayland was tomatoes and other salad vegetables, and the earlier the crop the higher the price. Smith therefore steadily moved to cultivation under glass, producing strawberries, lettuce, tomatoes and even melons – all crops whose wholesale price was good even with small quantities. Gradually he acquired the knowledge and skill to make his holding into a thriving business. Later he published handbooks on intensive cultivation,[4] although the picture they give of a scientifically managed market garden with intensive manuring, acres of cold frames, carefully regulated cloches and a large packing shed is perhaps not the pastoral image Smith or others had before them when setting off back to the land.

Within ten years Smith's reputation as 'an expert agriculturalist and enlightened man' was such that Mayland was chosen by Joseph Fels for one of his land settlement schemes. Fels, whom we shall meet again in the next chapter, was a wealthy American soap manufacturer who had come to Britain in 1901 to extend his business interests and pursue his ideas of land reform and single taxation. A follower of Henry George, he used his money in social experiments designed to 'bring the land and the people together'.[5] He was horrified by the extent of destitution in London and other big cities and believed that 'the key to the whole problem was simply that the worker, to have any advantageous position, must in the last resort be able to leave industry and secure a comfortable livelihood by the pursuit of agriculture. He saw that it was as a great alternative occupation that agriculture could supplement and balance industry and play its appropriate role in the life of a nation.'[6] He studied the rural development policies of Denmark, Belgium and France and came to the view that the future of Britain depended on 'the conservation of a strong and resourceful peasantry', together with 'the evolution of intensive culture with skilful and scientific methods'. He was therefore drawn to Thomas Smith.

In the preface to his first handbook on *French Gardening* (published in 1909 by Joseph Fels and the Utopia Press of Finsbury, with an introduction by Prince Kropotkin) Smith outlined Fels's many efforts to bring the people back to the land and explained that:

> it is not only the masses of paupers and the great army of the unemployed for whom land is urgently needed but that it is wanted as well for innumerable people neither pauper nor unemployed whose land hunger makes them yearn for the country, there to live and work on smallholdings of their own. Many of these have money enough to rent and work a little land but cannot realise their simple desire because of the land conditions that prevail in England.

Together, Smith and Fels revived the original Mayland scheme of independent smallholders, Fels providing the capital outlay and Smith the managerial expertise.

Nipsell's Farm, consisting of 600 acres to the north of Mayland, was bought in 1905 and twenty-one holdings of five to ten acres were carved from it, each provided with a house, outbuildings and newly planted fruit trees. Two acres were devoted to a demonstration French garden, to show the possibilities of intensive cultivation using large quantities of manure, water, glass and labour in the manner of Parisian market gardening, and a *maraîcheur* brought over from France. The rest of the land was run with hired labour by Smith, who, according to the title page of his book, rejoiced in the position of 'Supervisor of the Fels Small Holdings, Manager of the Fels Fruit Farm, Windmill Nurseries and French

Garden, Mayland'. Altogether the Mayland scheme cost Fels £35,000 for land (at £8 3s per acre) and improvements: roads, water pipes, fencing and a wharf to which London barges could deliver horse manure. The amenities of a village were also provided: schoolhouse, shop, post office, social club and co-operative packing shed for the smallholders' use. It is not surprising that there were over 1,200 applications for the twenty-one holdings, which more than justified Fels's belief in 'the desire on the part of the industrial labourer to enter agricultural life'.[7] In 1905 there were fourteen persons on the estate and 174 in 1910.

Despite all the advantages provided for them, the smallholders never succeeded in establishing their independence. Rents began at around £25 p.a., gradually increasing over the first few years, but other costs, particularly those of transport, were relatively high and wholesale prices low. As a result of the improvements made, the local rates on the Mayland property rose fivefold, while the price of surrounding land went up to £14 an acre, making it difficult to extend the scheme. Instead of becoming a model to be emulated all over Britain, Mayland remained an isolated, expensive example. Yet it is hard to assess the success or failure of the smallholdings. No doubt some of the settlers had been attracted by an over-rosy image of life on the land and either returned to the city or turned to other occupations in the Mayland area, using their land for domestic produce only. Smith was clearly an optimist: in his books there is no sense of disappointment or failure, although admittedly he deals almost entirely with the theory and practice of vegetable growing rather than the problems of land settlement schemes. Fels, however, certainly came to believe that Mayland had failed, that all smallholding schemes would fail as long as land was scarce and expensive and that his desire to abolish poverty in Britain required him to work for the abolition of monopoly ownership of land along the lines proposed by Henry George. Then, it might be possible to re-establish the peasant proprietor.

Similar problems were encountered at Cudworth in Surrey, where a smallholding scheme was started by Professor Long, who believed that 'the country labourer could have a yard of land for the price of a glass of beer' and found that it was not labourers but only members of the petit bourgeoisie – small shopkeepers, pensioned N.C.O.s, minor civil servants – who could afford even the smallest pieces of earth. 'If you stand on the top of Leith Hill,' wrote F.E. Green, himself a small farmer, 'your eye will be arrested, as it roams the Weald, by a number of red and white cottages some six miles to the south east.' This, he continued, was the Cudworth estate of some 400 acres,

> on which some forty or fifty families have erected houses and are working daily in the open air.
>
> It is interesting to note that every one of these families has come out of a town. A few of these back-to-the-land folk, it is true, need not work for their livelihood; but whether or not they are spurred by necessity, every one keeps some livestock and does some gardening, and the children, instead of being brought up in the Old Kent Road, Brixton, or Stoke Newington, are taught to plant a tree, to handle a hay-rake, or to milk a cow. They will live intimately with the wind, the clouds and Mother Earth.[8]

The holdings were small, about ten acres each, and were purchased by the occupier at between £20 and £25 per acre, to be repaid in ten years. According to Green, 'most of these back-to-the-landers made a gallant attempt at poultry farming at the start. It is curious to observe the close affinity that somehow seems to exist between the townsman-turned-farmer and the hen. Disillusionment soon follows . . .' Thereafter, the Cudworth cultivators turned to soft fruit, which made more money, despite the fact that the estate was over three miles from the nearest station and was surrounded by game preserves, which meant that 'every row of strawberries and every individual currant bush has to be closely netted'.[9]

The impulse to purchase such properties must have been encouraged by the books which were published on farming, gardening and fruit growing, it being apparently as vital to write about the subject as to practise it. A characteristic offering was issued by the simple-life publisher A.C. Fifield, under the title 'The Cottage Farm Series', appearing between 1906 and 1909. According to the publisher's note, the series was meant 'for those who dream of "a cottage and bit of land some day" ', and would consist of 'simply and honestly told stories of actual attempts to live on a small holding'. 'Whatever the present practical value of these stories,' Fifield added, 'I believe a useful purpose is served nowadays by stimulating the feeling of country life and such books undoubtedly feed the fancy.' The first of the little booklets was Harriet Martineau's account *My Farm of Two Acres*, originally published in 1859–60, and the second *Fork and Spade Husbandry* by John Sillett, Suffolk draper turned smallholder, originally issued in 1848. Then came F.E. Green's *How I Work My Small Farm*, the first contemporary account. The cover showed a picture of the author wearing a smock-frock.

Green's account is a mixture of the descriptive and the financial. He gives his accounts in detail, showing that the capital outlay on the property of sixteen acres came to £865 14s, to include land, buildings and stock. From a year's expenditure and income it may be seen that the dairy cows cost some £50 and brought in £132, the bees made a profit of exactly £8 10s and the pigs just over £9. Green evidently had an unpleasant experience with chickens; he wrote of their 'fateful kind of glamour' and the 'sporadic disease commonly known as hen fever'. Altogether, with some £34 spent on outside labour, the little farm's turnover of £219 yielded a net income of £47 10s 3d for the year. This was less than a pound a week – a low industrial income – to spend on household goods, fuel and recreation.

But what was this to the delights of country life, as 'milk pail in hand I walk down to the cowshed when the dew of the early morn casts its crystal beauty on every blade of grass and every leaf on the hedgerow' and where 'beehives stand at the foot of the fruit garden of black currants, between the row of standard damson trees'? But he issued a warning to:

> those delightful city folk who expect to find the conditions of country life sympathetic to the realisation of leading a simple life, that simplicity is as rare a quality in Arcadia as it is in the crowded market place. The business of conducting a small farm is very complex. One has to be a bit of a carpenter, a bit of a carman, a bit of an engineer, a bit of a bricklayer, a bit of a biologist, a bit of a botanist, a bit of a veterinary surgeon. . .[10]

The fourth booklet in the 'Cottage Farm Series' was *The Simple*

William Morris, bas-relief portrait by George Jack at Kelmscott, Oxfordshire

Conical tiled well in the garden of Red House, Bexley, Kent, designed by Philip Webb for William Morris

Kelmscott Manor (rear view), William Morris's house in Oxfordshire

John Ruskin, portrayed by Linley Sambourne in a cartoon published in *Punch*, 5 February 1876, depicting Ruskin's protest against the extension of a railway line through the Lake District, and his defence of all things pastoral

Edward Carpenter outside his home at Millthorpe, between Sheffield and Chesterfield. He is wearing a pair of the celebrated Indian-style sandals of his own making, and the jacket, knickerbockers, cravat and cummerbund of his own design

Kate Greenaway illustration for Browning's *Pied Piper of Hamelin*, 1888, showing an imagined English May scene

'At the Cottage Door,' from *Birket Foster's Pictures of English Landscape*, 1863, wood engraving by the Brothers Dalziel

'On Ide Hill', a water-colour by Helen Allingham, published in *Happy England,* 1903, a collection of paintings of country cottages and their inhabitants

Bas-relief over doorway of Lopping Hall, Loughton, Essex, depicting villagers exercising their traditional rights to lop branches for firewood in Epping Forest, between Martinmas and St George's Day

Mary Neal's Esperance Girls' Folk Dance team

A country couple at Hampton Lucy, Warwickshire in 1890 — probably posed for the sake of picturesqueness

Nellie Shaw, original Whiteway colonist and chronicler

Arnold Eiloart, one of the original settlers at Whiteway, wearing knickerbockers and sandals without socks, which so shocked the local people

Fels Fruit Farm, Mayland, Essex. Packing cos lettuce for dispatch to Covent Garden market, 1908

The unemployed on the land: workers at the Salvation Army's Farm Colony, Hadleigh, Essex

Starnthwaite Mill, Cumbria, site of the Home Colonisation Society's farm colony for unemployed city workers

Farmhouse at Whiteway Colony, Gloucestershire, where the first colonists lived

Hand-spinning and weaving craft revival at Winterslow, Wiltshire

Sidney Barnsley

Sidney Barnsley's house at Sapperton, Gloucestershire

Munstead Wood, house near Godalming designed by Edwin Lutyens for Gertrude Jekyll

Terracotta panel from Watts Memorial Chapel, Compton, Surrey, designed by Mrs G. F. Watts and made by Compton villagers. It was from the work on the Chapel that the Compton Potteries developed

Half-timbered Cheshire-style cottages built c. 1890 by W. H. Lever for workers at Port Sunlight soap factory in the Wirral

Early cultivation on a smallholding off Nevells Road, Letchworth Garden City

Life on Four Acres (1906) by F.A. Morton. Fred Morton was a young London clerk who had bought 'four acres of derelict clay land' in Essex and started to build himself a little cabin and live the simple life. In his book he described his original high hopes of 'dispensing with commercialism altogether, of making my own clothes from flax, of expressing illuminating oil from poppy seeds, and so forth', and his intention of sleeping out-of-doors in all weathers. In practice, he found it hard. The nights were damp or frosty, the ground cold and clayey. He had unhappy experiences with live-stock, as when one of the goats upset a beehive and never recovered from the stings, or when a donkey ruined his cabbage field, and he was lucky to finish the first season with 'a superabundance of parsnips', some small potatoes and a few dried broad beans to see him through the winter. But despite the many disasters, Morton's account was not discouraging. His spirit, as much as his subject, made his little book a best-seller of its kind. 'If something untoward occurs today,' he wrote, '– the cattle eat some promising crop or the crows take toll of the chickens – the promise of the morrow is yet entrancing. A dull rainy day is succeeded by a sunlit morn, and my spirits overflow.'[11] According to his publisher, Morton's work provoked letters of appreciation from hundreds of 'jaded and almost hopeless city folk', and a sequel was demanded. *Winning a Living on Four Acres* by Fred Morton appeared in 1909; in it our hero confessed that he was beginning to learn something about cultiva-tion, and stated confidently: 'My whole thoughts nowadays have as their basis the belief that country life is the only rational one.'

This theme was constantly before the reading public, nourishing their dreams of escape. A final representative example is taken from Tickner Edwardes's *The Lore of the Honey Bee* (1908) whose last chapter deals with 'Bee-Keeping and the Simple Life'. Here a bee-keeper, looking every inch a countryman with keen grey eyes and honest, sun-browned face, relates his history to his visitor:

He was a Londoner – he told me – at least that was his fate half a dozen years ago – a City clerk as pale as the ledger leaves that fluttered through his fingers from nine to six of the working day. And at home – in a dreary desert of house-tops called Nunhead . . . his sisters sewed for a living as white-faced as he. But one day, in an old second-hand bookshop, he lit upon a threepenny treasure – a book on the management of bees. He read it as his train crawled homeward on a stifling, freezing, fog-bound winter's night; and there and then, in the mean dirty cattle-box of a third–class carriage, in fancy the bee–garden was inaugurated, that has since developed into all I saw around me on that brave morning in June.

It took a long time, but at last:

> there came a day when the three of them shook the dust of Nunhead from their feet and took possession of the little tumble-down cottage with its bare half-acre of neglected ground. Well, those were hard times to begin with – he said, with an unaccountable relish in the recollection – but look now, how all has changed! He waved a triumphant, proudly proprietary arm around him. The cottage was sound and well-furnished throughout. The three or four hives with which he had started his business had multiplied into sixty or seventy, all made by his own hands.

Financially, profits averaged £2 per hive per year, which:

> was not a great deal, but there were only three of them, and their wants were simple. Their greatest needs – fresh air, peace and quiet, the healthful life of the country – these were to be had for nothing at all. And as for clothes – you never know, until you give over trying to keep up appearances, how very little appearances count in the world. At any rate, for them, the whole thing was a complete success . . . here was he, getting peace and plenty from half an acre; and as for the girls, they did nothing but laugh and sing all day long.[12]

With such an image before one, who would not dream of escaping from the city to a life on the land?

8

Farm Colonies

It was not long before the belief in the beneficial effects of tilling the soil was applied to that most acute urban problem – unemployment. In October 1894 a conference was convened at Holborn Town Hall in London under the title 'Land, Co-Operation and the Unemployed'. It was based on two contemporary observations: first, that 'in the last two decades about two million acres of English land have passed from arable use into the condition of permanent pasture', while the number of agricultural workers had dropped significantly. At the same time, far from the displaced labourers finding abundant employment in industry, it was evident that in the cities 'a large and to all appearances a growing number of workers are unable to secure constant employment and their physique and industrial character deteriorate under the ineffectual struggle for a decent maintenance'.[1]

'The concurrence of these two phenomena of unused land and unused labour-power,' continued the report of the conference, 'can scarcely fail to suggest the practical question: "how far is it possible to place this superfluous labour upon the vacant or half-cultivated land under such conditions as to make the land yield its increase and support the labourers and their families in decency and comfort?" '

This was not a rhetorical question. Indeed, the conference had been called to discuss and evaluate the various land resettlement schemes already in operation or plan. Seven years earlier the 1887 Mansion House Inquiry into the Condition of the Unemployed had set up a sub-committee on agricultural colonies as a possible contribution to improving the situation of those out of work. The most popular solution with the authorities was emigration overseas, but this was not the sovereign cure and there were those like Mr and Mrs George Lansbury who returned disillusioned after trying to find work in Australia. A remedy which kept people in Britain was a new and largely untried idea.

Among those who took up the colony idea was the Rev. Herbert Mills who, inspired by his discovery that the existing workhouse system was costly, degrading and ineffective in relieving poverty,[2] in 1892 launched the Home Colonisation Society with the object of establishing farm colonies in rural areas for volunteer workers from the ranks of the cities' unemployed. In place of wages, colonists would receive 'a rent-free house, three good meals supplied daily in the dining hall of the Society, a suit of clothing annually, education for the children and an allotment of land to each family consisting at first of one third of an acre, with lessons in the arts of bee-keeping, mushroom culture, basket-making, mat-making and various handicrafts'.[3] The rest of the land would be cultivated communally for self-sufficiency, and the colony would be internally self-governing. In theory nothing but the initial capital was required.

The first such colony was set up the same year at Starnthwaite near to Mills's home in the Lake District. Consisting of 130 acres of farmland and peatbog, it was intended as a model for the future, a means of eradicating unemployment and its consequences, 'crime, unbelief and prostitution'. When Mills reported to the Holborn Conference two years later, he said Starnthwaite had thirty residents, producing bacon, eggs, butter, peat moss, vegetables, milk and meat. He told the audience proudly, 'We have woven our own cloth and made our own clothing and built a new house and produced our own peat fuel.'[4] A water-wheel enabled them to grind grain and drive a circular saw. The colonists worked a normal eight-hour day and received, in addition to board and lodging, spending money of 2s 6d per week.

In fact, things had hardly gone so smoothly. Early in 1892 Mills had issued an invitation to the 'steady and industrious' out of work to join him in the new venture, promising 'we shall all live on the proceeds . . . and all sit down at the same table'.[5] The first of the many keen applicants were two young political activists who had led a protest on behalf of London's workless and were unlikely to obtain jobs again. They were joined by others from the Manchester region who were also active in labour matters, and by a lady graduate, Enid Stacy, whom Mills later alleged had falsely pretended to be destitute in order to be admitted to Starnthwaite.[6]

The main problem seems to have been Mills's volatile personality and lack of managerial experience. When criticized by the colonists, who were anxious for the experiment to succeed, he flew into a rage, declaring himself 'absolute master' and ordering them to do as they were told. The colonists, who believed they were being offered not just a chance to work but a share in the decisions as well, rebelled at this and, receiving no concessions from Mills, took their case to his Home Colonisation trustees. Mills responded with demands that all Starnthwaite residents sign a contract agreeing to his authority; those who refused to sign were immediately expelled. Demonstrating a strong sense of solidarity and organizing skills learnt in urban conditions, the colonists fought back, refusing to leave, although Mills cut off their food supplies. On 12 April 1893 he brought in the law and a group of hired roughs, who forcibly evicted the rebel colonists. Despite a protest meeting in Kendal and support from many quarters, they were unable to return to Starnthwaite. They were understandably bitter; as their foreman Dan Irving wrote: 'We claim that we have been misled and unfairly treated; having been drawn into this place in the belief that it was a commune, whereas it is an outdoor workhouse conducted on more arbitrary lines than any known to bumbledom.'[7]

The publicity they had generated, however, effectively undermined Mills's position, and the farm never recovered. In 1900 Starnthwaite was taken over by the English Land Colonisation Scheme, which offered no promises of democracy, but simply a rural training centre for men and boys decanted from the workhouse, with the object of teaching them 'self-respect and self-support, by the healthful influences of a simple country home with varied and interesting labour on the land, combined with a pleasant social life and a wise and loving discipline'.[8] This was a form of cheap labour the unemployed knew well, it being frequently made a condition for receiving relief and/or being recommended for passage-paid emigration schemes. In the 1980s Starnthwaite is still in similar use, as a home for young delinquents.

The rising militancy of the unemployed, illustrated in the Starnthwaite episode, was one reason why their plight aroused such concern, for in the late 1880s labour agitation led to protest marches and demonstrations in all the big cities – most alarmingly in London's Trafalgar Square, where in 1888 police and demonstrators joined battle, leading to the death of one young worker and the breaking of windows in Pall Mall clubs. The authorities responded by banning demonstrations from central London, so that the workless could gather no nearer the centres of power than Tower Hill. Both the statutory and charitable relief services tended to be harsh towards those capable of work but unable to find jobs, whom they deemed idle and undeserving. But such labels were not solutions.

One difficulty was that little was known or understood about the size and shape of the problem, or its causation; surveys and analyses of destitution were only just beginning. Perhaps because the urban poor were numerous and demanding, it was widely held that urban conditions created a 'demoralized residuum' who had succumbed to drink and were unlikely ever to work again. Another factor was held to be the influx into the cities of healthy young countrymen, who competed for jobs with weaker, city-bred workers. Then there was the question of remedies. There were those who favoured supervised, personal charity and those who preferred state intervention; those who advocated training in thrift and those who believed in public insurance; those who wanted to stop the poor from breeding and those who wanted to remove the surplus by emigration; those who wanted the Poor Law applied more rigorously and those who wanted it abolished altogether. The poor, by and large, were not asked for their opinion, but through their unions and friendly societies their demands were for steady work and higher wages to enable them to avoid having to ask for charity.

The religious element was naturally forward in most of these responses to the urban socio-economic situation in the late Victorian period. Many efforts to relieve or redeem the plight of the poor were directly inspired by piety – and one of the largest and most enduring was the Salvation Army, founded in the late 1870s on the basis of William Booth's evangelical conviction that the souls of the urban proletariat desperately needed saving for Christ. The Army concentrated its efforts on the lumpen portion of the population – the 'submerged tenth' in Booth's words. In 1890 he published his celebrated book *In Darkest England and the Way Out,* on the question of destitution and its remedy, for which he proposed a three-tier colony system: a city colony or refuge to collect recruits; a farm colony for retraining; and an overseas colony for eventual settlement. These ideas were not new, but Booth's proselytizing zeal and ability to attract support and funds were. In keeping with the authoritarian approach manifested in the quasi-military structures of his 'church', Booth explicitly rejected idealistic notions regarding farm colonies such as those being floated by Herbert Mills. He explained, citing no evidence, that 'broadly speaking your experimental communities fail because your Utopias all start upon the basis of equality and government by the vote of the majority'. Sooner or later, this meant that 'Utopia goes smash'. Booth added firmly: 'I shall avoid that rock'.[9] In his colonies respect and obedience were to be the rule.

At the end of his book was a full-colour pull-out chart depicting in graphic terms the comprehensive merits of his scheme. From a turbulent sea at the bottom of the picture tossing with the evils of homelessness, starvation, imprisonment, drunkenness, beggary and brothels, thousands of drowning souls are being rescued by the officers of the Salvation Army. The lighthouse represents the City Colony, to which these persons are taken and offered temporary shelter and training. They are then sent to the broad and leafy Farm Colony, occupying the central place on the page, there to work, according to the legend, in its 'Villages, Co-Operative Farms, Mills and Factories . . . far away from the neighbourhood of the public-house'. From 'Whitechapel-by-the-Sea' and other nearby ports, the rescued proceed to the Colony Across the Sea, pictured somewhat remotely on the edge of the chart but promising 'on the one hand, plenty of work, and on the other, abundance of food'.[10]

Within four months of launching its appeal, the Army had collected £100,000 towards its rescue mission. The money was spent on opening depots and relief stations in the cities and on purchasing a farm at Hadleigh near Southend in Essex. In fact the site consisted of three farms, then untenanted, with a total of 3,000 acres; later a tenth of this was sub-let to a local farmer. Possession was taken in May 1891, as a plaque commemorated:

THE SALVATION ARMY
DARKEST ENGLAND
The Castle and Park Farms with other
properties have been purchased by
General William Booth for the establishment
of the first Farm Colony and the
Elimination of the Submerged Tenth. [11]

Within a year there were over 300 colonists at Hadleigh, well away from public houses and other temptations, and all working busily in its fields, workshops and brickworks. The Army's sense of mission and determination meant that it did not flounder or fail in its immediate purpose, that of removing men from the city and setting them to work on the land. Visitors were many and most were impressed.

By 1905 the government was sufficiently interested in rural resettlement schemes to commission Rider Haggard to undertake a survey on its behalf. He found Hadleigh in a flourishing state despite some financial difficulties relating to under-capitalization. In his report he described:

> . . . the Hadleigh Colony with its 100 acres of fruit trees, its upland and marsh pastures, its brickworks and chicken farms and its market garden, from which Colony the total receipts for 1904 amounted, I am informed, to over £33,000.
> . . .now the population, including the Salvation Army officials and their families and certain employees directly associated with the undertaking, number over 500 souls . . . At the time of my visit there were employed on the Colony a further 200 persons, who had been sent hither by the Mansion House Relief Fund Committee. [12]

There was an adjoining settlement for alcoholics, also run by the Army.

The long-term residents at Hadleigh were divided into two classes, upper and lower, all newcomers starting on the lower rung which, not unlike the workhouse most were trying to avoid, was based on the notion of desert rather than need. Haggard explained the system: 'A man is raised in his grade if he works well and satisfactorily and his general character and conduct are proved to be good. If he is raised to this higher class dormitory he is also raised to a higher class dietary and receives food of rather better quality and more ample in quantity.'[13]

The purpose of Hadleigh Farm Colony was to teach the inmates the rudiments of agriculture to prepare them for emigration, and at the time of Haggard's visit it contained a poultry farm with 2,500 birds, a herd of 250 pigs and a market garden based in glasshouses where mint, tomatoes, lettuce, rhubarb and flowers were grown for sale. There was also a small herd of cows for milk and a fifteen-acre potato field. A small number of allotments were available to residents for growing their own produce to supplement the average wage of around three shillings a week. It is not clear whether the colony took only single men, for Haggard also mentions the existence of cottages on the estate and a colony school, which took most, but not all, of its pupils from the local village; the evidence, however, indicates that it was almost exclusively a 'bachelor' colony, and its purpose essentially transitional.

Commenting on the 'extraordinary results which can be attained by wretched men working on land which the ordinary agriculturalist would call wretched', Haggard found the farming yield impressive and the human reclamation scarcely less so. At the end of his report he wrote:

> It is a remarkable fact that there are no policemen on duty at Hadleigh Colony as, notwithstanding the rough nature of many of the inhabitants, they are not needed here. Indeed three years have passed since a drunk and disorderly case against any colonist was brought before the magistrates. This immunity from crime doubtless arises from the kind but strict discipline practised in the Colony, the moral tone which has grown up there, and from the circumstance that temperance is enforced. If by chance a man is found to be drunk he is warned, and should he repeat his offence he is sent off the place. There is practically no need for any other form of punishment.[14]

What the colonists thought of the strict discipline and enforced

sobriety is not recorded. They knew their place. Haggard claimed
to have talked with some of the men; his 'specimen conversation'
with one is given as follows:

Q. How long have you been here?
A. Four and a half years, sir.
Q. What were you before you came?
A. Sanitary engineer.
Q. Went astray, I suppose?
A. Yes.
Q. Not astray now? Doing all right?
A. Yes.
Q. You are superintendent of the laundry?
A. Yes.[15]

No doubt most of the men tolerated the rigours of the system in the
hope of being chosen for a promising emigration scheme. Booth,
on the other hand, thought he had found the answer. He pressed for
the state to establish a national scheme, staffed by the Army, to
achieve the objective set out in the title of a pamphlet he issued in
1904: *The Vagrant and the Unemployable; a Proposal for the Extension of
the Land and Industrial Colony System, whereby Vagrants may be
detained under suitable conditions and compelled to work.*

   A less ferocious type of Farm Colony was that established by the
Poor Law Guardians from Poplar in East London at Laindon in
Essex. Workhouse farms were common in rural areas, as W.H.
Roberts reported to the Holborn Town Hall conference. The one he
managed at Wyke near Winchester cultivated a mere seven acres,
producing potatoes and other vegetables for the inmates'
consumption, and keeping some pigs, but the Craiglockart farm in
Scotland had 100 acres of land and kept a dairy herd as well as large
vegetable fields.[16] The Laindon experiment was intended as an
alternative not an addition to the main establishment, and it came
about after several schemes had been canvassed by the East London
Poor Law unions during the 1890s as those seeking relief grew in
number and jobs remained unavailable to most of them. The Poplar
Guardians under George Lansbury's leadership put forward the
scheme for a farm, which would provide able men with productive
work at virtually no extra cost and at the same time teach them

some skills which might enable them to find jobs in healthier areas.

There was opposition to the plan, on the grounds that it fell outside the usual forms of workhouse relief and might increase expenditure and hence the local poor rate. On the other hand, unemployment was severe and many different remedial schemes were being proposed, at all levels. Under the Unemployed Workmen Act of 1905, the Central (Unemployed) Body (C.U.B.) was set up to encompass various options including direct works, farm colonies, assisted emigration and labour exchanges – which in theory were complementary but which in practice competed for political and financial support. Owing to an imminent election, the C.U.B. served mainly as a useful arena for social reformers to pursue their own ideas. Thus William Beveridge later described himself and Lansbury as 'the two wild young men of the C.U.B., he urging "back to the land" and I urging labour exchanges; the Minister in charge of us at the time. . . thought us both equally foolish'.[17]

Lansbury had a valuable ally however in the person of Joseph Fels, the benevolent capitalist who was already involved in the Mayland Small Holdings scheme in Essex. Lansbury was at first suspicious of this 'rich American' but was soon converted; as he later wrote, listening to Fels was 'like listening to one who has seen a great light'. To him, 'the freeing of land did not mean simply more potatoes or more strawberries . . . it represented the means by which the whole human race could be made free . . .'[18] Together Lansbury and Fels made a formidable team, Lansbury applying the political pressure, Fels the cash. The Poplar Guardians were thus enabled to set up a farm colony without raising the rates. Fels bought Sumpners Farm at Laindon, near Basildon, and leased it to the Guardians at a peppercorn rent. Possession was taken on 5 March 1904 and 200 Poplar men set to getting the land in good condition, erecting dormitories, etc. Their families were maintained at home while they were at Laindon, and the hope was that eventually some at least could be settled on the land permanently.

At the farm, fruit growing and market gardening were the main activities; Lansbury's biographer wrote of '100 acres of waste land being turned into orchards and garden'.[19] A small reservoir was dug, and kitchens, dining hall and laundry built. Under workhouse regulations it was not possible for the men to be paid for their labour, and so Fels offered to provide sixpence a week in pocket money, together with newspapers, books, board games and even a piano. Such extravagances were condemned by many on the grounds that the high standard of relief would discourage men from seeking work.

According to Mrs Fels, 'the success of the Colony was immediately manifest to all except those who believed that the workhouse test was a foundation of the British Empire',[20] and as a result Lansbury and Fels decided to extend the experiment. They found Hollesley Bay, a much larger estate of 1,300 acres in Suffolk formerly used as an agricultural training college for the sons of gentlemen, which Fels purchased for £40,000 and offered on a similar interest-free basis to the Central Unemployed Body. Over 500 men without jobs from all over London were soon at work. The scheme was intended to go further than Laindon by providing for a certain number of families to be settled on the estate in cottages (again thanks to Fels's financial assistance) with the aim of eventually becoming smallholders. This derived from Lansbury's vision of farm colonies not simply as a novel form of poor relief but as communities where people could be trained for a new life and which would be models for the substitution of co-operative for capitalist production.[21]

Hollesley Bay, like Laindon and Hadleigh, was visited by a constant stream of visitors. One group, escorted round by Lansbury, included the Rev. Samuel Barnett, formerly of St Jude's, Whitechapel, who twenty years earlier had advocated 'training farms' run by London workhouses for men willing to work for six months on the land 'in the hope of one day being accepted as fixed tenants of some portion of the reclaimed land, or of being emigrated';[22] his wife Henrietta Barnett, later founder of Hampstead Garden Suburb, where so many back-to-the-land ideas flourished; and Lord Carrington, enlightened landowner who had transformed a farm on his estate into 1–3 acre smallholdings for agricultural labourers to cultivate in their spare time.[23]

According to Mrs Barnett, there were 335 residents at Hollesley Bay at the time of their visit,

each one of whom had a past worthy of respect, but who had

been beaten in his fight. Each had a home, some woman who cared for him, some child to call him father. Each had voluntarily accepted discipline, exile from his family and the hardships of a rough communal life because he had been beckoned by purpose, driven by memories of despair. We saw all their work, the 4325 trees they had planted, the 943 sheep, the 397 pigs, the 437 poultry, the 147 stock, the dairies, the fields, the nurseries, the plantations, the gardens. . .

We saw their work and wondered, for did we not know these men in East London? Had we not experience of their lounging ways, their idle habits, their derision of industry, their unrighteous acceptance of the position of the disinherited? What had worked the miracle? Just the gift of hope, plus enough food, clean air, organised labour – surely the birthrights of every man . . .[24]

Encouraged by this success, Lansbury and Fels were going ahead with a plan for another farm colony when it was abruptly aborted by the change of government in early 1906. The incoming president of the Local Government Board, John Burns, had no liking for farm colonies. He at once forbade the C.U.B. to have anything to do with permanent resettlement schemes, and relegated Hollesley Bay to a country annex taking the overflow from the London workhouses. This in fact was the situation when the farm was visited by the Barnetts and the Rev. Samuel's account is noticeably less ecstatic than his wife's:

> The present condition of the Colony constitutes almost a tragedy. It is used simply as a workhouse, receiving parties of men for a few weeks and returning them at the end of the period little better prepared for their self-support. While Mr John Burns pours scorn on the experiment, here are elements of a tragedy or a scandal which has surely gone on long enough.[25]

Before Burns struck, the farm superintendent at Hollesley Bay had reported that the men were quick and eager to learn and he had 'no hesitation in asserting my belief that, if the way were opened for the establishment of co-operative smallholdings, we can quite successfully train suitable London men for this purpose'. There were, he was sure, many such London men 'keen to adopt country life and earn their living on the land'; these could easily be 'successfully trained for country life' despite the doubts of those who feared that city-bred persons could never adapt to village ways.[26]

The same fate met the Laindon colony, which became a workhouse out-station where men spent a maximum of eight weeks in desultory labour in order to retain their right to relief; it was not unfairly termed 'Poplar's pauper farm' by a local newspaper in 1909.[27] In 1928 it was taken over by the L.C.C. and remained an institution until after World War II. The land is now occupied by Dunton Park caravan site.[28]

Hollesley Bay became a borstal, memorably described in Brendan Behan's *Borstal Boy*. Hadleigh survives, in a semi-derelict state. During its early years it was a thriving business, producing and selling vegetables, flowers and home-produced bricks. But farmers' unions and others complained of unfair competition and the Army agreed to restrict operations, so Hadleigh settled down into its basic role as a rehabilitation unit. Inmates who responded might be sent overseas, but many, according to the Salvation Army magazine, 'grew to love the quiet country and the Army's strong protection' and asked to be allowed to stay on the land and be employed at regular wages.[29] As time went on a number of cottages were built to accommodate these former colonists and their families and by 1910 the estate was well equipped with specialist departments. During the 1914–18 war it was a military convalescent home, and then, as unemployment rose again in the 1920s and '30s it resumed its function as a farm settlement for the workless, combined with a training scheme for young men selected for emigration. Gradually its welfare role withered and although still run as a farm, its main use today is as a holiday site for Army families, close to Southend.

As a solution to the problems of unemployment and urban poverty, farm colonies, conceived as a means of turning thousands of industrial casualties into sturdy smallholders at home and overseas, had a less than lasting impact. Nor can their failure be blamed wholly on John Burns. Structural unemployment such as that suffered in London from 1880 onwards could not be cured by means of these; dock labour organization for example and the regulation of sweated trades were more significant moves. Yet it was true that market gardening for London consumption was one of the relatively few profitable sectors of the agricultural industry, as virtually all the farming schemes discussed in these chapters recognized, so it was not altogether unreasonable to believe that some of those who scratched a living in Whitechapel might be retrained and successfully redeployed on an Essex smallholding. But even in the rural areas where men had agricultural skills, the high price of land and the British system of land tenure hindered all attempts to create more smallholdings; a national policy would have been required to establish a yeoman peasantry. In countries where such policies were carried out – France, Denmark, Ireland for example – the rate of migration to the urban areas was slowed and real links were maintained between industrial workers and the family holding. The process of urbanization was not reversed however, and in general workers already established in the cities did not flock back to the land except on holiday. In England the allotment movement, aiming to provide a small area of ground for every landless village family, did have some success in enabling some rural workers to stay on the land. But neither allotments nor farm colonies emptied the workhouses.

Even Joseph Fels came to admit, reluctantly, that philanthropy could not prevail against the tide of monopoly capitalism. 'Everyone knows now,' he said late in his life, 'that "back to the land" is impossible so long as the fundamental land monopoly continues, because there is no land available for use except under conditions which make its use unprofitable. The long struggle to open the gate of the industrial prisons has made this abundantly clear.'[30] The city retained its inmates.

Part III
Rustic Arts and Crafts

The Guild Workshops,
Campden.

The Old Silk Mill, Chipping Campden

9

Handwork and Husbandry

The third strand in the back-to-the-land movement was the revival of handcrafts – the hoped-for return to pre-industrial production processes, where every article was the result of individual skill and artistry. There grew up an accretion of related ideas – the fitness of design to function, the beauty of peasant art, the happiness of the hand-worker, the ugliness of machine-made products – which formed the ideological and aesthetic framework for the Arts and Crafts movement. Ruskin first popularized the equation between the ugliness of the modern world and the degeneration of craft skills, between hand production in the medieval period and the happiness of the craftsman. As traditional manual skills fell out of use, the machine came to be blamed for the social problems that arose with industrialism. This was soon established as an accepted 'fact' by those with artistic leanings.

The architectural profession was particularly predisposed to these ideas, perhaps because its art form, building, was by this date heavily dependent on mechanization. From Pugin and other mid-century architects the later generation acquired views on the relation of beauty to the 'honesty' of the means of production, and a fondness for medieval styles which at its height was quite over-whelming. William Morris began his career in an architect's office and when in 1861 the firm later known as Morris and Co. was launched, it was with the intention of supplying beauty in interior decoration through artistic and not mechanical processes. The first prospectus offered domestic and ecclesiastical clients the best in:

> Mural Decoration, either in Pictures or in Pattern Work, or merely in the arrangement of Colours . . . Carving generally, as applied to Architecture . . . Stained Glass . . . Metal Work in all its branches, including Jewellery . . . Furniture, either depending for its beauty on its own design, on the application of materials hitherto overlooked, or in conjunction with Figure and Pattern Painting. Under this head is included Embroidery of all kinds, Stamped Leather, and ornamental work in other such materials, besides every article necessary for domestic use. . .[1]

These were the arts that were most favoured by the new generation of professional craftsmen.

To begin with, there was no great stress on hand production in the Morris firm, since most items were unique commissions that could be produced no other way. When later fabrics, wallpapers and basic furniture were produced, involving standard repetition, machinery was employed where useful, Morris himself not sharing Ruskin's hatred of the beast and knowing that automation could lighten the operative's toil and permit the exercise of other, more creative skills. But high quality remained a Morris hallmark, which could often only be achieved by hand and this, together with Morris's personal preference for mastering a craft before designing for it, set an example and influence. Not only did Morris get covered in dye at Thomas Wardle's works; he also taught himself the techniques of tapestry weaving and, when immersed in printing, both designed new typefaces and insisted on cutting the blocks himself.

It was from this example of the master craftsman, fusing idealism and practicality, fine art and thorough workmanship, that the Arts and Crafts movement was born. Like Morris, several of the pioneers studied architecture before turning to decorative art. The career of A.H. Mackmurdo is illustrative. The son of a wealthy chemical manufacturer whose fortune was founded on the new industrial processes so execrated by the arts and crafts people, at the age of eighteen Mackmurdo entered the office of the architect James Brookes, a Gothic revivalist who, his pupil wrote, 'was essentially a craftsman . . . (with) the sense that a craftsman must do every bit of work with his own hand . . . every detail to door hinge and prayer-book marker'.[2] Mackmurdo later accompanied Ruskin to France and Italy, sketching from nature and architecture; on his return he studied the craft techniques of carving, metalwork, embroidery and textile printing. In 1882 he began a new venture. 'I gathered round me,' he wrote, 'a number of artists and craftsmen who could supply all that was required for the decorations, furnishing and equipment of a house.'[3] This group was formally constituted as the Century Guild, and produced a range of original designs, some shown at the Liverpool International Exhibition in 1886, and gaining a number of commissions such as the decorations at Pownall Hall, Cheshire, before it disbanded in 1888.

It was as a discussion group rather than as a workshop that the Art Workers' Guild (its name indicative of the new emphasis) was founded in 1884, largely drawn from the architectural profession. Among the activities at its weekly meetings were demonstrations of newly discovered crafts. The architect James Maclaren, touring the country west of Birmingham to become acquainted with the vernacular building style of a region in which he had a commission, met Philip Clissett, a traditional chairmaker living in Bosbury, a Herefordshire village, who was described as 'a real survival of village industry, an old man who made rush-bottomed chairs with no other apparatus than his cottage oven for bending the wood'.[4] Maclaren made some sketches of slightly more elegant chairs and asked Clissett to make a few. The results were taken back to London to show the Art Workers' Guild, which promptly ordered a full set for its new meeting room. Having been several times re-seated, the Clissett chairs are still in use there.

From the Art Workers' Guild arose the Arts and Crafts Exhibition Society, which held its first show in London in 1888. The little catalogue contained short pieces on each of the crafts represented, and the outlook that informed them. That on ceramics describes in a high-sounding manner how man's first needs in domestic life, 'his first efforts at civilization came from Mother Earth, whose son he believed himself to be and his ashes or his bones returned to Earth enshrined in the fictile vases he created from their common clay . . . begun in the simplest fashion, fashioned by the simplest means, created from the commonest materials . . .' It ends with the words: 'to truly foster and forward the art the craftsman and the artist should where possible be united, at or least should work in common'.[5]

In pursuit of this last aim, the executor of each piece was named in the exhibition catalogue alongside the designer. This innovation would not, Morris pointed out, alter the economic structure through which the workmen, as a class, were exploited, but at least it acknowledged their contribution. A similar gap between creation and use was bemoaned by W.A.S. Benson writing on metalwork: 'the existing dissociation of the producing craftsman from the consumer is an evil for the arts', he asserted, citing the rise of the great department stores as a threat to good workmanship: 'the position of the village smith plying his calling in face of his customers might not suit every craft, but the services of the middleman are dearly bought'. He complained that the mass production of metalwork meant that 'the more ordinary wares have all life and feeling taken out of them by mechanical finish, an abrasive process being employed to remove every sign of tool marks . . .'[6]

Walter Crane, one of the founder members of the Arts and Crafts Exhibition Society, always insisted that 'the true work and basis of all arts lies in the handicrafts', while an equally influential figure, W.R. Lethaby, wrote 'a work of art is first of all a well-made thing'. Traditional crafts were vanishing: potters who could throw on the wheel were, it was claimed, a dying breed, along with hand weavers and spinners – but in the end, 'handwork is essential to the maintenance of quality'.[7] These principles were applied when the new Central School of Arts and Crafts was opened in 1896. Lethaby was joint principal and insisted that the students be drawn from the trades and be taught by practising designers in five main workshops: jewellery and metalwork; furniture and woodwork; dress design and embroidery; stained glass; book-binding and printing. He aimed to produce master-workmen, who were frequently and profitably recruited by manufacturers as designers rather than craftsmen. For within a few years the arts and crafts look had become so fashionable that it was produced in bulk by commercial firms, much to the fury of those making the genuine article.

In their enthusiasm for manual skill and their nostalgia for the pre-industrial workshop where there was 'no one who directs or merely finances what he cannot practise',[8] arts and crafts adherents sometimes over-emphasized their opposition to machinery. It was fashionable to dismiss machine-made goods as inferior, while the very smoothness and regularity which earlier generations of craftsmen and cabinet makers had striven for was rejected as lifeless and meretricious. Among the enlightened, rough homespun fabrics, furniture with the joins showing and handpainted pottery were preferred, the bumps and imperfections imparting a higher value to the article. The actual practitioners were usually less purist. Like Morris, they recognized that the enemy was not the machine itself, but the industrial and commercial pressures which led to men spending 'all their lives cutting mortise joints . . . or painting strips of pattern border – all one pattern, all day long, every day for years'.[9] Most arts and crafts workers welcomed machines which eliminated 'drudgery', such as power saws, and did not insist that their metals be mined and smelted by pre-industrial methods. For the finished product, however, manual skill was paramount.

If craftwork was the first principle, country living was the second. This is not self-evident: for all the castigation of the industrial system, most arts and crafts work was produced in the cities, particularly in London and Birmingham. The latter was the reputed source of all that the movement sought to banish in the way of cheap and nasty decorative ware, but as a manufacturing centre, it possessed the craft base necessary to sustain and benefit from new ideas and teachings from the school of art and a number of informal guilds and groups. In terms of its location, organization and membership the arts and crafts movement was predominantly urban.

But it saw itself as anti-urban, even pastoral – qualities which are conveyed in its iconography. The preceding generation of artists had looked back to an imagined medieval world; while not neglecting the Middle Ages, arts and craftsmen depicted timeless natural scenes and rustic images. The intention was not always archaic, for flowers and birds, which formed the basis of much arts and crafts design, do not change with the centuries; it is rather the absence of anything which could be said to reflect contemporary themes. Fresh daisies and buttercups adorned the tiles around the cast-iron fireplace, or the inlaid panels on the mechanical pianola; in mansion flats luxuriant leaves simulated the outdoor world in embroidered hangings or wallpapers. At Pownall Hall the front door had hinges of branching ironwork like bunched poppy-heads, while sunflowers in terracotta relief sprouted on the sides of School Board buildings. Pictorially, the Arts and Crafts movement is epitomized in the drawings of Kate Greenaway, with demure country maids in bonnets and bows, set in neat gardens or rustic interiors, or in the graphic work of Walter Crane, where slim girls in flowing garments dance over windy meadows, symbolizing spring and socialism. Thus the Arts and Crafts movement averted its eyes from the world it lived in.

For Ruskin had said that industry, by turning men into dehuman-ized extensions of the machine, prevented the achievement of good art. Morris had proclaimed that the present social and economic system would have to be abolished for beauty to be produced. Abolition, or even reform, of the existing system meant getting rid of the cities and the industrial and commercial conditions they had spawned. Art which aspired to the ideals of Ruskin and Morris could hardly be expected to embrace these conditions. In Crane's words, the Arts and Crafts movement was 'a revolt against the so-called industrial progress which provides shoddy ware, the cheapness of which is paid for by the lives of their producers and the degradation of their users'.[10] The country was clearly the only place in which the new art could flourish.

When William Morris thought of moving his firm from its cramped central London premises, he and William De Morgan toured possible sites in southern England,[11] eventually choosing a weather-boarded mill building on the Wandle at Merton in Surrey, on the south suburban edge of London. Here, from 1881, Morris employees produced printed chintz, woven silk, carpets, tapestries, tiles and stained glass. The water of the Wandle was used to wash the yarns, and a contemporary painting shows a very pastoral scene with ducks gliding on the river in front of the mill.[12] It is now part of an extremely untidy mixed industrial area.

A few years later, when Morris was active in the socialist cause, he chaired a Hammersmith branch meeting of the Socialist League at which two important figures were to meet. The speaker was Edward Carpenter, and among his audience was a young man from Cambridge, the artistically inclined Charles Robert Ashbee. Afterwards they were both invited to supper at Morris's house.

Three months later Ashbee was visiting Carpenter at Millthorpe. His aesthetic sense was somewhat dismayed at the ugly house his hero had had built for himself, but Carpenter told him that social conditions left little time for such considerations – what with 'black Chesterfield on the one hand and black Sheffield on the other'.[13] Ashbee visited John Furniss's community at Totley and came away inspired but sad at the lack of art in their lives; he began to dream of bringing beauty into the lives of working people. Encouraged by Carpenter – 'there is great work to be done and so few to do it' – he went to live at Toynbee Hall, the Rev. Samuel Barnett's slum settlement in Whitechapel, while training as an architect.

Lecturing to groups such as those working at the giant gasworks at Beckton on the edge of the river, Ashbee made the acquaintance of the British Working Man, as he put it. His class on Ruskin at Toynbee Hall proved popular, soon moving from study to practice; together the group painted a mural decoration of a ship – to illustrate the dual meaning of craft – and tried their hands at carving, modelling and plasterwork. Fired with enthusiasm and a discreet desire for closer comradeship with the more 'homogenic' of his young pupils, Ashbee decided to establish his class independently of Toynbee Hall, to put his larger ideas into practice.

The Guild and School of Handicraft, inaugurated in June 1888, had obvious affinities with other ventures, and Ashbee solicited the older generation's support. Burne-Jones and Holman Hunt were sympathetic to the young man with ideals of brotherhood, but Morris responded with 'a good deal of cold water', saying the idea was useless. 'I could not exchange a single argument with him,' wrote Ashbee after his visit on 4 December 1887, 'till I granted his whole position as a socialist, and then said, "Look you, I am going to forge a weapon with you, and thus I too work with you in the overthrow of society . . ." Morris replied: "The weapon is too small to be of value." '[14] Nevertheless, Ashbee raised funds and found premises. The members of the Guild were drawn from the surrounding community and the aim was summed up by Ashbee in 1900: 'We at Essex House have for the last 12 years or so been engaged in the making of things that we consider the public ought to want, provided meanwhile that the man that makes them is the happier in their making.'[15]

To start with there were three craftsmen: cabinet maker C.V. Adams and metalworkers J. Pearson and J. Williams. Six more joined in 1889–90 and by the end of ten years there were fifteen members, engaged in both production and teaching. The original wood and metal shops were extended into blacksmithing, enamelling, silversmithing and engraving, and evening classes were run for apprentices, other workmen and teachers in schools where handcrafts were on the curriculum. After 1895 the L.C.C. stopped sending such students to the classes and a valuable source of income came to an end.

The commercial work of the Guild depended to a large extent on fittings and furniture for the houses Ashbee designed in his architectural practice, and commissions from other architects and patrons. Their major triumph was the furnishing of a palace in Darmstadt designed by Baillie Scott for the Grand Duke of Hesse. The profits from the work do not appear to have been large, but were shared among the Guild members, workers also being paid for their labour. During the 1880s the radicalism of the labour movement amid recessionary cycles had given rise to a number of worker-co-operatives, providing the Guild with knowledge on which to build; its rules were drawn up by C.V. Adams, founder-member and committed trade unionist, and throughout its life the Guild was strengthened by the industrial experience of its workers. In 1898 the co-operative was reconstituted as a limited company to protect members from personal liability.

In 1891 the Guild moved into its own premises, a handsome Georgian building in the Mile End Road called Essex House, where its activities blossomed. As important as the craftwork was the social side of the Guild which flourished outside working hours. There were evening lectures delivered by artistic luminaries and weekly Guild suppers every Wednesday followed by folk songs and conviviality. There were dramatic productions of Jacobean plays, particularly those set in the City among apprentices and merchants, and – most importantly to the members – a Guild sports club with its own blazer in accordance with local custom.

The majority of Guild members were selected by Ashbee on the

basis of direct empathy rather than formal application, and for him
the most rewarding times were those spent on holiday with the lads.
He and his wife Janet rented a series of cottages where the cockney
craftsmen were introduced to the country and in the summer
Ashbee took a selected group on a river trip, rowing and swimming
by day, pitching camp in the evening and singing round the camp
fire – the epitome of outdoor, masculine comradeship. Such
pleasures were new and exhilarating to the young guildsmen.

Located as it was in Whitechapel, with its crowded tenements of
squalor and vice made notorious by the activities of Jack the Ripper,
the Guild of Handicraft was like an orchid in a cabbage patch. Its
name and its structure defied its surroundings, for the fraternity and
fair wages on which it was based could not have been further from
the sweated industries in courts and alleys all around. Ashbee saw
his Guild as a model of industrial reform: 'In our little microcosm at
Essex House,' he wrote, somewhat smugly, 'we practically have
for settlement all the leading problems of modern industry.' But he
did not mean to colonize the city from within. Instead he aimed at
removing the Guild to its proper home – the country. In the early
1890s a Guild offshoot was briefly established as a 'country centre'
at the newly-opened Abbotsholme School in Derbyshire, described
in Chapter 13. Eventually, in 1901, Ashbee decided that Chipping
Campden in the Cotswolds was the place for his Guild of Handicraft. There were those who argued forcefully in favour of
Letchworth Garden City, then being established, but the Ashbees
had visited Bourneville and found its newness uncomfortable.
Chipping Campden was a quiet, decayed market town, untouched
by the industrial revolution or anything later, with an old silk mill
for the Guild workshops and several empty houses for guildsmen's
residences. There was a wide main street lined with Cotswold stone
buildings, a medieval guildhall and market cross – an altogether
attractive setting for one of Ashbee's Elizabethan persuasion. He
saw Campden as the Guild's 'last Earthly Paradise'; heaven, he felt,
would seem very similar.[16]

Despite their country holidays, several of the guildsmen were not
in favour of leaving London. They were reluctant to leave family
and friends, fond of the bustle and activity, wary of the unknown.
The democratic nature of the Guild decreed, however, that it
should be a majority decision, and a party was taken down to

inspect the silk mill and the town before the votes were cast. Of the forty full members, thirty-three voted: twenty-two for Campden and eleven against. Ashbee rejoiced that 'the men themselves have decided that on the whole it is better to leave Babylon and go home to the land'.[17] 'Back to the land' was a phrase much heard at the time, he recalled later, adding: 'For those of us living in East London it had been neither a political tag nor an agricultural commonplace; it was a matter of necessity, instinct, life . . .' The Guild's country home, he concluded, was a definite protest against urban life: 'It was the great city we were out subconsciously to destroy.'[18]

The Guild of Handicraft moved to Campden in 1902. The dozen or so cabinet makers and woodcarvers had their workshop on the top floor of the Silk Mill, with some ten silversmiths making light fittings, tableware and church plate on the first floor, together with a small number of enamellers and about twelve jewellers. In an outbuilding three blacksmiths made ironwork screens, fire irons and gates, while in the adjoining powerhouse there were saws and planes for preparing wood. On the ground floor of the mill were the showroom, the general office, the Essex House Press (men and machines inherited from the Kelmscott Press in 1896 after Morris's death) and the drawing office. Ashbee appears to have designed all the Guild's products but the workmen were fully engaged in the artistic process through the high level of craft skill demanded. Commercial pressures were not intended to affect the execution of any work.

The Essex House traditions of sport and drama were maintained, and walking and cycling became popular, underlining the real change in lifestyle brought about by the move. Gardening also flourished as Guild members and their families settled into their new homes. A more ambitious project was the building of a swimming pool 150 feet long by 100 feet wide. This was opened in August 1903 with a summer gala for all Chipping Campden residents. Thus the self-exiled cockneys gained a new and pleasant life with no material loss. Craftsmen earned from 30s to 80s a week, while apprentices took home 10s – substantial wages in contemporary terms, and more or less guaranteed. By contrast, local wages were at a depressed rural level: the skilled stockman, the agricultural equivalent of the craftsman, earned only around £1 a week, while the general labourer was often on 2s 6d a day with a bonus only at harvest time. Poverty and anxiety were endemic.

Ashbee hoped to contribute to the revival of the rural community, and his sports and theatricals represented the reciprocal
intentions of the Guild towards the place in which it had settled. But
swimming pools and Shakespeare were all very well; more serious
needs, immediately apparent to the newcomers, were in basic areas
like housing, education and welfare. Bringing their experience of
urban conditions and industrial organization to the sleepy
Cotswold town, the Guild members were dismayed at the
condition of many of the local people. Charley Plunkett, fifty-year-
old polisher from the East End, at once started a 2d-a-week 'boot
club', a well-established urban expedient to help labouring families
meet one of their largest expenses. Archie Ramage, Glasgow-born
compositor, founded a local labour union and distributed Fabian
pamphlets to the Campden residents, for which he was denounced
by Lord Harrowby, who no doubt feared demands for better pay
from his employees and tenants. Ashbee, whose socialism was of
the romantic variety, set an example to the town's landlords by
restoring dilapidated cottages, and by providing the educational
resources he felt to be lacking in the district, which boasted a
grammar school for shopkeepers' sons and an elementary school for
the rest – neither offering, in his eyes, adequate training in the
'three Hs' of Hand, Heart and Head. He bought Elm Tree House,
an old malthouse in the High Street and converted it into the
Campden School of Arts and Crafts; this was formally opened in
December 1904 in the face of opposition from the town and with a
meagre grant from the county council.

As well as classes in carpentry, metalwork and other crafts, there
was training here in what the Ashbees considered neglected domestic crafts such as cookery and laundry, which were well attended by
the local women, a testament to their usefulness. Practical gardening was also taught, on small plots in the school's garden. It is a
measure of the rural decline of the time that such knowledge and
skills were sought from teachers and not from relatives and neighbours. In a paper on 'Country Schools of Arts and Crafts' Ashbee
wrote of prevailing social and economic conditions:

> What do people live on? What do they earn? What land have they
> that they can till? What is the family budget? What social ramifi-

cations are there with other grades of life? Is there a carpenter cousin, a sailor brother, a colonist away? We must look at the boys standing at the street corners and ask why they stand there and what we can do to stop it. We must ask at the same time why so many fields are covered with thistles and why the roofs of so many cottages are falling in. Any conscientious examination of local wants will quickly reveal what they are.[19]

So Ashbee set out to improve rural life. Not content just to live in the country, he wished to import art and culture. He also hoped to broaden horizons with intellectual discussion and debate, if the series of talks given at the School of Arts and Crafts in the winter of 1904–5 is anything to go by. The titles read like a litany of back-to-the-land themes, running through medievalism, early music, Pre-Raphaelite painting, William Morris, vernacular building styles and the Bourneville Village Trust. The Guild's metalshop foreman and founder-member W.A. White spoke on hammered brassware, while carver Alec Miller offered his own 'Notes on Craftsmanship from the writing of John Ruskin'. The 'Mr Adams' listed as giving a talk on 'The Garden City Movement' is surely Edward Carpenter's companion George Adams, who had moved to Letchworth to carry on the sandal-making business which had been started at Millthorpe. Seven weeks later Carpenter himself came to Campden to speak on 'Small Holdings and Life on the Land'.

This was, in its way, a prophetic title. For a few years the Guild of Handicraft flourished in Campden, vindicating all the ideals on which it was founded. But its financial base was never secure and from 1905 the position deteriorated. In 1908 attempts to raise new capital were abandoned and the Guild went into liquidation as a company, being reconstituted as a trust, whose objects were 'the encouragement of Craftsmanship in conjunction with Husbandry, with a view to enabling Craftsmen and their families to live a healthier and more reasonable life in the country and thus by means of the land to give them such economic security as shall make it possible for them to continue in the exercise of their crafts'.[20] The terms crafts and craftsmanship were defined as covering 'all such occupations with the hand, with or without the assistance of machinery, as are not usually carried on in large factories in towns' and husbandry as 'all these occupations on the land whether carried out individually or cooperatively . . . which shall best dovetail in with the occupations of Craftsmanship just defined and which shall primarily serve for the Craftsmen singly or collectively as sustenance'.

In order not to close the workshops altogether, Ashbee came to an agreement with none other than Joseph Fels, who put up the money to purchase seventy acres of land at nearby Broad Campden which with the workshops and other buildings comprised the property of the trust. The members of the former Guild were to use this land to supplement their income when there was low demand for their craftwork, which they carried on as independent businesses. This provision of smallholdings arose out of Ashbee's initial conviction that the failure of the Guild's high hopes was due to the move to the country. 'After six years working in the country,' he wrote, 'it was found to be impossible to do in a country district what we were able to do in London, that is to say, to carry on remuneratively our work in Arts and Crafts.'[21] In slack periods in London, men could be temporarily laid off to pick up casual work elsewhere; this was not possible in Campden and between commissions unsold stock quickly mounted, despite a saleroom in London.

But this was only part of the problem, which Ashbee later identified as competition, from machine production and from amateurs, both of which he classed as 'unfair'. With the popularization of arts and crafts design commercial firms had begun successfully to mass-produce goods with the hand-made look. The Cymric and Tudric ranges of metalware sold by Libertys, with simulated distressing to make them look hand-beaten, were particularly hated by Ashbee. The superior quality of hand-finished jewellery and furniture was not in doubt, but less discriminating customers were content with the same general effect at a much lower price. The problem of amateur competition also stemmed from the very success of the Arts and Crafts movement, which had encouraged people to practise craft skills. Some of the Guild workmen had in fact remonstrated with Ashbee for allowing private pupils in the workshops, aware that it would lead to undercutting; they had been 'rightly nervous of this competition of the amateur' who was ready to sell work at less than cost price.[22] The major problem, however, appears to have been under-capitalization, which could not be solved while retaining the Guild. As individual craftsmen, the continuing guildsmen seem to have competed more or less satisfactorily on the market and from 1909 to 1914 the workshops at Campden remained busy, with the exception of the printing press which had ceased operation in 1906.

In general the smallholding scheme was not a success, most of the craftsmen being indifferent cultivators, but old Charley Plunkett was an exception. Ashbee wrote in his *Memoirs* in 1914 that Plunkett was the happiest man he knew:

> When we started our land scheme he took an acre on the estate and in the face of gibes and taunts of hoary agriculturalists he made it by the sweat of his brow the model plot . . . His cabbages and potatoes are the best cabbages and potatoes, and he bakes his own bread. His pig is a wonderful pig . . .
>
> The old world of East London in which he spent the first fifty years of his life is a dark and rather terrible book closed for him happily and for ever. He has come out of it into green fields and sunshine. . .[23]

Thirty miles from Campden lived another group of craftsmen who might have disputed Ashbee's assessment of happiness, but who had also come out of the city into green fields and sunshine, albeit from a very different background. They had settled at Sapperton, to the west of Cirencester. Here were the workshops of Ernest Gimson and the brothers Ernest and Sidney Barnsley, architects, designers and furniture makers, where chairs, tables, chests, cabinets and ironwork were hand-crafted to a high standard by men working to simple yet exceptional designs. The lines were clean and pure, borrowed from cottage furniture and farm vehicles, and enlivened by a subtle use of detail and subdued but perfect decoration. Working on a smaller scale than the Guild of Handicraft and being of independent means, Gimson and the Barnsleys suffered from few financial crises, and the traditions they established have endured to the present in several lineally descended furniture-making concerns.

Ernest Gimson was born in 1884 in Leicester, where his father had established the Vulcan Works, a prosperous engineering business; his independence was thus dependent on the profitability of heavy industrial machinery – a fact not without irony in view of Gimson's chosen lifestyle. Family money also enabled him to train as an architect, a suitable profession for a socially rising young man. But it was another aspect of his inheritance that determined his future. Gimson senior had been a radical and a secularist and when William Morris visited Leicester in 1884 to lecture on art and socialism, it was at the Gimsons' house he stayed, talking late into the night with nineteen-year-old Ernest and his brother.[24] There were other visits and later Morris provided a letter of introduction to the London architect J.D. Sedding, in whose office Gimson met Ernest Barnsley. The latter's brother Sidney was also training as an architect under Richard Norman Shaw. The Barnsley family firm in Birmingham was one of the city's leading builders.

Gimson did not in fact share much of Morris's socialism, but he was closely involved in the work of S.P.A.B. and, more importantly, took up the great craftsman's interest in decorative work, especially that of the late medieval and Jacobean periods – no doubt inspired by lectures at the Art Workers' Guild. He learned the traditional methods of hand-modelling plasterwork and visited the chair bodger Philip Clissett at Bosbury to learn the basic techniques of chairmaking with steam and pole-lathe.

In 1890–2 Gimson and Sidney Barnsley joined W.R. Lethaby and a number of others in founding the firm of Kenton and Co., to produce 'furniture of good design and good workmanship' based on arts and crafts principles. The designs were more innovatory and modern than those of Morris and Co., Mackmurdo's Century Guild or Ashbee's Guild of Handicraft, but they aimed at the same ideals: honesty, beauty, fitness for function and fine workmanship, and their chests, standing cabinets and chairs followed traditional shapes. Many were made in oak and other plain woods, their simplicity relieved by chamfering or inlays. Although the firm was successful it soon split up, the partners returning to their main careers in architecture. Gimson and Barnsley however decided to continue with furniture making, and to move to the country. They persuaded Ernest Barnsley to join them. For some time, as Sidney Barnsley later told Philip Webb, the dream was 'to get hold of a few capable and trustworthy craftsmen and eventually have workshops in the country where we should all join together and form a nucleus around which in time others would attach themselves'.[25]

Like the Guild of Handicraft and the Whiteway Colony after them, Gimson and the Barnsleys chose to settle in Gloucestershire. They leased a decaying Elizabethan house at Pinbury Park, which was repaired and altered to accommodate the three men, together with Ernest Barnsley's family, and the workshop. Here from 1894 they worked together, learning and making furniture. Almost exclusively they used locally available woods – oak, ash, elm –with cherry or walnut inlays. By 1901 the orders had become more than they could execute themselves and several craftsmen and boys were employed at a second workshop, opened at Cirencester. The following year Pinbury House was reclaimed by the landlord, Lord Bathurst, whose wife took a liking to the way it had been restored, and the whole concern moved to Daneway House at nearby Sapperton. Here Lord Bathurst provided land for the three men to build themselves homes on the edge of the village. The houses are built of traditional materials –although Gimson's originally had a thatched roof, which is not usual in the district – and their owners/ architects were quietly flattered when visitors assumed they were several centuries old.

At Daneway House, a part–medieval domestic building which was used as a showroom with workshops in the outbuildings, Gimson and Ernest Barnsley entered into a formal partnership as designers and employers of a number of workmen making cabinets, chairs, wrought-iron fittings and other items. The Dutch foreman Peter van der Waals and some others migrated from else-where, while aspiring craftsmen and boys were taken on as trainees. By 1910 for example there were ten woodworkers working for Gimson at Daneway. The enterprise expanded: Edward Gardiner established a chair department, and a forge was established at Sapperton for Alfred Bucknall, son of the local blacksmith.

Sidney Barnsley did not join the partnership and that between Gimson and Ernest Barnsley was dissolved in 1905. Ernest Barnsley then returned to architectural work; his major commission was Rodmarton Manor, some miles to the south, where he built a splendid if somewhat extruded arts and crafts country mansion, using entirely local materials inside and out. The beams were made of hand-sawn oak, as was the panelling and other woodwork, while the iron-work was forged by the estate blacksmith. For some reason the prohibition on machinery extended to the construction process and no power lifting gear was used. This practice at any rate made work for some thirty or forty men, and Rodmarton took many years to build. It appears that no electricity was generally used inside the house; certainly some outdoor bedrooms on the first floor were provided, in keeping with the current taste for sleeping in the open air.

Ernest Gimson was also against machinery. According to Norman Jewson, who became part of the small community, working as Gimson's assistant and marrying Ernest Barnsley's daughter, Gimson 'hated mechanisation in any form and would allow no machinery of any sort in his workshops, not even a circular saw'. The Simple Life principles extended beyond Gimson's work:

> For the same reason he was proud of the fact that there was nothing made by machinery in his house except the plumbing, which was a concession to his wife! For him a log fire on the open hearth provided more comfort to the eye as well as the body than the stuffy heat of radiators . . . He preferred a rush-seated chair to an upholstered one, plain lime-washed walls to wallpapered, plain home-made food to imported luxuries . . .[26]

He adopted country ways and old-fashioned crafts, working in a smock in imitation of his rustic neighbours. He also took a keen, almost passionate interest in Nature and the surrounding country-side, as if nourished by his environment. Alfred Powell, artist and friend, described him as being 'quite alive to the entire necessity to himself and his work of the country and of this Gloucestershire country in particular. Without it he could not have had half the power.' Like many townbred persons, Gimson took great pleasure in learning the names and habits of wild flowers and animals – 'all that grew and changed in the earth'. 'He could not take them as a matter of course,' commented Powell, 'and so it seemed that his flowers, his trees, his grass, were richer in association and more memorable than other people's.'[27] In keeping with his high principles Gimson only visited London when he had to, and professed to feeling physically ill when obliged to approach the city. Yet he did not ignore the wider world. From Morris he derived his belief in the benefits of craftwork for all, convinced that healthy employment in the future lay in the abandoning of industrial

methods and in the return to craft production and agriculture where
every individual had useful work, time to do it well and leisure to
enjoy life. To this end he bought land near Sapperton in 1913 on
which he planned to build a craft village with houses and workshops
to attract skilled men, a project which came to nothing owing to the
war and Gimson's death soon afterwards.

To the existing village of Sapperton Gimson and his wife Emily
reintroduced country entertainment in a manner similar to
Ashbee's. They were interested in the recovery of old instruments
and music – both Arnold Dolmetsch and Cecil Sharp visited the
Gimson household – and Mrs Gimson played the piano in the
village hall for the local people to learn the country dances once
danced by their forebears. The traditions were not wholly lost, for
when songs and dances were presented to them, some local residents were able to recall and even perform them. A manuscript
notebook from Sapperton now at Arlington Mill Museum has the
text of a four-page mummers' play with the note 'Collected 1914',
and evidently resurrected in the village in response to the new
interest in the old traditions. The village hall at Sapperton was
designed by Gimson and paid for by Bathurst; it still has rush-seated
country chairs. Gimson also designed a memorial hall in William
Morris's village of Kelmscott.

Sidney Barnsley lived by an even purer ethic than Gimson – one
which Jewson said was too austere to be comfortable. Taking the
principle of closeness between artist and craftsman to its limit, he
refused to employ other workmen at all, designing and making
each item entirely by himself. Like Gimson he eschewed 'mod.
cons.' and chopped his own firewood which vanished all too
quickly; as he wrote in 1901:

> My winter store is just being hauled and when it is all piled up it
> looks sufficient for a lifetime. 16 tons a year I find I burn – and
> that means a good deal of sawing and carrying – still, as Thoreau
> says, it is economical in that one gets warmed twice – once in
> sawing it, and then in burning it, and the pleasure of splitting a
> big log and thinking of the future pleasure of watching it burn is
> worth a good deal.[28]

Perhaps because of his greater adherence to back-to-the-land principles, Sidney Barnsley's furniture possesses a more evident rusticity than that of Gimson and other arts and crafts designers. He made oak chests and coffers, which had once been standard furnishings in every home but were now regarded as old-fashioned and inconvenient. With curved tops and chamfered bars, other of Barnsley's pieces recall the farm carts of the period – and indeed the trade press remarked of one chest exhibited in 1896 that if put on wheels it would make a perfect covered wagon[29] – and farm implements such as the 'hayrake' stretchers beneath the long oak tables he made for Rodmarton Manor. Beds and dressers have headboards like haywains.[30]

Sidney Barnsley's son Edward carried on his father's work, moving in 1923 to take over the workshop of Geoffrey Lupton at Froxfield near Steep in Hampshire, where he is still (1982) living and working. This is close to Bedales School, where Edward and his sister were pupils and for which Gimson designed a hall like a tithe-barn. This was built in 1910 by Lupton, who had trained at the Daneway workshop, and was followed after the war by Gimson's last major work, Bedales Memorial Library, the building of which was undertaken by Lupton and Edward Barnsley, under Sidney Barnsley's supervision. The ironwork was made by Stevie Mustoe, who had trained under Alfred Bucknell at the Daneway forge, and sixty ladderback chairs of Gimson's design were provided by Edward Gardiner, who was thus enabled to resuscitate his workshop – which has continued to the present, now near Rugby under Neville Neal. At Chipping Campden, David Hart, grandson of one of the original guildsmen, still carries on work as a silversmith in the old Silk Mill workshop, apparently unchanged since Ashbee's time, and still prefers to craft every piece by hand. Elsewhere a latterday craft revival flourishes, frequently linked to contemporary dreams of country communes. So the arts and crafts tradition inspired by Morris and his disciples lives on.

10

Peasant Arts

Those urban designers and craftsmen who removed their workshops into the country mainly sought the benefits of rural life for themselves, though they often believed, like Ashbee, that their presence would benefit the countryside too. Other country-oriented reformers were anxious to establish rural workshops to benefit the people of the villages, and to dissuade them from leaving for the city. To this end they provided handcraft employment in a number of more or less benevolent schemes.

It was a Canute-like situation. By the early 1870s virtually all the small-scale industries which had locally manufactured and marketed cloth, baskets, utensils and other domestic goods had been displaced by factories using power-driven machinery and an expanding transport system which made it possible to distribute the goods on an almost national basis. A few specialized craft industries survived, as did a number of trades where costs were so low that it was hardly possible to undercut them. For the most part, however, Britain's industries had entered the modern world of standardized mass production with a labour force that worked away from home. Many viewed this process with dismay, attributing to it all kinds of contemporary malaises.

Ruskin was among the first to attempt to reverse this process by assisting craft-based rural industries. As we have seen, he provided financial backing to rescue the Isle of Man woollen industry at Laxey in 1876, and this was followed in 1884 by similar support for Albert Fleming, who wished to revive home spinning and weaving in the Lake District. Living not far from Ruskin, in Langdale, Fleming was a St George's Guild supporter, later described by Ruskin as 'my Master of the Rural Industries at Loughrigg'. In 1890 Fleming recalled the endeavour:

> I determined to try and bring the art back to the Westmoreland women. Scattered about on the fell side were many old women, too blind to sew and too old for hard work, but able to sit by the fireside and spin, if anyone would show them how, and buy their yarn. When I broached my scheme to a circle of practical relations a Babel of expostulation arose, wild as a Parsifal chorus. 'It won't pay; no one wants linen to last fifty years; it's fantastic, impracticable, sentimental and quixotic.' But to balance all this came a voice from Brantwood, saying 'Go ahead'; so I went ahead, hunted up an old woman who had spun half a century ago, and discovered some wheels of a different period. I got myself taught spinning, and then set to work to teach others. I tried my experiment here, in the Langdale Valley, in Westmoreland, half-way between Mr Ruskin's home at Coniston and Wordsworth's at Rydal.[1]

Fleming's first task was to ransack the country for old spinning wheels; they came from lumber rooms and garrets, and from as far as Stornoway and the Isle of Man, most unused for the past fifty years. A further fifteen were made by the village carpenter. A loom was discovered in Kendal, together with an old weaver who knew how to operate it. The first yards of linen produced were disappointing: 'I own it seemed terrible stuff, frightful in colour and of dreadful roughness, with huge lumps and knots', but Ruskin's *Seven Lamps* had pronounced that such irregularities were the honourable badges of all true handwork. The cloth sold without difficulty and Fleming recorded: 'To my great delight I found people did want real hand-made linen . . . orders and enquiries came from all parts of England.'[2]

Seven years later, the linen industry was under the supervision of Mrs Pepper, a local woman who had been one of the first recruits;

her husband worked in the Langdale slate quarries. Assisted by her mother, Mrs Pepper managed the business from a little cottage in Elterwater village, demonstrating and teaching spinning, weaving and embroidery, dealing with correspondence and handling sales.

The outworkers came in once a fortnight to bring their spun thread and collect more flax or silk, and their wages, which averaged 4s per week. It appears that 'Old John' the weaver had passed on, for the yarn was now sent away to be woven, except for some dress fabrics. When the linen returned, it was given out to another group of workers for embroidering in their own homes. Mrs Pepper at this date was experimenting with natural dyes, trying out local ingredients which had been superseded by chemicals: logwood for black, lichen for brown, heather for green.[3]

In 1917 the business was both thriving and stimulating: other schemes had been started locally. But in the 1920s, a survey of rural industries found that Langdale's reputation had been ruined and the enterprise had 'collapsed owing to the exposure of the fact that one of the weavers was selling factory-made materials as hand-woven'. The tradition, however, was being carried on elsewhere in the Lake District by weavers 'each claiming to be the present representatives of the original organization'. The report spoke darkly of secrecy, rivalry, accusations and rumours among the hand-loom industries of the area, commenting, somewhat unfairly, that these deficiencies were due to the fact that tourists were willing to pay high prices for the cloth. By this time, it appears, hand-weaving had taken the place of spinning as the major feature of the industry.[4]

Whatever criticisms might eventually be brought against it, the Langdale Linen Industry was successful enough to provoke several imitations. In Keswick another friend and follower of Ruskin, Miss Twelves, set up her Ruskin Linen Industry at St George's Cottage, employing local women to make homespun yarn, 'Greek lace' and 'art needlework'. In similar spirit Canon Rawnsley (of the National Trust) and his wife were helping to start the Keswick School of Handicraft, partly inspired by Ashbee's success in Whitechapel. Another homespun industry was established at Windermere. Outside the Lake District, home spinning and weaving were started at Winterslow, Wiltshire, and at Cullompton in Devon, followed by the Stonehenge Weaving Industry, all run by philanthropic ladies who wished to provide healthy employment for local women. There was no shortage of applicants even with wages as low as 4s a week, since all earnings contributed to the household economy and there were in most rural areas no alternative sources of employment for women beyond cleaning and washing for the gentry. Young girls, however, still moved away to service or to join relatives in town; spinning and weaving were not sufficiently profitable to keep them in the village.

The same was true of the lace associations which were also sponsored by benevolence, and which were found in various parts of the country, and especially in areas where the craft had traditionally been strongest – Devon, Buckinghamshire, Nottingham and Northampton. The aim was not so much to rediscover a lost skill but to prevent one from disappearing altogether. Pillow lace was still made at home according to traditional patterns, but by the 1870s it was rapidly being overtaken by machine-made work and the remaining labour force of outworkers was composed of old women, who still painstakingly produced hand-made lace for dealers. As it began to vanish, however, hand-made lace came to stand as an emblem of the old country values. The ancient village woman at her cottage door, viewed sentimentally, represented all that the industrial revolution was destroying.

The lace associations were generally founded by ladies of leisure and energy – the vicar's wife or lady of the manor – and patronized by the aristocracy, with the object of rescuing these craftswomen and preserving their skills. They undertook to supply patterns and materials and to buy the finished products. Standards were rigorous, as the only way to compete with factory-made lace was to offer designs too intricate for the machine, but failing eyesight or arthritic hands often made the work too demanding for the older lace-makers. The first lace association was started in 1874 by Miss Rose Hubbard at Winslow, in Berkshire, and employed some seventy women. In 1880 the Paulerspury lace industry was launched in Northamptonshire, followed by a similar scheme in Honiton, Devon, a traditional lace-making centre, in 1888, and the Midland Lace Association in 1891. The Buckinghamshire lace industry was revived at Maids Moreton; its object was to bring back 'the industry of beautiful old Buckinghamshire pillow lace which is rapidly dying out'.[5]

During the 1890s the lace associations flourished, royal patronage helping to popularize their wares and careful management keeping standards high. The aristocratic sponsors created a demand in the fashionable world – the Buckinghamshire association had four duchesses among its patrons – while the local ladies who supervised the work and the selling on a voluntary basis seem to have been efficient and resourceful. The Midland association was soon able to raise its prices and employ a full-time organizer; by 1910 it provided work for some 200 outworkers. The very proliferation of lace associations indicates their achievement: as late as 1897 a new one, the North Buckinghamshire Lace Association, was established, with some ten titles among its sponsor-list; its aims were to 'preserve and renew the best old designs', to 'discourage and stamp out as far as possible vulgar and degenerate forms of lace' and to 'provide employment in the country and prevent migration to large centres'. Its president, Lady Inglefield, cited Ruskin's distaste for machine-made goods as the major inspiration for her work.[6]

The women employed by the lace associations gained in income, in security and in status. Previously they had been at the mercy of the lace dealers, as one Oxfordshire organizer recalled: 'They earned three halfpence an hour in yarded lace and a penny an hour in borders and collars. All work had to be taken to a town seven miles away, the distance often walked. Sometimes the work was bought, sometimes not. When bought, half or the whole of its value was taken out in drapery goods.'[7] The lace associations, by contrast, paid on commission, provided good parchment patterns, and collected the finished lace. Although an exceptional case of a woman earning 20s a week was quoted, incomes from lace-making were generally low, but the security of regular work may have compensated for the rates paid, and it was widely accepted that lace-making kept many an old villager out of the workhouse – an achievement not to be despised when few rural households could afford to support unproductive members. And then there was some benefit in being part of a scheme which reached right up through the social scale, so that the humble lace-makers knew that their association had been asked to produce cuffs or borders for a royal wedding or a national display.

Although many of the associations hoped to teach the craft to a new generation of lace-makers, and illustrations from the period show classes of youngsters each with a lace-pillow and bobbins, the work did not attract younger workers – or perhaps lace went out of fashion and the demand withered. Another factor which contributed to the decline of hand-made lace may have been the introduction in 1908 of the 5s old-age pension for those over seventy with no other income, as this would have discouraged elderly lace-makers from carrying on their trade. Whatever the reasons, the lace industries declined and by the end of the 1920s most if not all were defunct. Perhaps the ageing of their organizers was also a factor. None of the schemes appears to have developed into a self-sufficient commercial enterprise.

Country women were an obvious group for such experiments in craft revival, but village men and boys were not neglected, and there were a number of small-scale wood- and metal-working ventures established on a voluntary basis by members of the benevolent gentry. A survey[8] in 1915–16 listed half a dozen, mostly extremely small. On the Rothschild estate at Wing, Buckinghamshire, there was a wood-working class where the men made small pieces of furniture, learning carving and inlay. The purpose of the class was said to be that of providing a useful occupation for winter evenings and a small extra income, but as the latter could more simply have been provided by raising the wages of the estate workers, for whom leisure was probably not a large problem, it is likely that the class's main function was to provide Mrs Leopold de Rothschild with a useful occupation and to add to her reputation for benevolence. In addition, it may have helped a small number of village lads to acquire a skill which would enable them to leave agricultural work, which was certainly not the object of the exercise.

At Failand near Bristol, Miss A. Ruth Fry started up a leatherworking class in 1895 for men under the age of thirty, drawn mainly from the ranks of farm and garden labourers in the neighbourhood. The group met one evening a week when instruction was given by Miss Fry and the work was completed at home. A room with free heating was provided and 'class funds' covered the cost of materials. Actual earnings were low (£70–80 was given as the annual value of goods sold, for a class of some thirty members) but no doubt many items were made for use, and for pleasure. For a voluntary evening class catering for members of perhaps the most depressed social group in Britain at that time to have lasted twenty years was no small achievement; it could hardly have been expected to survive the war, military conscription and higher wages.

Similar schemes were set up by Miss Grace Cheals at Friskney in Lincolnshire and by Mrs Waterhouse at Yattendon, Berkshire. The dominance of women in these projects is incidentally indicative of the restricted career outlets for 'ladies' at this period; those with energy and ideas often found fulfilment in philanthropy rather than employment, and they seem to have been capable managers. At Compton in Surrey, the wife of the highly successful Victorian painter G.F. Watts established a hand pottery employing local labour. This appears to have been a less favoured traditional craft – Lethaby lamented that the skill of throwing pots on a wheel had virtually died out – although it was later to prove both artistically and commercially profitable. At Compton Mrs Watts first designed a remarkable Byzantine-style chapel for the village's new burying-ground, decorated with terracotta tiles outside and semi-relief gesso inside. The work was accomplished by local people working under Mrs Watts's supervision, and when it was finished she opened the Compton Potteries, a commercial concern producing terracotta garden ware and odd hand-painted statuettes. This continued in business until 1954.

Not far from Compton is the small town of Haslemere, where a small cluster of craft revival schemes was concentrated. Here the St Edmundsbury Weaving Works was established in 1901 by Edmund Hunter, moving in 1908 to the new Garden City of Letchworth. And here was the self-styled Peasant Arts movement, led by Godfrey Blount in a heroic attempt to stave off industrial material-ism and build a new order based on country life and country crafts.

Godfrey Blount was a designer and teacher who was influenced by the desire of the Arts and Crafts movement to reintegrate the work of artist and artisan. In 1899 J.M. Dent published a handsome book by Blount entitled *Arbor Vitae*, a treatise on 'The Nature and Development of Imaginative Design for the Use of Teachers, Handicraftsmen and Others'. Here he asserted the primary import-ance of imagination, urging his readers not to think of the craft revival 'as a novel occupation for idle hours, or even as a philan-thropic trick to entice the labourer from the public house', but as 'the dawning of nobler conceptions of the charm of labour and of the unity of life'. Machine manufacture, Blount contended, affected the happiness of those who made such objects and those who used them, 'the mere revival of handicraft cannot redeem Art . . . it must be besides the carrier of a message and an angel of good tidings'.[9]

In 1898 the Peasant Arts Society had been located in Bayswater but it soon moved to the country address of St Cross, Haslemere. From here in 1903 Blount launched his 'New Crusade' in a 2d pamphlet issued by the Simple Life Press of Fleet Street. The Fellowship of the New Crusade was to unite 'all those who feel that the time has come to protest against the materialism of the present day and to try and restore nobler ideals of thought and life'. Members were to commit themselves to giving up 'useless, cruel and extravagant fashions'; to restoring country life and country crafts; to reviving traditional art forms; to opposing the use of machinery; and to meetings, publications and displays supporting these objects. He urged his readers: 'We should dress if possible in homespuns, and generally admire and use when we can get and afford them handmade boots, crockery, books and furniture.'[10] Blount wrote other pamphlets, whose titles are self-explanatory: *The Rustic Renaissance, The Gospel of Simplicity* and *For Our Country's Sake: An Essay setting forth the True Conditions under which a Return to the Land and the Revival of Country Life and Crafts are possible, and new Proposals for carrying out the same.* With support from sympathizers, the New Crusade hoped to establish a self-supporting craft workshop and school of handicraft, and a museum of traditional arts and crafts.

Despite his eloquence, few appeared to have responded to Blount's call. But a number of activities centred in Haslemere seem to have been inspired by his ideas. A collection of hand-made and decorated articles from all over Europe, especially Scandinavia, which by 1910 contained over 600 pieces, was made into the nucleus of the projected museum of traditional crafts by Dr Greville Macdonald, an original Peasant Arts associate, on condition that it did not go into a city museum; it was kept in private homes until being presented to the Haslemere Educational Museum, founded by Sir Jonathan Hutchinson, when the museum moved to new premises in 1924 and currently occupies two main rooms there devoted to Peasant Arts. The Peasant Arts Society launched a small magazine called the *Vineyard*, which was dedicated to rural life 'alike for its spiritual and economic value'. The *Vineyard* believed that 'fundamental in the upholding of England's greatness lies the restoration of the land to fruitful uses and of the essential crafts of the hand, as original rights and needs'.[11] In practice the *Vineyard* carried stores and verses written or chosen by the editor, Maud Egerton King. She and her husband Joseph King, later a Member of Parliament, were related to the Blounts and had been involved with the Peasant Arts Society since the Bayswater days, when Joseph King had written a booklet on how to design nesting boxes for birds. The Kings lived at Hill Farm, Haslemere, and later had a country mansion built nearby at Lower Birtley. Perhaps inspired by the Lake District weaving schemes, the Kings began a handloom weaving project for local girls in the town.

The work expanded and soon the Haslemere Homespun Weaving Industry, underwritten by Joseph King, was installed in a purpose-built weaving shed and studio in Foundry Road, beneath the railway and the gasworks, a somewhat less than pastoral location. The two large and picturesque wood and tile buildings are still to be seen,[12] with gothic-lettered nameplates identifying The Studio and The Olde Weaving House; the half-timbered effect was added by the present (1980) owner. Maud King and Ethel Blount both took an active part in the weaving work. At around the same time, Luther Hooper and Edmund Hunter were also setting up hand-weaving schemes in Haslemere, the former at the Green Bushes Weaving House and the latter at the St Edmundsbury Weaving Works at College Hill.

These weaving enterprises were accompanied by a woodworking project started by Romney Green in Foundry Meadow, and by a pottery set up by Radley Young about a mile away at Hammer. Little is known about these ventures, but the weaving appears to have been relatively successful. In 1908 Hunter was able to move his business to a new albeit small factory in Letchworth, and around 1910 the Peasant Arts movement experienced a sudden surge in popularity. It is unlikely that the Haslemere Hand Weaving Industry made much money, but the weavers were paid for their work, the goods were put up for sale in Haslemere High Street and later in a London showroom, and the business survived through to the 1920s. There was no shortage of local labour, and Mesdames Blount and King were convinced that it contributed to the cultural as well as the economic improvement of the rural worker. Early in 1912 they gave an account of 'Our Experience of the Influence of

Handicraft upon the Workers' in which they outlined the increase in manners as well as skill which was visible in their workforce: 'a girl coming into the Weaving House or Workroom interested in the work quickly becomes very proud of her growing skill and while gradually mastering a beautiful craft is also acquiring the splendid patience of the good handworker'.[13] They spoke proudly of the young woman who stayed after working hours to make the material for her own wedding dress, and of a young mother who had obtained a loom to work on at home.

The most successful part of the endeavour, however, appears to have been the junior branch, which met on Saturday afternoons after the weavers had gone home, when local children were invited to join the Wheel and Spindle Club. Here for three hours they practised teasing, carding, spinning and knitting. Ill-nourished, lumpish, uncouth and barely literate working-class girls were thus given an opportunity to learn the traditional crafts practised, as it was believed, by their grandmothers, and offered a vision of art and the future. In the authors' words: 'in an age of shoddy and showy dress, the little spinners are dreaming of a homespun grandeur, for which only the neighbour's sheep, the lichen and heather from the common at their doors, and their own busy hands are innocently accountable'.[14] After tea, the club practised folk songs and dances (Cecil Sharp was a paid-up Peasant Arts supporter) and listened to stories and plays. Miss Margaret Leith, who ran the Wheel and Spindle, firmly believed that pride in creative work would discourage delinquency.

1911–12 saw a revival of interest in the Peasant Arts Society and the resurrection of Blount's idea of a fellowship of supporters. A new manifesto committed members to be 'active propagandists to encourage everywhere the love of country life and handicrafts, and where possible to teach people to spin and weave and carve'. The annual subscription was 6s and in its first year's report the Peasant Arts Fellowship showed a membership of 189 and a budget of £200, largely from donations. Inexplicably, it had moved back to London, although the Blounts and the Kings were still prominent on the committee and most of the activities were based in Surrey. To complement the work of the weaving industry, Kate Sperling, 'a skilled and enthusiastic teacher of spinning, weaving and all the processes involved from preparing the fleece to completion of the fabric, including vegetable dyeing'[15] was in 1912 appointed as peripatetic instructor, employed either by the Peasant Arts Society or by local worthies who wished to introduce weaving into their district. Miss Sperling had no shortage of clients: her report on the year's work from October 1914 to September 1915 (when one would have imagined that people were otherwise preoccupied) shows a busy schedule, with the pupils ranging from the Countess of Plymouth and four companions to the vicar of Lenham in Kent, with twenty-six villagers and twenty-four children, including one 'cripple boy taught rug-making'.[16] To complement this work Ethel Blount wrote a shilling handbook, *The Story of Homespun Web: A Guide to Hand Spinning and Weaving* (1913), with illustrations by the author.

The first public meeting of the Peasant Arts Fellowship took place at Caxton Hall, London on 28 February 1912, when the audience heard G.K. Chesterton speak on 'The Peasant as the Basis of a Natural Society'; Philip Wickstead on 'The School and the Fields' (the aim of rural education to keep people on the land); Cecil Sharp on 'Peasant Expressions'; and Ethel Blount and Maud King on the Haslemere weaving workshops. Several of these topics recurred in the published Peasant Arts Papers, which formed the last main plank of the fellowship's activity. The British Library's collection of this series is sadly incomplete, but the titles indicate the Peasant Arts' priorities. Godfrey Blount continued his spiritual mission with essays on 'The Cause of Evil' – 'England is unsound because her people have forgotten agriculture for mechanical production and prefer to live feverishly in large towns to peacefully in the country' – and 'Art and Religion'. Founder member Greville Macdonald wrestled, on behalf of the fellowship, with the difficult problems concerning the permissible use of machinery, while the Rev. Baverstock looked at welfare considerations in 'The Condition of the Husbandman' and 'The Village and the Old Folk'. Mrs King produced five pamphlets altogether, on various topics including the residual May Day pursuits of the Haslemere children in 'Please Remember the Garland'. In 'Rag Time and Ring Time' she contrasted the noise and discord of contemporary pop music with the 'spring faces and spring graces' of Cecil Sharp's folk dancing group, while in 'The Red and Green Revolution' she took issue with 'revolutionary socialists', arguing that the 'green' Peasant Arts approach was the more radical. 'England is urbanised in heart, mind and deed,' she wrote, 'and to undo this is really revolutionary . . .'

As the Peasant Arts Guild, the group survived the War, despite the loss of 'several of our best spinners and weavers from our Haslemere workroom' owing to marriage with Canadian husbands (servicemen stationed in the area) and the departure of Peasant Arts carpenter John Beamish, a former miner who was offered 'the long-desired opportunity of cultivating his own land and carrying on his handicrafts at the same time'.[17] He continued to make the workshop looms. The Blounts were engaged in a new venture under the Peasant Arts umbrella, namely the production of hand-made wooden toys at the John Ruskin School of Handicraft in St George's Hall, Haslemere. The designs included old-fashioned windmills, merry-go-rounds, hobby horses, nativity scenes, old English villages and, later, hand-painted 'Talisman' pictures; all were for sale both in Haslemere and in Duke Street. There were plans to buy plots of land in the Haslemere district, where friends and supporters could build their own Simple Life houses, but this must have been blocked by the rising price of land. In 1927 the Peasant Arts enterprise was formally disbanded, Joseph King remaining honorary curator of the Peasant Arts collection until his death in 1943. Jonathan Hutchinson's daughter Ursula carried on the craft tradition with the Inval Weavers during the 1920s.

It is difficult to estimate to what extent any of these well-meant homespun and other traditional craft revival schemes helped to arrest the process of rural decline. By the 1920s, when most of them had gone out of business, the rural economy of areas like that around Haslemere had changed from that of the 'old West Surrey' known to Gertrude Jekyll into that of the 'Home Counties', with increased population and improved transport leading to the growth of service and tourist industries. A similar process, based largely on holidays, took place in the Lake District. At the same time, light industries were established in many parts of Britain outside the major conurbations, although areas where agriculture remained the only source of employment continued severely depressed until at least 1940. Not all of the new industries established in country districts were based on rural products, for with road transport and electric power it was as feasible to locate (say) a printing works in the country as in the city. In 1918 a survey by J.L. Green, *Village*

Industries, noted the recent appearance of 'the rural factory', established by enlightened or practical businessmen. One such was a lace-making plant set up, no doubt to the disgust of the home-based lace associations, at Shepton Mallet by Ernest Jardine, local landowner, employer and MP, who was described as a 'keen advocate of the rural reform movement' and who provided allotments for his tenant-worker-constituents. Jam factories were operated by both Chivers and Tiptree in country districts, while in Shropshire a toy factory produced wooden soldiers, trains and Noah's arks, probably on a more mechanized and competitive basis than Blount's John Ruskin School. Employment in these 'rural factories' was very welcome to local residents but a contradiction in terms to those who supported the Peasant Arts ideals, believing in country life and handcrafts, not in the export of the industrial system to the countryside.

Indeed, the missionaries of the movement were convinced that the restoration of handcrafts to country people was but the first step; as the Peasant Arts manifesto of 1911 put it, 'this Gospel is needed even more in towns'. The social and economic problems of the time, with which politicians grappled vainly, were only to be solved by a radically different form of progress – returning people from the cities back to 'Mother Earth' and rehumanizing them through handcrafts. As Blount put it in his tract *Rustic Renaissance*:

> Those of us who are in earnest, including perhaps a few politicians, are beginning to see that this country can only be saved physically, mentally and spiritually by cultivating it . . .
> A return to the country must imply the decay of the town. If it does not imply this it can be no true return. A return to the country with the corresponding decline of the town must also mean a return to the simplicity and handicraft because when the town ceases to be a burden on the countryman's back, he will have to make what he wants by hand in the country instead of having them made by machinery in the town . . . rural depopulation is our punishment . . . the city is our sin . . . No national revival or revification is possible till we repent of our sin . . .[18]

11

Halcyon Cottage and Wild Garden

From the combination of the middle-class drift to the country and the prominence of the architectural profession in the craft movement, there arose a characteristic building style based, not surprisingly, on the country cottage and old manor house. This led, in time, to architects rather than builders designing small houses, paving the way for subsequent developments in suburban estates, public housing and new towns. But its most immediate effect was the sudden scaling down of high Victorian ornateness and pretension in favour of plainness and simplicity, or 'sweetness and light'. The homes built in the suburbs and home counties for the new, country-loving bourgeoisie were designed in what is now known as the English vernacular style, representing the desire for roots, for a return to the village in form if not quite in fact. In contrast to the Victorian villa or Gothick mansion, ostentation and bombast were avoided, the ideal being a house which looked as if it had always been there, rather than one which proclaimed its new stylishness. The wealth of those who commissioned 'Olde Englishe' houses typically derived from commercial or professional pursuits that followed the industrial revolution, but they chose to ignore this, preferring faithful reproductions of the houses built by seventeenth-century squires and farmers.

Internally, the cluttered and ornamented Victorian furnishing style was rejected in favour of clean lines and bare boards. The inglenook, a necessary cottage feature when the front door opened straight into the living room, was revived for homes of all sizes, and if possible a hall and gallery were incorporated in emulation of the lifestyle of the late medieval period. Hand-made 'country-style' furniture came into fashion – Sussex chairs, probably made by Morris and Co., together with old-fashioned (and surely uncomfortable) high-backed settles, linen chests and tall cabinets. Such buildings and their interiors looked back to some of the oldest dwellings in England, consciously adopting half-timbered exteriors, small-paned windows, uneven gables, rustic porches, tile-hung walls and thatched roofs. In some cases the archaic ambitions of the architect were vetoed by the clients – as when Edward and Constance Garnett rejected the original plans for their new house at Limpsfield, which contained a great unceilinged hall with a central open fire, and insisted on a conventional L-shape, with normal rooms upstairs and down.[1] Generally speaking, the houses as built were spacious and comfortable; if they lacked 'mod.cons.' it was on the grounds of principle rather than expense.

Philip Webb was the pioneer of the English vernacular manner; indeed it may be reckoned to have begun with the Red House he designed for William Morris in 1860. The use of red brick (hence the name) was very unusual in a country house of that size at that date, and refers back to the Jacobean age, although the styling was distinct and new.

Webb liked old buildings – he was among the most active and longest-serving members of the S.P.A.B. – and particularly old bricks, especially 'seconds' because of their variety of colour and texture. The Victorian architectural convention decreed that 'the most uniform colour was the handsome thing to aim at', but Webb wanted his walls to look old and weathered from the start. To this end, according to one of his assistants, he 'always used lime-mortar pointing, never cement, and he got as many "dark-headers" into his walls as he could. He hated pressed bricks and dark pointing. He used to be very proud of his kitchen chimneys, which he often said were the best parts of his houses.'[2]

And although he built comfortable country houses for rich men and aristocrats, his image of perfection was 'a farm or manor house in fields and orchards. . .' Webb's last major work was Standen, built near East Grinstead, Sussex, for a prosperous solicitor. It is a very large yet curiously self-effacing house. There are architectural echoes from the Middle Ages, in the high square tower, right through to the contemporary, with a glass and ironwork conservatory. Inside was the same apparent lack of style: simple lines, high panelling painted white or blue-green, and less rather than more furniture. The decorations were by William Morris, Webb's oldest friend.

Comfort, rather than show, was Webb's first object; his buildings were intended to have the easy feeling that goes with long occupation, despite their newness. The inhabitants could thus feel themselves heirs of ancient England – although Webb had radical views and sympathy for the servants, and could be ferocious to clients. He believed in making kitchens and domestic offices as large and convenient as possible: 'if the client, as sometimes happened, suggested cutting them down, Webb would use his best arguments and offer to cut down the drawing room instead'.[3]

At the other end of the scale from Standen is the charming pair of bourgeois cottages built by Webb in 1876 in Redington Road, Hampstead. These are in fact among the earliest 'village-style' urban buildings and antedate the garden suburb type of house, which they closely resemble, by at least twenty-five years. Webb's influence was long-lasting: his integrity and modesty won him many followers. When he retired from architecture he moved to an old cottage in Sussex where he spent his time gardening, chopping firewood and drawing water up a seventy-four-foot well.[4]

One of the first places where ideas derived from Webb were put into practice was Bedford Park, built around 1880 as the first 'artistic' suburb on the then edge of West London where the new electric railway ran from the City and West End. This was a commercial venture, aiming to attract well-to-do and 'progressive' tenants, and including several houses with studios. A stock of about thirty designs was used, mainly in 'Queen Anne' style, mostly in red brick and distributed about the estate so that the effect is varied, although today the site seems somewhat cramped and it is hard to re-create the enthusiasm Bedford Park aroused in its time. Then, it was in marked contrast to the rows of suburban terraces and villas spreading outward from London; now, its very influence has undermined its impact. Visitors flocked to Bedford Park, with its air 'of a village or a small country town where nothing had happened for at least a hundred years'.[5] W.B. Yeats, whose family lived there, later recalled 'the crooked ostentatiously picturesque streets with great trees casting great shadows' as well as the conscious nostalgia of some of the buildings: a co-operative store looking like an olde worlde village shoppe, and a pub named 'The Tabard' after the inn of Chaucer's *Canterbury Tales,* which was nevertheless a normal Victorian public house.[6] Within yards of both shop and tavern, the electric railway rumbled.

The designer of both these buildings and principal architect at Bedford Park was Richard Norman Shaw who, although rarely an arts and crafts architect in the usual sense of the term – he built great flamboyant hotels and the mock-baronial Scotland Yard – was also known for several smaller half-timbered or tile-hung houses in and around London for private clients. In Hampstead he designed a picturesque 'cottage' some three storeys high for Kate Greenaway, whose 'back-to-the-village' illustrations were in tune with the pastoral movement.

It was a group of Shaw's pupils who came together to start the Art Workers' Guild and to form the nucleus of the Arts and Crafts movement, with the initial aim of bringing architecture back into touch with old crafts and traditional forms of building. It became almost an article of faith that old houses were better than new – except when new houses could be built in the same way as the old. There emerged a veritable passion for natural or traditional materials; as Edward Prior wrote of 'Nature's own textures':

> We may borrow from her and show the grain and figure of her works, the ordered roughness of her crystallisation in granite or sandstone, or the veining of her marbles. . . our work in each must take a character from the material. . . as evidence of our delight in texture, we may leave our wood or stone as it comes from the chisel or the saw, to show the fracture the tool has made. . .[7]

Prior, who is best known as the designer of 'butterfly-shaped' houses, made his buildings look as though they grew from their environment. The same is true of Ernest Gimson's architectural work, which he never wholly neglected even after his move to the

Cotswolds. In 1898 Gimson designed the amazing Stoneywell Cottage in Leicestershire, built on a sloping rocky outcrop from local stone; the house seems to grow from the ground. It is a highly picturesque, even inconvenient dwelling, with a great open fireplace for cooking in the kitchen, and a tiny bedroom which could only be reached by a ladder. But it so re-created the authentic feeling of an age-old rural cottage that, it is said, a local resident, returning to the district after some absence, remarked of Stoneywell: 'Odd that I should have forgotten that old cottage.'[8]

The distinction between tradition and revivalism is a narrow one, and many of the 'rustic' houses built in this period were crude 'Tudorbethan' replicas. Those architects whose work is still admired – and is now enjoying a great revival of its own, as the flood of exhibitions, books, television programmes and talks on Edwardian architecture indicates – were those who were not designing from the past but the present and even, on some occasions, for the post-industrial future. C.F.A. Voysey, for example, is regarded both as a traditionalist and a pioneer of modernism. His Walnut Tree Farm, built near Malvern in 1890 to replace a timber-frame farmhouse that still stood (and which Voysey refused to demolish) is a new house incorporating many older features without becoming a pastiche. On the entrance elevation the roof sweeps down to the eaves at almost shoulder height, and the gables are made of black and white timbering typical of the area.

Voysey's principles of domestic architecture were: 'Repose, Cheerfulness, Simplicity, Breadth, Warmth, Quietness in a Storm, Economy of Upkeep, Evidence of Protection, Even-ness of Temperature, and making the house a frame for its inmates'.[9] Like Webb and virtually every arts and crafts architect worthy of the title, he designed every detail of the house, down to door hinges and window fastenings. Though he was also a designer of wallpaper, he was not over-eager for decoration in his houses; colour, however, was admitted and the result was the kind of rich simplicity evident in this description of the house Voysey built for himself at Chorleywood in Hertfordshire.

Grey slates pave the path up to the front door and continue through the hall to the kitchen and offices – providing easily cleaned surfaces where they are most needed. All over the house there is a low picture-rail with a deep frieze above. In Voysey's day the friezes and ceilings were distempered white; some walls were papered with Eltonbury silk fibre paper, which had a slightly textured finish (purple in the hall, staircase and upper landing and green in the dining room) others were papered with papers of Voysey's own design (in the study, schoolroom and bedrooms). Except for the stair-rail, which was unstained, unpolished oak, the woodwork was all enamelled white. In the hall was a peacock-blue rug; on the stairs a grey-green carpet; in other rooms patterned carpets of Voysey's own design. The whole of the first floor had fitted green cork carpet tiles wall to wall. All the curtains were bright Turkey red.[10]

Although not the most admired, the most representative and in some unfortunate ways the most influential of this generation of architects was M.H. Ballie-Scott, who designed prolifically for the owner who wanted a new/old dwelling in Surrey or Hampshire. Ballie-Scott believed in cottages, barns and medieval halls, suitably adapted for contemporary times, with a large living area surrounded by smaller spaces and, if possible, a musicians' gallery. His designs were much in demand, and he was a rare example of an internationally known architect whose practice was not in London; he started in the Isle of Man and then moved to Bedford. Among Scott's prestigious commissions was one for a house for the Grand Duke of Hesse at Darmstadt in Germany, for which Scott in turn commissioned Ashbee's Guild of Handicraft for all the interior furnishings and fittings. His most notable construction must, however, have been the tree-house retreat he built for Crown Princess Marie of Romania. This was supported by the trunks of growing trees in the forest – a literal demonstration of 'back to Nature'. Internally, it was a kind of gorgeous hide-out, decorated in golden yellow and blue; externally, it blended into the surrounding wood.

A more conventional but still comparable house was Blackwell in the Lake District, designed by Scott in 1898–9. Here the interior is centred around a two-storeyed timber hall and gallery as in an Elizabethan manor, with a bay-windowed drawing room like a late medieval solar. Decoratively, Nature is brought into the house through slender columns rising like saplings to foliated capitals, surmounted by a deep frieze of branches laden with carved fruit in bas-relief. This tendency to bring Nature indoors was a conscious one; elsewhere he wrote: 'In a room where the walls are covered with foliage and glimpses of the sky, the ceiling may develop into a blue-sky without cloud and set with circling swallows. . .' But, he warned, there should not also be a frieze of flowers apparently blooming above the tree-tops.[11] At Blackwell the actual effect was inevitably rather petrified and bizarre. The primary purpose of a dwelling-house, after all, is to keep Nature on the outside, not invite it in.

After these somewhat extravagant designs, Ballie-Scott's work quietened, as he concentrated more on work for more ordinary purposes. In 1906 a collection of designs for smaller homes was published, all more or less based on his country cottage ideal, containing attractive water-colours as well as plans and elevations. The text of *Houses and Gardens* gives his pastoral views clearly:

Those who dwell amidst the vulgar and impossible artistry of modern villadom may visit now and then some ancient village, and in the cottages and farmhouses there be conscious of a beauty which makes their own homes appear a trivial and frivolous affair; but such beauty is generally held to be incompatible with modern ideas of comfort and sanitation . . .

The man who . . . is wise enough to regard the small house as a large cottage rather than a restricted mansion, will demand planning and furniture on totally opposite principles to those usually followed. . . The very simplicity and unpretentiousness of his surroundings are eloquent in suggestions for the ritual of his daily life. . . When he asks a friend to dinner he does not seek to impress his guests by the multitude of his courses nor the magnificence of his plate. He may indeed be quietly proud of the homely beauty of his surroundings, but it is a pride which is based not on their costliness, nor on their price in the market but rather on such qualities as fitness of their uses and beauty of line, colour or texture.[12]

Typical of Scott's work are the designs illustrated for Springcot, Heather Cottage, and Halcyon Cottage, the names indicative of the rustic orientation of both architect and client – although it is a bit disconcerting to discover that a 'cottage' may contain five or six bedrooms plus servants' quarters. Heather Cottage at Sunningdale is really a manor, with an open timber-frame roof and high wall-panelling. Halcyon Cottage, which Scott said had been built 'in a site within sixteen miles of London' but which has never been located, was costed at only £525 for four bedrooms and a servants' attic. A large central living room on the ground floor looked out onto a lawn and pergola, and could be screened from the traffic of the house by a curtained recess. Also on the ground floor were a study and 'the usual kitchen premises'. Scott's sketches show a traditional rural dwelling, with exposed beams, small-paned windows and ancient oak dresser: the perfect country residence for an Edwardian commuter.

Designing new houses to look old was but one step from making old houses new. 'An Old House Remodelled' in *Houses and Gardens* shows Scott's own residence at Fenlake near Bedford. Here Scott adapted an older building, 'forming a hall by the removal of a partition. The fireplace in the room so formed was then removed and the brick arch which formed its structural basis left exposed. A coarse sacking was then fixed on the walls as a background for the old furniture.'[13] The modern passion for restoring old cottages, uncovering fireplaces and taking out walls, re-furnishing with natural fibres and old wood, may thus be dated at least as far back as 1900. In his later years Ballie-Scott became increasingly occupied with old buildings, so that architectural historians lose interest in his work. One new house built at Westhall Hill in Burford was actually constructed from the stone and timber salvaged from a nearby ruin. During the 1920s he restored a fifteenth-century farmhouse near Edenbridge in Kent for his own use. It was set so deep in the country that it was difficult to find, being 'approached by a narrow lane, then another, and along a minor road leading from a small village, set in flowery meadows, pasture and woodland'. Scott himself became increasingly reluctant to leave this earthly paradise for his architectural office; he preferred to stay permanently where things were 'pure, time-defying and pre-industrial revolution'.[14] And his home was old-fashioned in more than appearance: for many years no modern conveniences apart from a small bathroom were installed, the lighting being by candle. In the end, however,

the twentieth century and Mrs Scott prevailed, and electricity was
installed.

With the halcyon cottage went a new style of garden, conceived,
like so much else in this book, in reaction to prevailing mid-
Victorian fashions.

The far-flung exploration that accompanied the extension of the
British Empire in the early nineteenth century brought many new
plants from both temperate and tropical regions. At the same time
technological developments and rising wealth made large-scale
greenhouse cultivation possible, particularly among the richer
classes. Together with the availability of cheap manual labour and
the contemporary liking for ornate display, these factors produced
the garden phenomenon known as 'bedding-out' where strong-
coloured but tender plants are nurtured under glass for planting out
in sequence during the summer. Greenhouse cultivation also
permitted the development of forced early flowering and the raising
of artificially large blooms. And these standards filtered down the
social scale as gardening spread to the suburbs: a good garden was
showy and expensive, radiating money and effort spent on plants,
labour and equipment. An example of what this meant is seen in the
'Complete Plan of a Villa Garden' published in the 1870s in *The
Amateur's Flower Garden* for the well-to-do householder, where the
villa possesses an octagonal greenhouse, an outdoor fernery with
water-wheel, an indoor fernery with ten fountains, a forcing house,
an orchid house and a garden full of azaleas.

A return to naturalness was inevitable, and it was led by William
Robinson, a tireless proselytizer and editor of numerous gardening
magazines, whose views on gardening eventually became as
entrenched as those he had displaced. The story goes that as a young
gardener on a large estate in Ireland, Robinson had quit his
employment, turning off the greenhouse boilers and opening the
shutters on a January night – an apocryphal episode emblematic of
his hatred of bedding-out and forcing. Ten years later he issued his
call to combat in *The Wild Garden,* subtitled 'Or our Groves and
Gardens made beautiful by the Naturalisation of Hardy Exotic
Plants; being one way onwards from the Dark Ages of Flower
Gardening, with suggestions for the Regeneration of the Bare

Borders of the London Parks'.[15]

In this much-reprinted volume, Robinson argued that herbaceous flora from all over the northern hemisphere should be planted in conditions where they could 'thrive without further care'; the result was 'more artistic and delightful' than all the formal beds. A typical 'wild' effect was the showing of bulbs and spring flowers like anemones in drifts under trees at the end of a lawn, or in the grass borders of a smaller garden. The prevailing passion for close-cropped turf (patent mowing machines having appeared at about the same time as cheaper greenhouses) was denounced. Elsewhere in the garden, hardy plants like lilies, forget-me-nots, delphiniums and lupins were favoured, together with some distinctly robust species like michaelmas daisies and cow parsley ('for rough places only'). It was Robinson who first observed that climbing plants are rarely seen to advantage when pinned to walls; instead, he suggested, 'One of the happiest ways of using them is that of training them in a free manner over trees. . . nothing is more beautiful than a veil of clematis montana suspended from the branch' or a holly festooned with honeysuckle. For alpines, he suggested 'wild gardening, on walls, rocks, or ruins'.

The wild garden, strictly speaking, was intended for the more distant parts of the demesne; closer to the house, a more traditional garden was preferred, and *The English Flower Garden* (1883) was the title of one of Robinson's most popular works. Here the products of hothouse and forcing bed were again dismissed in favour of hardy, varied plants. In his own garden at Gravetye Manor, an Elizabethan building, Robinson argued that the age of the house precluded garish colour; instead he planted beds full of tea roses (hitherto neglected in favour of begonias and the like) with carnations and daisies. In the further reaches of his extensive estate he put his 'wild' ideas into practice. Incidentally, as a pugnacious property-owner, he contested local residents' rights to age-old footpaths through Gravetye, which had previously been a farm. Not all was sweet rural harmony: there were often conflicts between different manifestations of pastoralism.

The new flower garden as popularized by Robinson looked back to styles which had almost vanished except among those who could not afford to follow fashion. The cottage garden was already the subject of sentimental attention in the water-colours of Birket

Foster, Helen Allingham and others, and as fashion swung from formalism, so the cottage style was adopted by gardeners in other social classes.[16] By the end of the century, Gertrude Jekyll recalled the old days of bedding-out 'when that and only that meant gardening to most people' compared with the present, when 'the old garden flowers are again honoured and loved and every encouragement freely offered to those who will improve old kinds and bring forward others'.[17] Indeed, the fashion swung so fiercely that many visitors to the Jekyll garden expressed surprise at seeing 'horrid bedding plants' like geraniums. On the contrary, she replied: 'I love geraniums. There are no plants to come near them for pot or box or stone basket, or for massing in any sheltered place in hottest sunshine; and I love their strangely-pleasant smell and their beautiful modern colouring. . .'[18]

Colour was the guiding principle in Gertrude Jekyll's garden design, combined with imagination and common sense. In *Home and Garden* she wrote:

In all free or half-wild garden planting, good and distinct effect . . . is seldom planned or planted except by the garden artist who understands what is technically known as 'drawing'. But by planting with the natural lines of stratification we have only to follow the splendid drawing of Nature herself, and the picture cannot fail to come right.[19]

At the same time:

No year passes that one does not observe some charming combination of plants that one had not intentionally put together. Even though I am always trying to think of some such happy mixtures, others come of themselves. This year the best of these chances was a group of pale sulphur hollyhock seen against yews that were garlanded with clematis flammula; tender yellow and yellow-white and deepest green; upright spire of hollyhock, cloud-like mass of clematis, low-toned sombre ground of solemn yew. . .[20]

Some of her favourite effects were those created by 'wild' planting:

stretches of daffodils in one part of the copse, while another is carpeted with lily-of-the-valley. A cool bank is covered with gaultheria, and just where I thought they would look well as little jewels of beauty, are spreading patches of trillium and the great yellow dog-tooth violet. . .where the wood joins the garden some bold groups of flowering plants are allowed, as of mullein in one part and foxglove in another; for when standing in the free part of the garden, it is pleasant to project the sight far into the wood, and to let the garden influences penetrate here and there, the better to join the one to the other.[21]

Here, the impulsive 'Return to Nature' is checked; the natural world is not allowed to invade the garden, much less the house. Instead, the careful cultivator extends the garden, bringing Nature itself within the bounds of the homestead.

Her own garden at Munstead Wood, described here, was created before the house that it was to complement. Built by Edwin Lutyens at the start of his career, it is one of the finest houses of its period. Miss Jekyll was delighted; she wrote:

Does it often happen to people who have been in a new house only a year and a half, to feel as if they had never lived anywhere else? How it may be with others, I know not, but my own little new-built house is so restful, so satisfying, so kindly sympathetic, that so it seems to me. . .

. . . it is designed and built in the thorough and honest spirit of the good work of old days, and the body of it, so fashioned and feared has, as it were, taken to itself the soul of a more ancient dwelling place. . .

Everything about it is strong and serviceable, and looks and feels as if it would wear and endure for ever.[22]

Trees were incorporated in the fabric in an altogether more natural manner than those of the carved capitals at Baillie-Scott's Blackwell, for heavy oak timber-work formed a structural part of the house: posts, beams, stairs and floors, as well as doors, window frames and banisters, being made of 'good English oak, grown in the neighbourhood'. As the owner wrote: 'there is the actual living interest of knowing where the trees one's house is built of really grew'. The 'three great beams' across the sitting room:

> were growing fifteen years ago a mile and a half away, on the
> outer edge of a fir wood just above a hazel–fringed hollow lane,
> on whose steep sandy sides, here and there level enough to bear a
> patch of vegetation, grew tall bracken and great foxgloves and
> the finest wild Canterbury bells I ever saw. . .
>
> I am glad to know that my beams are these same old friends,
> and that the pleasure that I had in watching them green and
> growing is not destroyed but only changed as I see them
> stretching above me as grand beams of solid English oak. . .[23]

Truly, this house grew from the countryside in which it was
planted.

ARENARIA BALEARICA, self-planted on wall
at Great Tew.

From William Robinson's *The Wild Garden*, first
published 1870

Part IV

Pioneers of the New Life

Letchworth's Reputation depicted by Louis Weirter for
The Citizen, 1909

12

Rational Dress and Diet

It seemed hardly right to emerge from a rose-covered porch attired in stovepipe hat and stiff collar, or to tend the sweet-peas in tight corset and trailing skirt; the Simple Life in a country cottage required an appropriate style of clothing.

Fashionable dress for the bourgeois classes in the late nineteenth century was about as elaborate and uncomfortable as it was possible to be – a perverse declaration of wealth and status that gave its wearers no advantage except that of belonging visibly to a superior caste, since the upkeep of a fashionable wardrobe required considerable money and time, in the services of dressmakers, tailors, laundrywomen and domestic servants. For the sake of a spurious respectability, clothes had to be changed frequently, with morning, afternoon and evening dress donned at the appropriate hour. For this, for the doing and undoing of innumerable buttons and hooks, and for the starching of linen accessories, a personal maid or man-servant might be required. Recalling her childhood in Cambridge during the 1880s and '90s, Gwen Raverat confessed to envying girls with maids when it came to clothes.

She also listed the many layers of garment to which young girls might be subject: woollen combinations, sometimes with frilly cotton combs on top; stays and suspenders, with stockings and cotton drawers; short petticoat, long petticoat and bodice; blouse

and skirt, belt and high button boots.[1] Out of doors, hats were
obligatory even in the garden and gloves if going further afield.
Heavy, full skirts made walking difficult and games virtually
impossible, with the exception of croquet – which may account for
its popularity. Boned corsets were the chief torture, however, when
fashion decreed that every lady aspire to an hour-glass waist and
only the naturally slender were ever at ease. Writing in 1885 Ada S.
Ballin described the results as 'admired deformities', remarking: 'It
is no rare thing to meet ladies so tightly-laced that they positively
cannot lean back in a chair or on a sofa, for if they did they would
suffocate. I know many a girl who can hardly dance because the
agony which exercise causes her in the cramped state of her body is
too great.'[2] Gentlemen suffered somewhat less than ladies, but high
stiff collars and cuffs, hard hats and tight black coats were not the
most comfortable of garments, and evening dress was particularly
formal.

The tyranny of this clothing, maintained for the sake of propriety
and property, was obviously incompatible with any form of the
Simple Life. It was incompatible with comfort, too, and many
people were happy to reject it without dispensing with their servants or seeking out a smallholding. Artists, of course, had long
been excused formal dress, though even they were expected to
conform when dining out. William Morris – who gleefully celebrated his resignation from the directorship of the mining company
which provided his income by sitting on his top hat – was
renowned as the wearer of soft blue cotton shirts like those of a
workman. Edward Carpenter knew he had finally escaped from the
duress of respectability when after settling at Millthorpe he threw
away his dress clothes – an event marked in his autobiography by
italics. Henceforth, if invited to dine out, he explained the position
to his hosts; the response might be a regretful withdrawal of the
invitation, for which Carpenter was not sorry, or an assurance that
he was welcome whatever his clothes. For women the moment of
liberation came when they threw away their stays – an act
comparable to that of 'burning one's bra' in the early 1970s. Janet
Ashbee discarded her corset on a beach soon after her marriage in
1898,[3] while as a plump teenager Gwen Darwin repeatedly and
defiantly took off her stays when 'forcibly corseted' by her mother
and governess.[4]

During the late 1870s the 'aesthetic' dress allowed women to enjoy a short break from tight-lacing, in a style derived from both the quasi-medieval Pre-Raphaelite ladies painted by Morris's friends Burne-Jones and Rossetti, and from the oriental designs and fabrics popularized by Liberty and Co. from 1875 onwards. Silks from India, fine wool from Kashmir, shantung from China and crêpe and satin from Japan displaced thick woollens and stiffened cotton and alpaca, and loose gowns came into fashion, some hanging straight and some draped and clinging. Strong aniline dyes had arrived in 1859 introducing bright pinks and purples which could be dazzling under artificial light; twenty years later the aesthetic movement returned to vegetable dyes and the 'greenery-yallery' effect caricatured by W.S. Gilbert in *Patience* (1881). The flattering tea-gown was one enduring result, although illustrations from the later 1880s suggest that corsets were still *de rigeur* beneath the soft drapery.

By this date in fact tight lacing had become so extreme that waists of over twenty inches were considered ugly and many young women with a natural waist of twenty-five or twenty-six inches squeezed themselves inside stays with a circumference of fifteen or sixteen inches. The time was ripe for a more radical reaction, and to meet this need the Rational Dress Society was founded in 1881, followed the next year by a Hygienic Wearing Apparel Exhibition in Kensington. The aims and objects of the Rational Dress Society were 'to promote the adoption, according to individual taste and convenience, of a style of dress, based upon considerations of health, comfort and beauty, and to deprecate constant changes of fashion which cannot be recommended on any of these grounds'. It specifically protested against tight corsets, high-heeled or narrow-toed footwear, heavy skirts and cloaks which constricted the arms. The annual subscription was 2s 6d.

The R.D.S. sought to promote its objects through 'drawing room meetings', through pamphlets and through the sale of paper patterns. The leading light was Viscountess Harberton, who argued the case forcefully in a twopenny pamphlet entitled *Reasons for Reform in Dress* (*c.* 1884) opening with a keynote quotation from William Morris on decoration being beautiful only if in accord with Nature. In fashionable female dress, Lady Harberton asserted:

not only are the true lines of Nature ignored but they are
positively reversed. . . A woman's waist in Nature's scheme is
broad and flat. Are the bodies of most of the dresses we see
calculated to set off this sort of figure? Are they not, on the
contrary, designed expressly for a round waist, sloping in like the
letter V from under the arms, thus contradicting Nature's lines
directly?[5]

Pointing out that 'women have to catch trains and get about quickly
in all weathers' but that tight stays and skirts weighing up to six
pounds on top of heavy undergarments (elsewhere it was stated that
underclothing should on no account exceed seven pounds in
weight) made women effectively immobile if not invalid, Lady
Harberton insisted that 'a change in the dress of women *must*
come. . . Any form of dress which does not look its best on the
perfect natural figure is faulty and our ingenuity should be applied
to altering such a dress until we get one which does look right under
these conditions instead of as heretofore labouring to alter the
human form to suit the dress.' The forthright Viscountess herself
designed a divided skirt which was only half a yard around the
ankles and extremely convenient for walking.

It was important to have titled persons in such a movement
because of the anxieties dress reform aroused, and other well-
known personalities in the R.D.S. were Marie Stopes and Mrs
Oscar Wilde. Meetings were very popular and full of animated
discussion. 'Indecency!' exclaimed Constance Wilde when replying
to a question on the divided skirt, 'when you look unblushingly on
young girls with arms and necks bare, a mere strap across the
shoulder to prevent the bodice from slipping completely down. . .'
Yet it was considered improper, she continued, 'to say "God has
made us with two legs and not one and we wish for freedom to use
these two legs." Believe me, there is no indecency here!'[6]

However, most women found themselves unable to wear the
'trouser-dress' as it was and covered it with a long skirt, thus
apparently destroying the whole purpose. One such rational outfit
shows a long jacket and waistcoat over a blouse, surmounting a
loose skirt on top of kilted trousers; made of 'pale grey beige' or fine
wool, it was claimed to weigh only three pounds. Another example
of rational clothing were baby's garments designed by Mr Day of

the Royal Hospital for Women and Children, consisting of a long flannel vest, a longer calico shirt and a robe or wrapper on top. All three fastened down the front and could be put on the infant at the same time.[7]

The Rational Dress Society itself had two shops or depots where it was possible to examine and purchase rational clothes and patterns. It also issued a newsletter with articles and correspondence. One item nicely illustrates the impact of dress reform on the ordinary mortal. 'After reading your Gazette,' wrote 'Minnie', 'I feel sure I am quite wrongly dressed.' She asked for suggestions that 'would not make me look peculiar or dowdy', adding 'I have always worn stays . . . my waist measures 22 in. Is that too small? My height is 5ft 4in. I am very well and strong. . .' Although she ended her letter with 'Hoping you will be able to help me', she received a distinctly unsympathetic reply from the editor.[8]

In order to oppose injurious fashions more forcefully, the R.D.S. laid great stress on the 'hygienic' nature of rational clothing. It was argued that tight-lacing displaced the internal organs and that heavy garments led to curvature of the spine and a host of other deformities. Nor were men exempt from the ill-effects. 'The tall stiff hat, whether silk or felt, is a most insanitary article,' wrote Mrs Ada Ballin. 'It presses on the arteries entering the scalp and so lessens its blood supply, interfering with the nutrition of the hair' and thus causing baldness. She deplored the new City custom of wearing hats inside the office as well as in the street and advocated ventilation holes or preferably going bareheaded. 'The poor,' she commented, 'if cleanly, have very good heads of hair'; they rarely wore hats.[9]

The major 'scientific' principle associated with rational dress was that of the beneficence of wool, a theory that originated with Dr Gustav Jaeger of Stuttgart who, as a professor of physiology, was presumed to know what he was talking about. According to Jaeger, wool clothing was health-giving because it encouraged the noxious gases emanating from the body to evaporate, while clothes made from vegetable fibres attracted poisonous substances, especially when wet or cold, and made the body more susceptible to disease. The rationale for this was that animal wool was designed by Nature to keep animals well and warm whereas vegetable fibre 'is not a natural clothing material' and only human perversity had led to the creation of linen and cotton. (One wonders what would have been thought of synthetic fibres.) The exposition of Jaeger's ideas – which he claimed had transformed him from an obese, dyspeptic invalid into a healthy, energetic individual – was published in Britain as *Essays on Health Culture,* translated by his disciple Lewis R.S. Tomalin, and is an amazing book, building several chapters of nonsensical theory on to the animal–vegetable dichotomy, verified by a process of 'nerve-measurement' and followed by a garment-by-garment account of the 'Sanitary Woollen System' of clothing which Jaeger devised to put his ideas into practice. The book finishes with assorted observations on camel hair, writer's cramp (caused by the vegetable nature of paper and cured by a woollen pad placed under the writing hand) and other such matters. As expounded by Jaeger, the Sanitary Woollen System was rigorous:

> It is most important to bear in mind that it is not enough to wear wool next to the skin and any other material over it. If at any point underclothing or lining, or padding or stiffening of vegetable fibre, or of silk, intervene between the body and the outer atmosphere, an obstacle is set up to the free passage of the exhalation from the skin, with the result that the noxious portion of the exhalation settles in the vegetable fibre, which consequently becomes mal-odorous; and everything mal-odorous is prejudicial to the health. . .
>
> All material, therefore, manufactured of or adulterated with vegetable fibre should be discarded, whether in the form of underclothing or of linings or pockets etc., to the outer clothing. The same principle holds good for Bedding. . .[10]

Jaeger clothing was designed for men and the pioneer garment was the sanitary wool shirt, made of stockinette and fastened on the shoulder with a double layer across the chest. Drawers were 'a necessary evil'; far better to bring the shirt tail through the legs and safety-pin it to the front. Normal trousers were an 'unaesthetic monstrosity' and should be replaced by close-fitting knitted leggings held up by sanitary woollen braces. They were worn with a close-fitting unlined coat, soft hat or cap, and woollen gloves, plus woollen handkerchief. All garments were to be made of natural yarn, as dyes were poisonous substances, and the total effect could be extraordinary. In the early days of the craze, Bernard Shaw, young and penurious in London, saved up ten pounds to buy a Jaeger suit in the belief that it would keep him healthy for the rest of his life. With his spindly figure and red hair and beard, he was described as looking like a forked radish.

The only garment which seems to have defeated the good doctor was the collar. Made out of wool, it tended to go yellow with washing, which was 'undoubtedly an obstacle to its more general adoption'. An even more serious problem, it was admitted, 'is the inevitable tendency of the Woollen Collar to shrink'. Woollen boots were considered beneficial – 'Imprisoned in impervious leather the feet cannot *breathe*' – but impractical, and a broad boot something like the 'earth shoe' of the 1970s was designed. Socks with toes completed the costume. For night–time, the correct mode was a woollen sleeping suit with feet, woollen sheets and blankets and pillows with a horsehair mattress. If of wood (vegetable) the bed should be varnished to keep the poisonous vapours at bay, and placed with the head towards the open window. Here is the origin of that nursery edict that one should always sleep with the window open – and of the apparently traditional belief in 'wool next to the skin'. Less amusing to quote are Jaeger's assertions that proper woollen clothing would reduce the high rate of infant mortality in contemporary cities.

The British Jaeger clothing company – now a West End fashion store – was established by Tomalin in 1883 and a cult following of 'Woolleners' adopted the strange garments, which were soon assimilated into the dress reform movement. Despite their efforts, however, enthusiasts were invariably looked upon as freaks and frumps. This led, in 1890, to the launching of a new group called the Healthy and Artistic Dress Union. This was formed by Dr Sophie Bryant, headmistress of the North London Collegiate School, and aimed at bringing beauty as well as rationality into modern clothing. It was supported by a number of Royal Academicians, friends of the painter Henry Holiday, who was a leading figure in the H.A.D.U., and by a number of titled ladies.[11]

All these attempts at dress reform failed, in their own eyes, to convert the masses but they nevertheless helped the general movement towards greater ease and comfort. From the 1890s onwards the accepted 'progressive' attire for middle-class men was soft shirt, soft tie, Norfolk–type jacket and knickerbockers. With the addition of fisherman's jerseys, this was more or less the uniform chosen for the new schools at Abbotsholme and Bedales, at a time when public school boys were still dressed in Eton collars and top hats, and it soon became familiar and acceptable wear in town, at least during the daytime. As late as 1913 Rupert Brooke defied convention when he wore a soft grey flannel shirt to an after–dinner gathering at W.B. Yeats's London flat.[12] Women were expected to wear hats when out of doors; that the women of the Whiteway commune went bareheaded was sure proof of their immorality. Men wearing smocks in imitation of shepherds and carters were considered merely eccentric.

Sandals featured largely in the literature and beliefs of dress reform and the connection with back–to–nature cranks, vegetarians, hippies and 'whole–earthers' of several generations persists to this day. They were adopted because of the stiff and often uncomfortable boots and shoes then available, and from the notion that feet needed to 'breathe'. The sandal craze appears to have begun when Edward Carpenter acquired the pattern of an Indian sandal from his friend Harold Cox of the ill-fated Craig Farm, and was taught how to make it up by a Sheffield comrade who was also a bootmaker by trade. When George and Lucy Adams moved to Millthorpe to look after the housekeeping and help with the cultivation, George also took to sandal-making (his own father had been a cobbler). On leaving Millthorpe he first moved back to Sheffield where he carried on his new craft; an advertisement in 1892 in *Seed-Time*, the journal of the Fellowship of the New Life in its pre–Brotherhood days reads as follows:

SANDALS

Leather Sandals, made from a pattern used in Cashmere can be worn either with or without stockings, and are suitable for indoor use at all times, and for outdoors in dry weather. They are pleasant to wear and elegant in appearance, and by restoring freedom and circulation to the foot, render it in a short time as healthy and vital as the hand. To persons suffering from cold feet they are specially recommended. The best materials only are

used, and the sandals are very durable.
Price 10s 6d a pair; lower terms for children. Orders
may be sent to either of the undersigned:
George E Adams, 94, Colver Road, Sheffield.
Edward Carpenter, Holmesfield, Chesterfield.

In 1897 the dress reformist W.A. Macdonald was excluded from the British Museum Reading Room for wearing sandals; Carpenter and others signed a protest letter to the press in his defence.[13]

Women also espoused sandals, although this was less remarkable, as far as the rest of the population was concerned, than the short skirts and loose scarves adopted by 'progressive' women. By the early 1900s those who attached themselves to what would now be termed libertarian ideas had probably all shed their stays and were wearing far more comfortable clothes than their mothers. It should be remembered, however, that rational dress had very little impact on high fashion, which continued to devise extremely unnatural styles for its wealthy clients. Shortly before the First World War, the hobble skirt was in vogue, presumably to demonstrate that rich women had no need of legs but went everywhere by carriage. Those who preferred natural exercise – and they were a growing number, as country walks, cycling and modern sports were taken up – wore comfortable blouses and loose skirts, which could be exchanged for knickerbockers when walking or cycling.

Thus the overall effect of the rational dress movement was in favour of freedom and naturalness against the artificiality and discomfort imposed on women and to a lesser extent men by the arbiters of fashionable wear. Perhaps because fashion in dress is a particularly irrational matter, the results were often as formal and uncomfortable as the clothes they were intended to replace. Certainly the same rigid, prescriptive approach prevailed and it was not until the stern admonitions of the Rational Dress Society and Dr Jaeger had had time to mellow that a genuinely freer and easier style of dress, which enabled individuals to find their own style in a more or less natural manner, was introduced and accepted. The following account of the clothing designed and worn by Dorelia John, wife of Augustus, at her home Alderney Manor from 1911 onwards illustrates the happy results of dress reform allied to creative talent. For the numerous children in the John household, Dorelia designed a kind of uniform: long belted smocks over corduroy knickerbockers with red socks for the boys, and long, loose natural woollen dresses with saffron socks for the girls. As for herself:

> She was a skilled dressmaker. From cotton velveteen or shantung in bright dyes and shimmering surfaces; from unusual prints, often Indian or Mediterranean in origin, she evolved clothes that followed the movement of the body, timelessly, like classic draperies. Her long flowing dresses that reached the ground with their high waistline and long sleeves topped by a broad-brimmed straw hat, its sweeping line like those of the French peasants, became a uniform adopted by nearly all the girls at art colleges, and a symbol, in their metropolitan surroundings, of an unsevered connection with country things, with the very substance of the country. [14]

Dress reform was closely linked to diet reform, sharing the concern with health and hygiene; dietary reform meant 'No Flesh Eating' or vegetarianism. Modern vegetarianism appears to have surfaced in England in the late 1840s and spread to Europe and the United States before re-emerging strongly in Britain during the 1880s. This sketchy history is confirmed by the distribution of entries in the British Library catalogue, which shows a huge increase in books, pamphlets and periodicals relating to vegetarianism in the last twenty years of the century. A pioneer work was Howard Williams's *The Ethics of Diet* (1883), which by the use of quotations sought to demonstrate that a long list of eminent persons from Buddha and Pythagoras to Swedenborg and Shelley had been vegetarians, and that renouncing meat did not therefore lead to mental and physical enfeeblement, as was commonly supposed.

The Vegetarian Society, founded in 1850 and based in Manchester, was joined by many other local and national groups in the years 1880 to 1890, and there was a rash of new vegetarian periodicals. The *Vegetarian Messenger* started a new series in 1887, the weekly *Vegetarian* was launched in 1888, followed by the *Hygienic Review* in 1893 and *Humanity* in 1895. The last-named was edited by Henry Salt, one of the original practitioners of the Simple Life, who devoted most of his energies to combating cruelty and what he considered barbaric social practices such as hanging and flogging. In his autobiography *Seventy Years Among Savages,* published in 1921, Salt recalled:

> Forty years ago, the possibility of living healthily on a non–flesh diet was by no means so generally admitted as it is now; and consequently very naive and artless objections used to be advanced against abstinence from butcher's meat. Mr Kegan Paul told me that he had once heard a lady say to F.W. Newman: 'But, Professor, don't you feel very weak?', to which the Professor sturdily replied: 'Madam, feel my calves'.[15]

Salt spent a good deal of his time advocating vegetarianism and exposing the arguments of those who opposed it – for although it was a practice which hardly hurt or inconvenienced others it was vigorously and often foolishly attacked because of the fact that, as Salt recognized, 'the cannibal conscience is somewhat guilty and ill at ease'. In 1892 Salt published his most forceful book, *Animals' Rights,* arguing against all killing of animals (except in times of absolute necessity such as famine). This included not only butchery for food purposes but also all forms of game hunting and shooting whether for trophies or skins. This was a period of great popularity in field sports in Britain, owing to the increase in wealthy gentlemen for whom it formed a pleasant and expensive recreation. With the depression in agriculture, a large acreage of arable land had been turned over to game as a more profitable form of husbandry, thousands of birds being reared each year to be shot down by shooting parties. In Salt's view, hunting was equally obnoxious and he waged a special campaign against the Royal Buckhounds, a stag hunt anciently associated with the crown (the Queen's distaste for stag-hunting led to the disbanding of the Buckhounds in 1901). If killing for sport was unacceptable to Salt and his supporters in the Humanitarian League, the pursuit of exotic feathers, furs and skins for use in 'murderous millinery' and haute couture was simply 'reckless barbarism', and with a far-sighted view that today's conservationists must wish had been more widely heeded, they protested that such unnecessary slaughter of animals would lead to the rapid extermination of several species. Vivisection was equally abhorrent, as were the primitive methods of killing employed in contemporary slaughterhouses.

Unfortunately, developments in animal husbandry, canning, shipping and cold storage towards the end of the nineteenth century meant that, in general, more people could afford to eat more meat. For the richer classes there appears to have been something of an explosion in the amount and variety of fish, flesh and fowl eaten, with dinners regularly including all three items in multi-course meals. For the poor, who could rarely afford it, meat was a symbol of well-being, and it was therefore mostly from among the ranks of the middle classes that vegetarians emerged, revolted by the over-indulgence and selfish contempt for the less fortunate they saw around them. Within a short while vegetarianism was virtually obligatory amongst those holding 'advanced' views, particularly those inclined to ideas of Simplification. Like Salt, Carpenter and Shaw were early and well-known converts, although Carpenter hated dogmatism and chose not to shun meat absolutely, believing that an occasional taste helped to temper the soul, and the palate. Amongst those holding back-to-the-land beliefs, vegetarianism was usually a primary article of faith from the beginning, and owed nothing to the difficulties of stock-rearing on small farms. Most of the agrarian communes were as firmly committed to no meat as to self-sufficient cultivation; Tolstoy, from whom many notions were adopted, himself practised vegetarianism and an un-aristocratic plainness of diet which was eagerly copied.

Enthusiasts of vegetarianism preached their cause throughout the 1880s in a number of influential places. There was a vegetarian restaurant at the 1884 International Health Exhibition and at the 1886 Liverpool Exhibition, and an international vegetarian conference at the 1893 Chicago World's Fair. The growth in interest was reflected in the number of local groups which sprang up in Britain and the United States and no doubt in Europe as well. By the mid-1890s there were some thirty affiliated groups in Britian, not forgetting Ireland and New South Wales. There were vegetarian rambling clubs and vegetarian cycling clubs and vegetarian athletic clubs, all dedicated to the belief that vegetarianism was conducive to good health. In June 1894 the Northern Heights Vegetarian Society of Hornsey held a picnic in Tetherdown Woods, with speeches, open-air music and drama and vegetarian refreshments. A prominent member of this Society was R.K. Goodrich, who went on to found the Methwold Fruit Farm Colony and supply his former friends and companions weekly hampers of fresh fruit and vegetables.

Vegetarianism could become almost a faith, replacing more conventional beliefs and having a strong flavour of the millennium. 'Thus only,' wrote A.F. Hills in the *Hygienic Review* in an article on 'Vital Food', 'can the fountains of vitality be replenished. It is not enough to abstain from the indulgence in dead and stimulating foods; under the new gospel of vegetarianism we listen to the beatitudes of Vital Food and Vital Drink. It is good to give up the conventional carnality of carrion; it is better to adopt the living luxury of the kindly fruits of the earth.'[16]

Another article asserted that vegetarianism led not only to personal health but to social improvements:

> If money were not spent on meat, tobacco,opium, alcohol, tea, coffee and other poisons, what wonders would ensue!
>
> You could eat fruit with every meal and set farmers to work planting orchards; you could have fresh vegetables and treble the number of gardeners; money to buy books and time and brains clear for reading them; bakers might learn to provide genuine wholemeal bread and every child could sip a cup of milk with every meal . . . Picture to yourself such a reformed city, where fruiterers, bakers, florists displace butchers, dramsellers, druggists and tobacconists . . .[17]

The popularity of vegetarianism, even among those who were not wholehearted believers, is indicated in the number of vegetarian restaurants that opened in the big cities for clients who preferred non-meat dishes together with what would today be termed health foods – brown bread, salads, fresh fruit desserts. In 1894 there were fourteen such restaurants in London, five in Manchester and one each in Dublin and Belfast. Several vegetarian holiday guest-houses advertised in the various magazines – among them the vegetarian farm run by Mr and Mrs Hebditch at New Cross near Ilminster. Their enthusiasm for diet reform had led the Hebditches into fruit farming, and they built up a flourishing business supplying hampers of vegetarian food: fruit, vegetables, jam, butter, cream, eggs (how vegetarian are these?) together with twenty-eight pounds of wheatmeal flour for four shillings. There were a number of vegetarian nursing homes for convalescent patients, while across the Atlantic, Dr J.H. Kellogg of cornflake fame was supervisor of a vegetarian sanatorium in Michigan. Mapleton's Nut Food Co. Ltd., founded by the former leader of the Norton Colony, ran advertisements declaring: 'Animal Food is dangerous in any form and just now the Cow is under suspicion. Nuts and Fruit are man's natural diet.'[18]

The celebrated yeast extract Marmite was invented to provide a vegetarian alternative to beef broth and gravy, and a substance named Proteid Food was advertised by its inventor Eustace Miles as: 'Wonderfully sustaining. Free from Uric Acid. Rich in Phosphates. The best Food for the Brain and Nerves. Easily digested. Ilb, post free, 1/7.' This has apparently not survived.

Eustace Miles ran a well patronized health food restaurant in Chandos Street, off the Strand in London, which features in the memoirs and biographies of many literary figures of the Edwardian era; while sufficiently respectable for ladies to lunch there unaccompanied, it also appears to have flirted with advanced ideas on relations between the sexes. Each table was equipped with a small flag, which if raised signalled to other customers that the person concerned wished to converse, a device regarded as highly daring in an age when rigorous chaperoning was the rule. Eustace Miles was a self-appointed health instructor; as well as running the restaurant, he issued books of vegetarian recipes and physical exercises, and pamphlets on 'Control and Self-Expression', 'How to Remember', 'Breathing' and 'Let's Play the Game'. In *The Eustace Miles System of Physical Culture with Hints as to Diet* (1907) he elaborated ten dietary principles, covering economy, digestibility, compactness, speed of preparation, variety and 'cleansing power', ending with a paragraph on the problems caused by too rigid adherence to a reformed diet, which 'nearly always means that the person must be cut off from social life and fellowship'. Miles recommended compromise:

The reformer who is almost exactly like other people, except that he is rather healthier, has a great deal more influence among the best people than the reformer who makes a point of being as unlike them as possible: for example, the reformer who wears no hat, has very long hair, wears no collar or tie or waistcoat, and wears no socks but only sandals, and who perhaps, confines his diet to fruit and nuts and salads.[19]

Where might such an apparition be found? Not only in the person of G.B. Shaw, but in the pages of the *Open Road,* a small vegetarian magazine previously entitled *Ye Crank,* edited by the return-to-nature publishers Florence and C.W. Daniel.

Doubtless a reformed and simplified diet did much to improve the health of certain individuals – and many prominent vegetarians lived healthily on into advanced old age – but far greater claims were made by some adherents. Along with the return to manual labour or craft production, vegetarianism was seen as bringing wide benefits, even a cure for bloated urbanism, as a correspondent to the *Vegetarian Review* outlined in 1895:

> Steadily and surely enough England is becoming a huge desert, picked out here and there with big manufacturing centres. London alone represents something like five millions of souls. Manchester and Liverpool are gradually becoming merged and the rural districts are going to decay. And no-one seems able to suggest a remedy. Will Vegetarianism help in the matter? I think it will and in this wise. The ordinary man or woman thinks only of food as an article to be purchased at the nearest cheesemongers or butchers, whilst the vegetarian recognises the fact – simple enough in all conscience – that man depends for his food upon his mother Earth, and that the greater the gulf between him and the direct production of his food the more dangerous his position becomes . . .[20]

A prescient sentiment, looking forward some seventy years to the 'Whole Earth' movement (which also adopted vegetarianism) but sadly not specifying how vegetarianism could stop industrialization.

A topic which is strictly speaking not connected with diet or dress reform yet seems somehow to occur in the same context – and also features in that 1960s compendium the *Whole Earth Catalogue* – is sanitary reform. This has nothing to do, as one might expect, with the great Victorian advances in urban sewage disposal, clean water and efficient drainage systems which did so much to reduce urban mortality during the nineteenth century. Indeed this seems to have been a regressive, contrary movement, for it advocated a return to 'natural' methods of waste disposal, mainly through the use of earth closets.

The chief advocate of earth over water in sewage treatment was one George Vivian Poore, M.D., F.R.C.P., who in 1893 published *Essays in Rural Hygiene,* where he argued first against over-concentration of population in cities, and secondly against water-borne sewage, which he believed was founded on a scientific error, and was likely to cause disease, river pollution and the contamination of springs and wells. In a chapter entitled 'The Living Earth' he demonstrated the power of topsoil to absorb and break down all organic matter into compost. In 'The House', he described 'the many evils which are practically inseparable from what are known as modern sanitary fittings', and insisted that 'no house can be securely and permanently wholesome unless it have tolerably direct relations with cultivable land'. In 'Personal Experiences', he described the property he held in Andover, and how he had converted a row of cottages from water closets back to the earth closet system, the contents being removed daily and dug into his own adjoining garden. As a result, the dwellings were more hygienic, there being no more blockages, breakages and seepings from the sewage pipes, which had hitherto emptied into a small stream, while 'the fertility and beauty of the garden have been enormously increased, and its value, which was depreciated by its filthy surroundings, has probably rather more than recovered'. This account was accompanied by photographs of the succulent soft fruit produced in the said garden.

In a suburban villa on the outskirts of London, Dr Poore also experimented by removing the water closet and cesspool and installing an earth closet, whose contents were buried every day just beneath the surface of the garden. Dirty water from kitchen and bathroom was disposed of by means of an elaborate system of pipes running from the house to the shrubbery and altogether, Dr Poore concluded, it was a great satisfaction to know that a natural system of waste disposal was being used, with no risk of self-infection from faulty plumbing, nor of public pollution through the discharge of sewage into rivers and streams. Since the majority of domestic and industrial waste at this date went more or less untreated into rivers, this was not a small consideration. However, public health regulations were against Dr Poore: increasingly it became obligatory to connect houses to the main sewage systems, and private waste disposal was not looked on favourably. A number of 'earth enthusiasts' took up the cause of the earth closet, however, notably the founders of the new schools at Abbotsholme and Bedales, where the lavatory contents were systematically used as fertilizer for the vegetable beds. It is possible that the practice was more widespread, particularly in the dwellings inhabited by back-to-the-land enthusiasts, but by the nature of the subject little information is available.

Rational, Artistic and Modern Costumes.

LOUISE BARRY,

152, REGENT STREET.

Speciality **RATIONAL DRESS**, as supplied to Viscountess Harberton. Light, stylish skirts without the additional weight of foundation lining. Fashionable Modern Costumes. Estimates Reasonable. Perfect Fit.

Ladies' Material accepted if required.

Advertisements from the *Rational Dress Society Gazette*, 1888

13

New Schools

The movement towards greater freedom and naturalism which accompanied the cult of the countryside touched on virtually all aspects of life and society, with a direct and visible, if limited, impact on the field of education. Here, reaction against the corseting formalism and competitiveness characteristic of high Victorian schooling emerged as a call for the radical reform of teaching, and once launched, it developed into that educational current generally identified with the 'progressive' schools, although such ideas have now become pedagogically mainstream.

In fact, when the demand for alternatives arose, the 'typical' public school with all its traditions and conventions had been only recently established. Most of the major foundations were either started or reformed in mid-century, in response to the growing demand from the professions and the colonial service. Perhaps owing to the relatively rapid turnover of pupils, however, they had already begun to ossify. Very formal teaching and a strict system of rules and privileges was the basis of all private schools, and the same ethic was carried over into the public sector, where from 1870 onwards education for all was provided through a mixture of 'church' and 'board' schools. In both types, the curriculum comprised facts to be memorized and learning was enforced with disciplinary punishments and beating. The public schools placed most emphasis on classics and games, the state schools stressed basic but accurate numeracy and regular handwriting, but neither offered much to the hand or the heart, as Ashbee complained. Both had their activities determined by the purposes they were designed to serve – in the case of the state schools, the expansion of commerce and public administration in the wake of industrialism, with the accompanying demand for clerks and manual workers sufficiently educated to read instructions, keep records and make their own calculations. The independent schools were there to train potential managers and leaders, for the diplomatic service and armed forces down through industry and trade. Educational content was less important than learning how to give and take orders, and co-operation was discouraged except on the sports field, where team games were developed to encourage the corporate spirit and provide for the largest number of boys the greatest amount of exercise with the smallest amount of supervision (rugby football, it is thought, being developed for just this purpose).

Boys were, of course, the only pupils in such schools. While state schools were generally though not always mixed, the sons and daughters of the upper and middle classes were kept apart in education as in other ways. This was due in part to ideas of propriety, which strengthened as the nineteenth century progressed, partly because the public schools were mostly boarding establishments, and partly because girls were thought to require a different type of education, based on accomplishments rather than authority. However, as potential customers increased – owing to the growing number of colonial administrators and army families living abroad – so schools were founded to cater for their daughters, copying the public school model. The idea of co-education was rarely contemplated.

At its best, the Victorian public school offered an education that was both rigorous and humane, as many distinguished products demonstrated. Many men, however, believed that they had survived despite their schooldays, which were often emotionally terrifying, sometimes physically brutal and almost always narrow and snobbish. Beating by prefects and staff was commonplace, and discipline was maintained by a combination of exhaustive time-tabling, so that every moment of the day had its ordained activity, and multiple regulations whereby harmless activities like putting one's hands into one's pockets or leaving less than a half-inch margin were punishable offences. To add to the normal difficulties of adolescence, the enclosed nature of boarding school led to a great deal of clandestine emotional and sexual activity, which was harmful to some because fiercely frowned upon and therefore guilt-inducing.

J.H. Badley, one of the pioneers of the new school movement, later assessed his own experience as a boy at Rugby in the early 1880s in the following terms:

> To Greek and Latin more working periods were allotted than to all other subjects altogether, and the scanty time given to these others was not turned to good effect by living methods of teaching. French, for example, was taught in the same way as a dead language . . . History was a matter of dates, battles and political changes . . . In the few periods given to Mathematics I seem in retrospect to have done nothing but learn Euclid by rote, or attempt conjuring tricks (which might or might not come off) . . . Science was an optional subject, commonly regarded as merely a relaxation . . .
>
>   At best it was a training at second-hand in that it was entirely bookish, teaching us to look at everything through others' eyes . . .

Although not entirely regretting his classical training, Badley then summed up his education:

> I am conscious of the loss I have suffered throughout life from the fact that during some of the most formulative years my mental development was so narrowly circumscribed, and that much of whatever potentialities I possessed had so little nourishment and guidance. It was, eventually, the realisation of this loss that made me desirous of broadening the scope of education and making available for others what was lacking in the experience of so many of my generation.[1]

Strictly speaking, the pioneer of the new school movement was Cecil Reddie, who in 1889 founded his school Abbotsholme near Ashbourne in Derbyshire. Reddie was a science graduate who studied in Germany and taught at Fettes and Clifton before raising sufficient support to start his own establishment, on radically different lines. There were within the existing educational system those who felt that innovation was needed and that the Empire's ascendancy was threatened by other nations, such as Germany, where more adventurous schools were already in being, but the main impetus to Reddie's ideas was provided by Edward Carpenter and others on the socialist side, who desired a less class-based school system for the happier development of all. Both Carpenter and Reddie were associated with the Fellowship of the New Life, that seed-bed of alternative thinking, which in 1886 issued an outline of the type of school it sought. This was one which would 'secure the harmonious development of all the faculties of the child, by guiding and influencing its spontaneous energies and efforts, and providing healthy environment and nutriment for its expanding life'.[2] The following year Carpenter visited Reddie at Clifton and the idea was taken further. One suggestion was that Reddie should join forces with R.F. (Bob) Muirhead, mathematics teacher and Socialist League member from Glasgow, who was a close friend of Carpenter's, to set up a school near Millthorpe.

Reddie stayed at Millthorpe from April to October 1888, absorbing Carpenter's influence and working out his ideas. The influence was both intellectual and emotional, enabling Reddie to come to terms with his own strong desire for masculine affection (which he seems successfully to have sublimated through teaching) which clearly contributed to his notions of how a school should be run.[3] The following New Year's Eve Reddie and Muirhead drew up a detailed outline of the new school they proposed to start.

Money was raised from the four partners in the venture: Reddie, who gave a modest £88, Muirhead, Carpenter and William Cassels, who contributed £2,000 to purchase a large house, renamed Abbotsholme, above the river Dove. Cassels is described as a disciple of Ruskin's educational ideas (which were not dissimilar to Reddie's, particularly in respect of their elitist approach); as someone with some practical as opposed to classroom experience, he was to take charge of the 'outdoor' side of the school. Muirhead was in charge of 'engineering and maths'. Before the opening of the school in the autumn of 1889 Carpenter withdrew from active management, although he continued to give moral and material support, and as a result of personal friction, Muirhead and Cassels also resigned at the end of the first term, taking their investments with them. It was not an auspicious start but on Carpenter's reputation and Reddie's impressive though autocratic personality the school survived, with most of its ideals unchanged.

Although Abbotsholme was claimed by the New Life Fellowship, which announced its opening in the first issue of its magazine, noting that the educational atmosphere would aim to stimulate the dormant aesthetic sensibilities of the average boy and that religious services would be unsectarian, it was largely Carpenter's ideas that prevailed. Foremost of these was the belief in the importance of being close to Nature. Thus the setting of the school in the country among hills and woods with the river close by was an essential feature of the new school; natural educational development could not take place in an unnatural or ugly (urban) environment. In a lecture in 1901 Reddie explained that as the city was a bad influence, so:

> In order to avoid the ill effects of modern town life, its unwholesome physical surroundings, with the distractions of its intellectual activity and the dangers of its moral atmosphere, a school should be remote from towns and placed amid the wholesome, beautiful, simple, and fundamentally instructive surroundings of the country. In this way our boys can see the world as it was before towns existed; and they can come into contact with the fundamental industry of agriculture, the prerequisite of all civilised life.

He went on to link this, less originally, with education, saying that 'contact with Nature and Nature's laws . . . is the best introduction to the whole field of Nature Knowledge and Natural Science', and that:

> out in the fields, in the garden, among the trees, on the river, [the boys] can perform those simple operations which give man the mastery of Nature. As the circle of the year revolves they see the procession of the seasons, the procession of the flowers, the sequence of ploughing, sowing, reaping, – all serving as a background and foundation to their subsequent study of civilisation.[4]

This pastoral element made the school unique, although there were other innovations. In the classroom teaching methods were advanced, with the emphasis on the living languages English, German and French, together with mathematics and science. The daily timetable was divided into three parts: the morning for class-work, the afternoon for outdoor activities or manual work, and the evening for music, art and recreation. Social and spiritual development was deemed as important as academic progress, and although he did not advertise the fact too explicitly, Reddie planned to explain the facts of life and feeling to his pupils in a systematic and non-punitive way, to ensure that they were not ashamed or ignorant of their own bodies and emotions. This was in keeping with the advanced ideas of the time. Estate work was equally radical. According to Carpenter, the sons of the upper and middle classes who would form the school's pupils should learn the manual tasks – gardening, cookery, woodwork – normally done for them by servants. The school would be run on the lines of a Millthorpe smallholding, cultivating vegetables for its own consumption, keeping cows, and carrying out its own carpentry, tailoring and leatherwork (including boot- and sandal-making). Several of these projects did not materialize, but overall the pattern was decidedly new. Vegetables were indeed grown and harvested by the boys; all classes were suspended during haymaking; digging, wood-chopping and fencing were perennial tasks; and there were livestock and bees to be looked after. Such a mixture of farm and school was unknown in England. Defending the use of pupils as free labour, Reddie wrote in 1900:

> Why should they not help to pick the fruit that they themselves are going to eat; to dig the potatoes they planted and will them-selves devour; or mow the grass and make and carry the hay which feed the cattle that yield them milk and cream and butter? . . . Our practice, however, is to let every boy according to his size and strength, his intelligence and aptitude, do that which he can do best . . . in order that he may know what work is, and may go through a complete curriculum embracing, as far as possible, all that is necessary to be done on the place.[5]

Still following Carpenter, and to a lesser extent Ashbee, who had stayed at Millthorpe in 1886 shortly before Reddie, the new school had a strong arts and crafts element. Carving, carpentry, metal-work and such other crafts as could be mustered were taught, with the idea that as far as possible the boys themselves should decorate and embellish the school; beautiful surroundings indoors and out would contribute to the scholastic flowering of each pupil.

As outlined, the new school was conceived as the educational complement to the agrarian and craft communities dreamt of by Ruskin and Morris, with the homogenic aspect added by Carpenter; not surprisingly, it held in the early years features from all the impulses described in this book. Some of the connections were direct: as well as supplying ideas, Ashbee joined Reddie around 1890 in establishing a short-lived 'country centre' of the Guild of Handicraft at Abbotsholme, to which guildsman and cabinet-maker H. Phillips was dispatched from Whitechapel, to make furniture for the new school. The agricultural side was run by a resident farm manager. 'On the farm the livestock had been steadily increasing,' wrote Reddie of the early years, possibly with some hyperbole. 'Horses, cows, fowls, pigs, ducks and bees but especially the horses and the poultry have been partially tended by the boys,' he added, indicating that the serious farm work was not done by pupils.[6] At one stage the man in charge of the farm was called Pearson – a name which may indicate a connection with St George's Farm at Totley, where the Pearson family were then living with John Furniss and other 'communists'. It is possible that Carpenter's links with both farm and school helped him to supply Reddie with a farm manager who both knew his job and sympa-thized with the communal aims of the school.

The other main feature of Abbotsholme was its preoccupation with health and hygiene, fresh air, fresh vegetables, naked bathing and 'rational' clothing. This was quite unlike the stuffy conditions, poor food supplemented by 'tuck' and formal attire then common to most public schools. Reddie's ideas on dress largely derived from Carpenter, and were favoured by enlightened parents, though they were somewhat unusual in others' eyes. Abbotsholme boys, Reddie pronounced 'are expected to wear as little clothing as is compatible with health, comfort and decency; to wear, as far as possible, nothing tight and nothing but wool, which keeps sweet and will not burn, in addition to being both warm and light. They are also expected to avoid, as far as possible, all dyed garments and all peculiarities dictated by shifting fashion.'[7] The school suit was Reddie's own choice of clothes and one which he never varied: Norfolk jacket with four outer pockets and a belt, worn over a soft woollen shirt and thick knickerbockers with knee socks and sturdy boots. One of the original pupils recalled how they assembled in 1889 in this unusual uniform, with a variety of headgear, as Reddie had forgotten to design a school hat. Several mothers had dispatched their sons with bowlers, apparently feeling that these would redress the informality of the jackets, but deerstalkers and prep. school caps also featured, together with a couple of dark blue French berets, which Reddie immediately adopted for the whole school. Outdoors, the boys appear to have worn woollen jerseys and long flannel shorts – without underwear, which must have been somewhat rough – donning jackets and berets on outside excursions.[8]

Reddie had decided views on every aspect of school organization, and current ideas on hygiene fuelled his talent for elaborate rules and explanations. In 1893 he drew up a set of regulations to be framed and hung in each dormitory, which included in their seventeen paragraphs the following admonitions:

> As everyone should sleep as nearly as possible in the open air, the windows of a sleeping chamber should be wide open the entire night, except in *very* cold, wet or windy weather . . .
>
> Good ventilation promotes the oxygenation and the healthy circulation of the blood, which warms the body. The pure air of heaven also hardens the body against disease, and prevents effeminacy.

The boys were further instructed never, ever, to sleep with their heads under the bedclothes (as some were doubtless doing to keep warm) and always to lie on their side, never front or back. The dormitories evidently gave Reddie some trouble, for in 1903 he penned another disquisition on 'The Educative Value of Life in Dormitory', which dealt with undressing. Noting that 'in many schools a great deal of mischief takes place in Dormitory', he discussed the problem:

While there is something wholesome, physically, intellectually
and morally, in nakedness, there is something paralysing in the
terror from which many people suffer of being seen without their
Clothes. On the other hand, it is not desirable that a Boy should
have to dress and undress before a crowd. The number seven hits
the happy mean.

He then blamed 'three-quarters, if not all, of the evil thoughts and
evil actions of youngsters', to say nothing of 'nearly all the vice
which everyone deplores' (i.e. homosexuality) on the desperate
Victorian attempts to conceal all bodies from view. At
Abbotsholme the opposite approach was used, to great success, in
Reddie's view:

> The natural curiosity with regard to the body, which all boys
> feel, is satisfied and can only be satisfied properly, by allowing
> them to see the bodies of others in a natural and wholesome way
> . . . at all times, but particularly in the Dormitory and during the
> open-air bathing in the river, they are encouraged to act as if they
> were unaware whether clothed or not.[9]

An illustrated booklet on the school issued in 1904 has photographs
depicting this 'natural, simple and modest' approach, one showing
three discreetly naked figures washing in large basins in the dormitory and the other a long shot of nude swimming in the river. This
was in fact no novelty: Gwen Raverat described the public bathing
places on the river at Cambridge in the late 1890s, through which
ladies had to pass with their parasols lowered over their faces.

A genuine innovation at Abbotsholme was the abolition of prizes
and places for competitive work. It was Reddie's belief, shared by
all who worked with him, that boys should aim at personal progress
not at outdoing others. Therefore, he wrote, 'the New School is not
intended to "cram" boys for the capture of prizes and scholarships.
This is at present a serious evil in our schools.'[10] What is now called
mixed-ability teaching was practised up to the age of fifteen; boys
were encouraged to work co-operatively and to underline this the
school song was adapted from Whitman's *The Love of Comrades*,
which had also inspired Carpenter. At the same time Reddie was no
egalitarian: he envisaged his school turning out leaders, fitting

young men from the ruling classes to guide and enlarge the Empire, endowed with a natural authority. A few years later Baden Powell was aiming in the same direction with his Boy Scouts. Abbotsholme was accordingly organized into senior, middle and junior bands, each with reciprocal duties. Outstanding lads were awarded positions of status; but where other schools had School Captain or Head of Cricket, Abbotsholme had Captain of Hay-making, whose task was to organize squads of boys to bring in the hay in record time.

Schoolboys and haymaking are not images naturally connected in the English mind, and their conjunction is an emblem of all that was original in the new school movement. Many pupils found the vigorous outdoor life, with its elements of adventure and its spartan living arrangements, inspiring and enjoyable, although it could certainly be tough. One frail thirteen-year-old by the name of Lytton Strachey, who joined the school in 1893, lasted only two terms, despite his desire to emulate the others' hardiness.[11] The Unwin family were more successful, several brothers and cousins attending the school and one joining the staff. In his autobiography, Sir Stanley Unwin recalled arriving at Abbotsholme wearing 'nature-form' boots fitted to the natural shape of the foot. Once over the first term and its terrifying swimming sessions, he enjoyed the regime. A photo shows him lined up with ten other boys with spades over their shoulders, ready for an afternoon's potato digging.[12]

Also chronicled was the beginning of the disintegration of Abbotsholme under Reddie. His powerfully eccentric personality became unstable, paranoiac and obsessional until the great 'C.R.', as he was known, turned into absolute dictator of his small kingdom. His first breakdown came, significantly, at haymaking time. This, according to Maitland Radford, another pupil, was 'a mixture of a great lark and a demonstration of loyalty to C.R.'[13] It was Abbotsholme's main festival. In the summer of 1900 Reddie, who was already on the verge of mania and threatening to sack all the staff, crossed verbal swords with one of the older pupils, Norman Wilkinson, then Stanley Unwin's dormitory head and later a celebrated theatre designer, who appears to have matched Reddie in individualism. Wilkinson declined to render tribute to haymaking, telling his headmaster that the boys were being used as cheap labour to harvest a crop for the benefit of the school's owner, i.e. Reddie. 'After all,' he was heard to say to C.R., 'it's your hay.' Wrath descended and the festival was blighted. 'I have a vision of C.R. standing up after lunch,' wrote Stanley Unwin, 'and yelling something about *my* hay, and again *my* hay, and of a master intervening incoherently and being told to sit down.'[14]

Such breakdowns, followed by months of recuperation and a refusal to admit that all was not well, became increasingly frequent. This, combined with Reddie's fiercely pro-German sentiments during the First World War, led to the virtual demise of the school. In 1927, however, it was rescued by a group of former pupils who finally persuaded Reddie to hand over to a limited company and a new head, he himself being guaranteed a pension on condition that he did not approach the school again. Nearly seventy, he retired to Welwyn Garden City, a confirmed crank, where he pursued his obsessions – the introduction of a perpetual calendar, and a campaign to abolish capital letters, for which he sought parliamentary support.

J.H. Badley was one of Dr Reddie's original lieutenants at Abbotsholme. After a conventional education at Rugby and Cambridge, he heard of the new school venture from Lowes Dickinson and, being already an admirer of Carpenter, he contacted Reddie with enthusiasm and was offered a job. After three years in which, Badley claimed, he learnt both how to run a school and how not to, he married Amy Garrett, from a prominent feminist family, who shared his views on education. Reddie did not accept married members of staff, and Badley was thus obliged to leave. He and Amy had in any case developed their own ideas and so in the autumn of 1892 they proposed to set up what was intended as a kind of offshoot or colony of Abbotsholme. Reddie, who thought they ought to run a preparatory school under his direction, was angry with this apparently rival establishment. For the rest of his life he regarded it and its founder with great hostility.

In outlook this second new school was very close to Abbotsholme. On the same grounds – that the city was antipathetic to true education – Badley chose to site his school in the country. He found an old mansion, Bedales, near Haywards Heath in Sussex –

conveniently close to the Surrey and Sussex uplands where many members of the intelligentsia and Arts and Crafts movement had settled and were now rearing children. The values of the new school happily complemented their own. In one major respect, however, Bedales differed from its predecessor, by fostering the atmosphere not of an Outward Bound camp but of a large family. Reddie suffered rather than welcomed women as matrons and so forth; Badley regarded their presence as essential to a natural community. The family feeling was reinforced when, as happened more than once, staff members married each other, or children were born – starting with the Badleys' own son. Although Mrs Badley took no direct part in the running of the school (and in termtime her husband, known as The Chief, slept in a cupboard-sized room near the dormitories) her presence was stimulating: a militant suffragette in the pre-war years, she helped to make Bedales a mixed school, in marked contrast to most other boarding establishments. Because of lack of suitable accommodation and staff, it was in fact four years before the first girls joined the school in 1898. It was, Badley wrote in an essay on the subject, physically and morally necessary for girls to be freed from irksome and cramping restrictions on what ought to be natural and healthy development, and for boys to learn not to be rough and crude. Both girls and boys had much to teach each other.[15]

Following Reddie's outline, the timetable at Bedales began with a brisk wash in cold water, with a short run before breakfast and then classes until lunchtime. The afternoon activities alternated between games (once the pitches had been levelled and prepared with pupil labour) or work in the garden, workshop or art room. Unlike other schools, there was a fair amount of free time, to be spent in constructive activities, and in the first year those chosen were listed under the following headings: running; Swedish wood carving; bookbinding; bird stuffing; Animal Society. After the first year, during which the part-time teacher demonstrated how to skin a squirrel to make a hat or muff, and how to stuff an owl, the stuffers, as they were known, suffered from a lack of corpses, the only ones available in quantity being mice and sparrows, until a friendly local keeper undertook to supply dead predators. This must rank as an unusual school activity, but one which certainly appealed to the boys. The Animal Society was for pupils to look after live animals;

in 1894 the members owned between them eighteen rabbits, eight
hens and seven guinea pigs. From the start boys were also
encouraged to cultivate their own little gardens, in keeping with the
close-to-the-earth approach, although in view of all the other
activities it is hardly surprising that in the summer of 1895 only two
boys were recorded as digging their own plots.[16]

Estate and farm work were integral parts of the curriculum at
Bedales. In place of games or gardening, boys could also spend a
week at a time helping at the farm, which supplied the school with
produce and where the school horse, who pulled the cart and rolled
the cricket pitch, was stabled. In the first few terms a great deal of
the maintenance and alterations to the estate were done by staff and
pupils working together, and if a new item was needed, such as a
shed or path, the pupils were put to its planning and construction,
under supervision. Haymaking was also an essential event on the
school calendar, although lacking the emotional value invested in it
by Reddie. The outdoor activities appear to have mattered more at
Bedales than what went on in the classroom, and the first external
inspector, who was the hardly impartial Lowes Dickinson, drew
attention in the winter of 1895–6 to weakness on the academic side,
criticizing spelling, handwriting and other aspects. Badley admitted
that there 'has hitherto been too little written work and this must
now be altered'. For some time the school avoided all public
examinations (in the early years pupils tended to leave at sixteen
in order to proceed elsewhere, for formal qualifications), but
eventually succumbed. As the numbers increased the approach to
both lessons and activities became more organized, and sport began
to feature more prominently in the reports.

Inevitably, during the early years when staff and pupils formed a
small community of interest and activity, Bedales most approached
the back-to-the-land ideal of a school in the country where children
could learn from nature under the impulse of creative inclination
and where manual skills were encouraged equally with intellectual
ones. There were rigours too, since a certain severity lay behind this
version of the Simple Life, as Francis Scott, one of the first pupils,
remembered:

First in my mind are the dormitories with every window open in
all weathers and, as a point of honour, or was it bravado? our bath

water poured into each little sitz-bath under the open window before we got into bed, and not infrequently in consequence a slab of ice to remove in the morning and a sponge which was made to function only with much difficulty and at the expense of fingers not far removed from ice themselves.

Our outdoor activities open up memories of much gathering of garden leaves and work with spade and hoe, of that duty peculiar to Bedales, the weekly task-force detailed off to clean earth closets, of first enthusiasm for the week of haymaking rather subdued by later blisters and sun-baked fields.[17]

The earth closets were not in fact peculiar to Bedales, having been brought by Badley from Abbotsholme and being popular, as we have seen, in certain enlightened circles. Whether because they were thought to be more 'hygienic' than water closets, or because of the high costs of adapting the plumbing to cope with the numbers in the old country houses where both new schools were originally situated, a line of earth closets was installed in the grounds, using a deep trench system. In a literal interpretation of back to nature, when full the contents were transferred by barrow to the gardens and fields as manure, and the trenches used again.

Within ten years the staff and students at Bedales had expanded sufficiently for new premises to be needed and a site was secured outside Petersfield in Hampshire where the present school was built, bringing its name with it. The move, which took place in 1900, kept the pioneer spirit alive through the multitude of tasks to be done, including digging out a swimming pool (open air bathing was almost an article of faith in the new school movement although since girls were involved at Bedales swimming suits were presumably worn). The neglected gardens also required immediate attention. The first term was spent making paths, the second in digging over the ground thoroughly and sowing seeds, and the third in weeding and transplanting. 'The beans are now in pod,' concluded the school report happily, 'and the love-in-a-mist is nearly out.'[18]

The gardens were put to pedagogic as well as pastoral use, as the following report on nature study illustrates. The 'discovery' method of teaching and learning is now so well established in our schools that it is hard to imagine how different it was at the time from the conventional memorizing approach. At Bedales in the summer of 1900:

> Botany has been the class subject this Term for IIB2 and all of these do gardening in the afternoon sets. From the descriptions given of classwork it will be gathered that we do simple plant physiology, mostly experimental, which is assisted by the work in the gardens – the garden work providing us with flowers etc for study and suggesting occasional problems and experiments. Any boy who wishes has a garden of his own. . .

One pupil from IIB2 contributed his own account:

> In the Summer Term we watch the growth of plants from the seed, as beans and barley. Also we examine flowers and learn about their different parts, and take notes about them. We go out of doors sometimes to watch the trees and plants. We did several experiments to find whether there was starch in a plant by means of iodine . . . We took a fresh bean and sliced it up. Then we put it into a beaker and boiled it, and poured off the bean water and added some iodine to it, which turned the water dark blue. This is a proof to show there is starch in a fresh bean . . .[19]

The craft element was developed at Bedales through the workshop sessions and leisure activities. One of the first pupils was Geoffrey Lupton, to be found in the pages of the early school reports making himself a toolbox and then constructing a shed for the use of the school. On leaving Bedales, Lupton went to train in the workshops at Daneway under Ernest Gimson before returning to Hampshire where he set up his own workshop at Froxfield on the ridge above Steep. Here he built several houses, including one for Edward Thomas and his family, who had settled at Steep in order to be able to send their children to Bedales as day pupils. Later Lupton built the school hall and library, both designed by Gimson. His workshop was later taken over by Edward Barnsley.

Bedales was and is a very successful school which has always attracted plenty of pupils. In the early years, when its ideas were unfamiliar and tinged with unconventionality, its customers were largely drawn from those who already shared its outlook. Other educational reformers were encouraged, and a number of schools followed where Reddie and Badley led. In 1897 King Alfred's School in Hampstead was founded to cater for the sons and daughters of progressive parents living in north-west London. It was described in its first prospectus as 'A Proposed Rational School'. The first head was Charles Rice, who had taught at Bedales and was to return there; the second was John Powell, a strong supporter of women's rights and co-education; and the third was Joseph Wicksteed, son of the Rev. Phillip Wicksteed who in the 1880s had been involved with the Labour Church and various utopian socialist activities. Situated in the London suburbs, King Alfred's hardly qualifies for the back-to-the-land label, but it fits the same tradition – which continues through schools like St Christopher's, Summerhill, Dartington and the Rudolf Steiner schools right up to the 'free schools' established in 1970s. New schools and 'alternative' currents have a natural affinity.

14

The Garden City

The Garden City was the culmination of the back-to-the-land movement, the vindication of its ideas and aspirations. Here the impulse was not backwardly nostalgic but forward-looking – not to repudiate the city and return to a pre-industrial way of life, but to build a new society incorporating all the features of the good life. And in the Garden City, as it was built at Letchworth, congregated all the aspects of that life as it was planned and practised by those whose ideas have been described in previous chapters of this book.

Model villages, built by benevolent employers and landowners for their workers and tenants, have a long and respectable history in Britain; New Lanark and Saltaire were among the earliest such responses to industrialism, although they remained isolated examples of what might be done. And when in 1888, W.H. Lever set out to build houses for the employees at his new soap factory of Port Sunlight near Birkenhead, it was in no sense an unprecedented development. Enlightened employers were very often concerned about the quality of housing provided by speculative builders at rents working people could afford, and about the overcrowding and squalor that ensued. What was remarkable about Lever's plan was the nature of his vision for Port Sunlight's housing estate. He saw it as a village, green and spacious, self-contained yet open and tranquil, quite cut off from the industrial world surrounding it. On one side the village is bounded by the factory, with its tall block, chimneys, wharves and railway sidings, where the Lever soaps, which between 1890 and 1910 came to dominate the market, were developed and manufactured in accordance with the efficient and profitable practices of modern capitalism. Although the works was and is crucial to Port Sunlight's existence, it is not visible from the houses, being shielded by a neo-classical façade that forms a physical and symbolic barrier separating village from factory. To the west of the village runs the mainline railway, and to the east lies the new Chester Road and the industrial areas of the Wirral's north bank – Ellesmere Port, Stanlow, Runcorn.

Amid this environment, Port Sunlight is an extraordinary place, its 130 acres laid out graciously with half-timbered or tile-hung cottages fronting wide lawns and tree-lined pathways. Within a smallish area there is a great variety of house styles, including curly Flemish gables and the elaborate black and white patterning seen in Cheshire manor houses of the seventeenth century. A large number of amenities are provided for Port Sunlight's 3,000 residents, including a red sandstone village church, a large Tudor-style coaching inn, a big hall for social functions, a turreted Lyceum now housing the men's club, a half-timbered library, an arts and crafts school building and various other halls and clubs. Lastly, but in no sense least, is the Lady Lever Art Gallery, a small Renaissance temple set amidst lawns and fountains, containing an extensive collection of British painting, eighteenth-century furniture, sculpture, Chinese pottery, Wedgwood ware, porcelain, enamels and tapestries. The failure or inability of the working class to appreciate 'art' was a cause of great concern to their benevolent superiors in the last years of the nineteenth century; like others, Lord Lever (as he became) seems to have believed that this deficiency was due merely to lack of opportunity, to be remedied by placing works of art on the people's doorstep. The culture represented by the objects on display, however, remains more or less inaccessible to those who live around it, just as the neo-classical stone gallery is set apart by its appearance from the brick and timber English vernacular houses on all sides. Nothing could be more unlikely in an ordinary village.

For even today, nearly a hundred years on, Port Sunlight is a startling place to visit, something like a film set, depicting a Platonic type of English country life, leafy and leisurely but far too self-conscious for comfort.

Bournville, founded by the Cadbury cocoa and chocolate firm, is less arresting, largely because the building styles are less various and flamboyant. The company had moved its factory from the centre of Birmingham in 1879, but the employees remained until in 1895 George Cadbury decided to build a model village close to the works, with the aim of 'alleviating the evils which arise from the insanitary and insufficient housing accommodation supplied to large numbers of the working classes' and offering urban workers 'some of the advantages of outdoor village life, with opportunities for the natural and healthful occupation of cultivating the soil'.[1] He had observed the conditions in working-class areas of Birmingham for many years and had come to believe that the biggest problem was the lack of healthy leisure activities. His conclusion was that:

> the only practical thing was to bring the factory worker out on to the land, that he might pursue the most natural and healthful of all recreations, that of gardening. It was impossible for working men to be healthy and have healthy children, when after being confined all day in factories they spent their evenings in an institute, club room or public house . . . it was equally to the advantage of their moral life that they should be brought into contact with Nature . . .[2]

On the one hand, 'the cultivation of the soil is certainly the best antidote to the sedentary occupations of those working in large towns', while on the other, if offered gardens, the proletariat would at once forsake the public houses as their recreation. This was 'proved' at Bournville, where in 1906 it was noted that nearly every householder spent his leisure time gardening, and there was not one liquor outlet in the whole place. George Cadbury also believed that the workers would be healthier on a more vegetarian diet, encouraged by growing their own produce to eat less meat, and that they would also be richer. In practice the garden produce at Bournville in 1901 was valued at an average of 1s 11d per week, a sum roughly equivalent to a wage increase of ½d per hour.

A total of 925 houses were built at Bournville, not occupied exclusively by Cadbury's workers but by any who applied. In 1901 just two fifths of the tenants worked at the Bournville factory, while a similar proportion worked in Birmingham (four miles away by rail, workman's fare 2d return). Fifty per cent of householders were factory workers, thirteen per cent clerks and sales representatives, and the remainder manual workers in various outdoor or small workshop trades. As at Port Sunlight, large open spaces were retained, to which were added a social centre, the Quaker meeting house, a library and adult education centre named Ruskin Hall and a local school for 540 pupils. In the school basement were purpose-built classrooms for instruction in cookery, laundry and handcrafts; on the top of the sixty-foot tower was a stone map identifying the surrounding landscape; and in the school grounds were garden plots for instruction and practice in vegetable growing.

The architectural aim was to build the cheapest and most con-venient cottages in the soundest possible manner consistent with economy, avoiding the unsightly effect of rows of cramped artisans' dwellings erected by jerry builders, with fanciful cornices and capitals at the front and squalid yards at the back. What was required was houses of different sizes irregularly positioned, as seen 'in so many well-known old villages' but nevertheless at rents the workers could afford. Solid foundations and modern sanitation, including baths, were deemed essential despite being largely un-known in actual cottages at this time. The cheapest and smallest Bournville cottage, meant for building in blocks of eight, had three bedrooms (the smallest 7' ⋎ 8'), a large living room, scullery with cupboard bath and boiler and 600 square yards of garden. Its cost was estimated at £135 and it had no ornamentation beyond its own 'homely simplicity' of which, it was claimed, the tenants showed themselves quite appreciative. Each dwelling at Bournville had its own backyard, with coal shed, tool shed, washing line and lavatory approached from the outside, as was considered hygienic. Had Cadbury or his architect favoured the earth closet system, building regulations made modern water-sewage arrangements obligatory. As most of the houses were very compact, not to say small, with frontage of under twenty feet, to compensate the total plot length might be up to 200 feet, allowing two thirds of this for cultivation and a wide grass verge in front. The gardens were laid out when the houses were prepared for occupation, with ash and gravel paths, lawns, vegetable plots and even little orchards at the end. With the fitted cupboards and gas cookers provided indoors, the Bournville gardens were supplied with:

eight apple and pear trees, assorted according to the nature of the
soil, which, in addition to bearing fruit, form a desirable screen
between houses which are back to back; twelve gooseberry
bushes, one Victoria plum, six creepers for the houses including
Gloire de Dijon and William Allen Richardson roses, wistaria,
honeysuckle, clematis, ivy in a number of varieties, white and
yellow jasmine etc., according to the aspect as well as one or two
forest trees, so placed as to frame the building. Hedges of thorn
divide the houses and form road boundaries.

The cost of laying out gardens ranged from about £7 to £10 each.[3]

The garden village idea was soon taken further, as a national
solution to the problems of the inner city, by the garden city
concept launched by Ebenezer Howard. According to Howard,
who spent the major part of his working life as a shorthand reporter
and part-time inventor, the garden city notion sprang into his head
as a result of reading Edward Bellamy's *Looking Backward*, a utopian
fantasy of American life in the year 2000, but the examples of Port
Sunlight and Bournville, together with the emergent town-
planning movement, are inescapable sources, whether Howard
wanted to admit them or not. Intriguingly, Howard's biographer in
1933 quoted him as saying that by 1898 he had 'already taken part in
two very small social experiments unsuccessfully'; it would be
interesting to know what these were.

In the middle years of the nineteenth century a number of proposals for ideal towns were put forward, following from Robert
Owen's industrial villages and including the projected 'City of
Health', to be named Hygeia, outlined by the sanitary reformer Dr
Ward Richardson in 1875. This was to have had 100,000 inhabitants, a grid pattern of streets washed down daily, and no public
houses or tobacconists. Howard's not dissimilar views were developed over several months in 1897–8, during which he and his wife
lectured to any available audience, gradually building up a body of
supporters. In October 1898 with the aid of a benefactor, Howard
published *Tomorrow: A Peaceful Path to Real Reform* (reissued three
years later under the more explicit title *Garden Cities of Tomorrow*) in
which the idea of the garden city is sketched out under the argument
that 'there should be an earnest attempt made to organise a migra-
tory movement of population from our overcrowded centres to

sparsely settled rural districts'.[4]

Howard's ingenious diagrams – particularly that showing three magnets of Town, Country and Town-Country – are frequently reproduced in histories of urban planning or architecture. The Town-Country magnet, naturally, is shown as having no draw-backs, promising both beauty of nature and social opportunity, both low rents and high wages, pure air and peace. The diagrammatic plan of the garden city showed it occupying 1,000 acres and surrounded by 5,000 acres of farmland containing, among other things, cow pastures, allotments, agricultural college, children's homes, fruit farms, asylums for the blind and a farm for epileptics. Inside the circular city, which is ringed by a railway line, is a layer of industry and commerce around concentric residential circles pierced by boulevards and avenues leading to a central park, civic buildings and a cultural area. The total population was scheduled at 32,000 – the size of a very small town.

Howard's book was a vision rather than a blueprint, and this quality contributed to its impact, the nature of which is well illustrated in this commentary:

> The idea is nothing less than a vision of a transformed English industrial civilisation . . . There is no antagonism to any class . . . No abolition of anything in particular except slum dwellings and overcrowded industrial districts and these disappear like a dissolving view . . . The migration of industrial population into the country takes place within the usual forms of law and by the usual methods of road and rail, motors and trains. Factories – no longer 'dark Satanic mills' – have become sightly buildings, standing in gardens . . . A transvaluation of values has somehow been effected. Where foxes and partridges have been the principal occupiers of land in parks and preserves the land is carrying its complement of modest homes; red-cheeked children have taken the place of bright-plumaged birds . . . England is looking sober, prosperous, thrifty – as though the bad dream of the industrial revolution had somehow no more permanence . . . the dream is broken, the ugly nineteenth century has been wiped off the slate . . .[5]

The idea was for the first garden city to be built as a model, with others following and clusters growing up around London. Eventually the population remaining in the capital would be temporarily rehoused while London itself was demolished and reconstructed as a garden city itself. What a dream of the de-urbanized future!

The publication of Howard's book stimulated the founding of the Garden City Association, which held its first meeting on 10 June 1899 in the offices of the Land Nationalisation Society. A dozen people attended, Howard spoke briefly and the association was proposed by J. Bruce Wallace, of the Brotherhood Church – who was associated with the ill-fated Purleigh Colony, then in the throes of disintegration. From this meeting sub-committees were set up to look at various aspects of planning, sites, finance and publicity, and membership (subscription 1s) rose. A year later the association formed the Garden City Ltd., a company offering a first issue of 5,000 shares and promising a five per cent dividend, but this proved optimistic and few shares were purchased. Instead, in 1901 a full-time secretary was employed, whose first task was to organize a garden city conference, held at Bournville, and attended by 300 people from local authorities, churches, trade unions and co-operatives, who shared a common interest in the formation of new towns and estates. The following year a second conference was held, this time at Port Sunlight, attended by 1,000 delegates; support was clearly growing. Those who were attracted were social reformers, who wanted to rescue the poor from the slums; land reformers, who wanted to abolish private ownership of land; utopian socialists, who saw in the garden city the realization of their hopes for co-operative endeavour; and all kinds of pastoral idealists whose minds leapt forward to the instant achievement of their perfect vegetarian, sandal-wearing, arts-and-crafts, allotment-tending country community. Surely, the garden city would bring into being the conditions foreshadowed by Ruskin's Guild of St George, by Morris's *News From Nowhere*, and by Carpenter's Millthorpe smallholding.

A new Garden City Company was formed with a share capital of £20,000 and the aim of establishing garden cities in any part of the United Kingdom. The directors were Ralph Neville (lawyer), Edward Cadbury (chocolate manufacturer), Howard Pearsall (civil engineer), Franklin Thomasson (cotton spinner), Thomas Purvis Ritzema (newspaper proprietor), Aneurin Williams (ironmaster) and Ebenezer Howard. The major subscribers to the share issue were George Cadbury (1,000), W.H. Lever (1,000), Alfred Harmsworth (1,000) and J.P. Thomasson (1,000). The whole amount of £20,000 was raised in four months.

A site was found at Letchworth, in Hertfordshire – a total of 3,818 acres, costing £155,587 and skilfully negotiated so that no owner was canny enough to hold out. Surveys guaranteed the healthiness of the locality – disease being believed to be associated as much with place as with poverty or lack of sanitation. Communications were good, and the Great Northern Railway Company was willing to build a new station for the new town; the journey to London took only forty-two minutes.

Plans for the development of the new settlement were then invited, and Raymond Unwin and Barry Parker, practising jointly in Derbyshire,[6] were appointed Letchworth's consultant architects. In accordance with prevailing ideas, the industrial area was placed to the north-east, carefully separated from the residential areas (but closest to the cheapest housing), the civic buildings were placed on the highest land of the estate near the centre, and as far as possible all trees, hedges and streams were retained in their natural state. Parker and Unwin shared many contemporary progressive views, Unwin being a former member of the Socialist League and a current member of the Fabian Society – he delivered a paper on garden city housing to the 1901 Bournville conference – and Parker an esteemed member of the Arts and Crafts movement; their provenance was perfect. They continued in partnership, doubling up as consultants to the Rowntree garden estate at New Earswick, York, until 1914 but by 1906 Unwin had already transferred most of his work to the new Hampstead Garden Suburb in north London. In the 1920s Parker was to plan Wythenshaw, the model overspill area for Manchester, built on garden city lines.

At Letchworth, the new city, which was so far unnamed, was inaugurated on 9 October 1903. Detailed surveys and plans followed before construction began in the summer of 1904 with roads, sewerage and water supplies; gas and electricity came later. The name Letchworth Garden City had been chosen (other suggestions being Wellworth, Homeworth and Alseopolis – from the Greek words for garden and city) by the company's shareholders. The tenant farmers in occupation of the agricultural land on which

the new city was to be sited were promised that no more than ten
per cent of their holdings would be taken for building in any year,
so residential development was gradual. In the first year fifty plots
were let alongside existing roads for the first houses. The Garden
City Company itself only owned the land – houses and factories
had to be erected by individuals and companies acting as lease-
holders, and special regulations applied so that all plans were
approved by Parker and Unwin. Sites varied in size, but nowhere
was a density of more than twelve houses to the acre permitted.
Workmen's homes were built for rent by companies or housing
associations.

The earliest houses, such as those built by Parker and Unwin for
themselves and for Howard in 1904, set a kind of garden city
standard, with roughcast walls, dormer windows and tall chimneys. They look very like the homes Ernest Gimson and the
Barnsleys built for themselves at Sapperton. Inside, Unwin's living
room, with obligatory ingle-nook, contained rush-seated country
chairs from his native Derbyshire, a plain trestle table and hard-
backed settles. Two portraits hung over his desk – those of William
Morris and Edward Carpenter. A later feature of Parker's houses
was a tower added in 1913 to provide balconies for sleeping out in
fine weather.

Early in 1905 the *Spectator* magazine and the Country Gentlemen's Association (which moved its headquarters to Letchworth)
sponsored a Cheap Cottage Exhibition which incidentally
increased the area under development. Plots were allocated to the
north of the estate and competitors invited to construct dwellings
suitable for farm labourers at a cost of no more than £150. Over a
hundred houses were built, by architects, builders and contractors,
to a variety of plans, some traditional and some notably progressive
in conception such as the 'round' or polygonal house made from
Cubitt's prefabricated concrete parts. The houses were let as soon as
finished, on condition that they were open to the public for three
months from 25 July 1905. As over 60,000 visitors came to the
Cheap Cottage Exhibition, the long-suffering tenants perhaps
regretted this clause in their agreements. Looking at the pro-
miscuous mix of housing thus erected, the Letchworth authorities
were somewhat appalled at their own action and tried to disown the
'cheap cottage' reputation, which was not at all the image they

aimed for; two years later an urban cottage exhibition was held in a small area to the south of the town centre, as a practical demonstration of town planning rather than cheap building.

The most expensive cottages were located to the south-west of the town, and attracted those who, in the words of a Letchworth historian, were 'the enthusiasts who had been looking forward for years to the founding of the town. They came to it in a spirit of adventure, they discovered it as though it were a new land . . .'[7] And in its early years Letchworth indeed became renowned as the home of crazes of all kinds. This reputation was resented by the majority of respectable, conventional residents, but it was probably inevitable given the lifestyles of a handful of prominent personalities. Today's judgment depends on whether they are now seen as cranks or pioneers, more or less deluded or in possession of creative dreams – a judgment which must ultimately be made too about the other subjects in this book, for one way and another the enthusiasms chronicled here found their way to and flourished in the garden city.

Country lovers were weaned off the Surrey uplands and discovered the modest but still unspoiled beauties of the north Hertfordshire landscape, conveniently situated halfway between London and Cambridge – within a stone's throw, one guesses, of the house at Howards End. They explored the footpaths, walked up the easternmost edges of the Chiltern Hills, and found ancient, undisturbed English villages. Here they had their new cottages built to the old look (but with all mod. cons.). Baillie-Scott himself undertook several commissions for clients moving to Letchworth, as well as entering the Cheap Cottages Exhibition (his entry was disqualified for exceeding the cost limits). All his houses here had 'open-plan' interiors based on the late medieval hall – a style that also appealed to Unwin and Parker.

Every house in Letchworth has a garden, naturally, as did many of the factories and public buildings, so the place soon became renowned for its horticulture. As one commentator said: 'There are roads in Letchworth where every house has a rose garden, for roses grow in Letchworth clay as freely as gorse on a common.' He continued:

The town garden which lies four square inside a belt of

Lombardy poplars is a botanical garden and a flower show all summer. You can go there and learn the names and scents of new plants for your own herbaceous borders . . . Letchworth came into existence just at the right time for herbaceous borders. Miss Jekyll had published her evangel which shattered the idea of the garden as a place which ought to be made to look like a dining room carpet. She had opened the gates of a garden of Eden where behind borders of arabis and forget-me-not, irises and lupins, campanulas, montbretia, sweet sultan, verbena, gladiolus, dahlias, sweetpeas, michaelmas daisies, anchusas and paeonies, anemones and phloxes, delphiniums and chrysanthemums may in their season vie with one another in friendly rivalry as to which can get most sunshine . . .[8]

A neat footnote records that all these plants were actually to be found in a Letchworth border.

The residential development of the garden city necessarily obliterated a good deal of the farmland and countryside which was so deeply venerated, without apparent anguish on the part of promoters or residents. It was not, after all, possible to build the new city and preserve the countryside at the same time and in the same place. As far as possible the natural features of the area were saved: Norton Common to the north of the estate, for example, was kept intact – and reopened to the public having been previously enclosed for rough shooting. This 'wild stretch of country divided by a little stream, rich in bird life and in wild flowers, with magnificent hawthorns and other trees' was of 'inestimable value to the town', wrote C.B. Purdom, the original estate manager. Without the common, Letchworth 'would lack a great deal of the peculiar rural atmosphere, which no gardens or even open fields, could bring to it . . . it is a part of the town and its influence pervades it. It is like a crown of untamed nature or, rather, like a heart of virgin sweetness which will ever keep the town pure . . .'[9] To the south of the centre the Pix brook was retained as a kind of rustic walkway, while many footpaths wound into and out of the town. The ancient Icknield Way ran across the site, and some householders thus had an address which would have been old in the time of the Romans. With the abundant trees and hedges and wide grass verges throughout the town, it may be felt that little has been lost in Letchworth; the overall effect, if not exactly rustic, is certainly that of an over-whelmingly green town.

There were plenty of allotments and smallholdings too, for those who dreamed of cottage farming amidst congenial society. Although it is not evident how they did so, it is apparent that some of Letchworth's original inhabitants moved there with the idea of being self-supporting on their own plots, with perhaps some craft work or casual jobs thrown in to make ends meet or pay the (very low) local rates. The following account was written in 1930 by one of the first residents:

> Thirty years ago I was in a London factory, artificial light most of the time, and wife in rooms with children. It worried me what would happen if I got out of work. We determined to emigrate; went on the *Ruapehu,* a New Zealand ship, saw the accommo-dation and were preparing to go. Got stock of clothes, needles and cottons, tools, woodman's axe, and what we thought might be wanted. Then came the Garden City movement, and instead of leaving all friends and relatives, we built a cottage here for £300 and rented 2¼ acres of ground.

The aim, evidently, was self-sufficiency, but:

> I got other occupation here after 3 years, always kept at work as we had to borrow money for house etc. Others who could dig or prune or the hundred and one jobs there are to do, have been employed at various times to help, the income being too small to develop, and knowledge and aptitude on my own part not enough, never having had a garden before.
>
> The result is that on this ground some £3,000 have been spent in wages in 25 years, about £1,000 in seeds, manure, ground rent (there is no ownership of land other than secure lease from First Garden City) greenhouse, bees, ducks, fowls, trees, plants, bushes, stringbaskets, and all kinds of things, nearly all of which has been got back in produce. . . . I can't sing – was turned out of every singing class I went in, and that was many, up to 30 years old – but have been able to show how to bring a family of eight children up, and keep a bit of old England cultivated as it should be.

We can hear the blackbird, thrush and cuckoo, gather a cherry or a strawberry, apple or nut, blackberry or flower and say to the flying motorists scurrying past on the Hitchin–Cambridge road, 'You are going nowhere better'.

With this the author, W. (Bill) G. Furmston, signed himself off, but could not resist a postscript pointing out that he had written his letter at home in the afternoon and adding:

We have sought not to make a business, i.e. take other's, but to cultivate a piece of England thinking England should grow her own food and that here is the cure for our troubles – Housing, Employment, Safety. Dependence for food on other countries is dangerous; the submarines sank food last time. Next time it may never leave the other shores.[10]

The residents of Letchworth took to gardening, like those of Bournville, not only out of patriotism or in preference to the pub but because there was no licensed house. Associating drink with city slums and depravation, Letchworth pioneers were nearly all teetotal. As industry and its employees arrived in the town, the demand arose for a local pub, the nearest inns being in the old villages of Norton and William on the edge of the estate. Other residents also favoured the opening of a hotel, where guests might stay. Both ideas ran into opposition from the temperance side, and in 1907 the Garden City Company held a referendum of all adult residents on whether or not an establishment selling alcohol should be admitted. By 631 votes to 544 the drinkers lost and the town remained dry. Polls were taken again in 1908 and 1912, with the same result. It was, however, recognized that the public house fulfilled other functions as well, and so a teetotal pub named the Skittles Inn was opened as an experiment. It was financed by two Garden City directors, manufacturers Aneurin Williams and Edward Cadbury, and advertised itself as

A PUBLIC HOUSE (Unlicensed)
conducted on the lines of the Old-Fashioned Inns
The *Liberty Hall* of the Letchworth worker
Fellowship; Rest; & Recreation
Good Meals and an extensive variety of Beverages.

The man behind the bar, dispensing cocoa and Cydrax and other non-intoxicating liquors, was Bill Furmston.

There was in addition a Food Reform Restaurant and Simple Life Hotel (which sounds rather uncomfortable) in Leys Avenue, which catered for vegetarian visitors. The associated Health Food Store was advertised as 'under the personal supervision of the proprietor who is a life vegetarian'.[11] Vegetarianism was strongly associated in the popular mind with garden cities, as was dress reform and eccentric habits like wearing no hats or going barefoot. A cartoon of 1909 shows a group of Edwardian tourists visiting Letchworth like a zoo, to look at the inmates with their long hair and beards, digging cabbages and feeding on nuts and fruit, much as a hippy colony might have been depicted in the late 1960s. Notices direct the way to the 'Hairy Headed Banana Munchers' and the 'Sandle (*sic*) Footed Raisin Shifters', as well as to the 'Non Tox Pub' and the 'Single Life Hotel' where 'French Polished Rice' is 'Always Ready'.[12] Mrs Austin, one of the original residents, recalled the early days when interviewed in 1966. 'We wore sandals of course,' she said. 'I'm still wearing them. There were a great percentage of vegetarians and Healthy Life people. The dress of some of them was a bit unorthodox. We used to wear jibbas' – long loose unshaped Arab-style garments favoured by progressive women – 'and Mr Muir he used to go round in a smock.' A photo of artist Andrew Muir in the Garden City Museum shows him in smock and sandals and little else. According to Mrs Austin, he also 'used to bring his knitting to work', but what the job was she did not specify.[13] The sandals came from the source: George Adams, Carpenter's friend and partner at Millthorpe. Through Carpenter Adams had met Raymond Unwin, then practising in Buxton, and moved to Letchworth as soon as it was launched, living in a house designed by Unwin on Croft Lane. At Letchworth his sandals were much in demand and a pair made by him to the original design is preserved in the Garden City Museum; they belonged to Edith Booth, local headteacher and cousin of Unwin's.

Craftwork was also prominent in the new city. The success of Letchworth depended, as its board of directors knew well, on its ability to attract employment in manufacturing industry (despite the antagonism of its more idealistic supporters to everything associated with these words). The Garden City Company thus set out to attract industries by means of low rents, spacious premises, good transport links and new housing for the workforce, and appropriately enough among the first firms to accept the invitation were several with strong craft elements, whose products would have delighted William Morris himself. The most important of these were in printing and bookbinding. In 1907 W.H. Smith moved its binding department from central London to Letchworth under the management of the eminent bookbinder Douglas Cockerell. Following Morris and Ashbee, bookbinding was a favoured fine craft, its products much in demand among the intelligentsia. Having left W.H. Smith for the Ministry of Munitions in 1914, Cockerell returned to hand binding in the 1920s, setting up a small practice in Norton Way with his son Sydney, producing books for collectors and rebinding and repairing rare manuscripts for cathedrals and libraries. Here the *Codex Sinaiaticus* was bound for the British Museum in 1935. Sydney Cockerell, who was born in Letchworth in 1906, revived and developed the old practice of marbling endpapers. Fine printing was done at Letchworth by the Arden Press, by J.M. Dent and by the Garden City Press – a co-operative set up by Aneurin Williams within a few months of Letchworth's foundation; it is still in business.

There were also a number of engineering firms who moved their works to Letchworth, and by 1913 several small companies were engaged in the growing business of motor-car manufacture. The most prominent factory, however, was one whose products ought never to have been associated with Letchworth at all: the Spirella Company Ltd., makers, according to the proud legend along the side of the enormous building, of 'High Grade Corsets'. This British subsidiary of an American company which had patented a kind of spiral wire to replace whalebone was set up in Letchworth in 1910 and such, apparently, was the importance of the 'catch' that it was given permission to erect a huge and very visible factory close to the town centre, instead of being tucked away in the eastern industrial area with the other factories. The Spirella building thus dominates Letchworth in a disturbing way despite its fine appearance. A graphic depiction of it drawn in 1922 shows it as Castle Corset looking down from on high over the houses and churches and other buildings of the town. The factory was important because it provided work for girls whose fathers and brothers were employed in printing and engineering and other exclusively male trades, and its size suggests that it must have been the largest local employer – although there is something ironic in Letchworth's largest female labour force being engaged in making articles which the rest of the Garden City's jibba-clad women abhorred. A contemporary Spirella advertisement asserted, however, that 'Our Healthful Modish Corsets and Waists are endorsed by Physicians, Physical Trainers and Dress Reformers everywhere'.[14] It was not until the 1960s that the corset trade declined drastically in a new era of liberation, and today much of the Spirella building is sublet to other manufacturers.

The Spirella factory was notable, however, for its excellent working conditions, with high workrooms, warm-air heating and deflected light. Bathrooms were provided for the workers and at the top of the building were a canteen, rest room and roof garden; dances and other social activities were also organized by the company – altogether a model Factory As It Might Be, after Morris's description, and living proof that industrial conditions were not inevitably drab, overcrowded and unhealthy.

A more suitable industry for Letchworth was the St Edmundsbury Weaving Works, one of the clutch of handloom revival industries described in Chapters 9 and 10. It was around 1900 that the artist and designer Edmund Hunter, son of a wine merchant, and his wife Dorothea, cousin to W.B. Yeats, decided to set up their own craft workshop producing fine silk textiles to original designs. Dorothea had taken up weaving along with her enthusiasm for ancient Celtic art and lore, and through the workshop she aspired to rekindle a love of tradition and symbolism. With her cousin, she was a member of the esoteric Order of the Golden Dawn, and later both Hunters were deeply involved in Theosophy. The name St Edmundsbury Weavers was derived from Bury St Edmunds, where the Hunter family came from, and the site chosen for the enterprise was Haslemere in Surrey, where Godfrey and Ethel Blount and Maud and Joseph King were already engaged in craft revival operations.

The Hunters began in collaboration with Luther Hooper, an authority on handlooms and weaving, who opened the Green Bushes Weaving House in 1901, but soon separated to build their own workroom on College Hill. A works scrapbook kept by

Edmund Hunter begins on 1 June 1902.[15] The chief employee was a
master weaver from the old Spitalfields silk industry, and three or
four other skilled workers made up the labour force. The work was
of high quality and at the other end of the scale from that produced
by most other hand weaving ventures; instead of lumpy, natural-
coloured cloth or plain white linen, St Edmundsbury produced
superb and richly-hued silk textiles, mainly for ecclesiastical commissions. The company benefited from royal patronage, where
cost was no object. In 1902 Queen Alexandra ordered red silk
hangings for the private chapel at Buckingham Palace, followed by
a resplendent white and gold altar cloth. In general the fabrics were
designed by Edmund Hunter, aiming at a quality and richness of
effect not attainable from machine production and reminiscent of
the finest damasks of earlier ages; many were shown and awarded in
international exhibitions. Illustrative, if not typical products were
altar silks for the 1911 coronation in Westminster Abbey. Modelled
on a fifteenth-century damask frontal from the church at Ashbee's
Chipping Campden, it was designed by W.R. Lethaby and sent to
St Edmundsbury to be woven before going to May Morris at her
father's firm for embroidering with gold and silver thread. Hunter's
own designs appear to derive from William Morris, with dense,
strong colours and flat patterns, often featuring leaves and birds but
depicted in a more linear manner than on Morris's crowded fabrics.
Motifs were sometimes taken from Nature, as in the 'Vineyard'
design, and sometimes from the mystical subjects dear to the
Hunters, like the signs of the Zodiac, or heraldic animals. Certain
fabrics suggest Persian inspiration.

The expensive commissions were accompanied by other bread-
and-butter work, which kept the looms occupied; among other
such jobs St Edmundsbury designed and wove linings for Burberry
raincoats. This was uneconomic on handlooms, and in 1907–8 the
Hunters were faced with the dilemma of whether to expand their
enterprise and include power looms in order to keep the whole
venture financially viable. To do so entailed a move, and it was
partly because of the opportunity to relocate at Letchworth that the
decision was taken. In 1908 the firm moved to the garden city
where, with Parker's assistance, Hunter designed and had built the
new St Edmundsbury Weaving Works in Ridge Road, and a house
for his family. The Hunters shared many of the ideals manifest at

Letchworth and were particularly impressed by the quality of the housing available for their employees. The number of looms was increased from four to ten, and by 1920 the workforce numbered twenty. St Edmundsbury flourished in its new home, producing cotton damasks, bedspreads, dress lengths and silk scarves on the power looms, and carrying out special orders on the handlooms; Hunter believed there was no loss in quality when machines were used for a relatively simple piece of work and certainly the examples which survive are very fine.

The family and the firm soon became integrated into the life of the new community; in 1909 Edmund designed a vivid appliqued banner for the First Garden City to be carried in the May Day procession, showing a strangely Arab-looking walled town only half visible behind a tree of plenty holding flowers, fruit and birds in its branches. The Hunters' second son Alec also became a designer and joined his father in the firm; with his wife Margaret he founded the Letchworth Morris Men, the inhabitants of the garden city being naturally disposed towards the folk revival. The Letchworth morris side soon acquired a reputation as one of the premier teams in Britain and subsequently Alec Hunter was elected first Squire of the Morris Ring, as the national body and its president were designated. One of his designs for a St Edmundsbury fabric is based on the figure of a morris man.

In the post-war period the firm produced upholstery fabrics for the furniture designer and manufacturer Gordon Russell (who extended the tradition of the Cotswold craft furniture-maker into mass production and general sale) and woven worsted-and-cotton covers for an edition of Shakespeare published by the Nonesuch Press. But as with all small companies, capital was a recurring problem and in 1927 the commercial fabric manufacturer Morton Sundour offered to take over St Edmundsbury, with the Hunters setting up a new unit in Edinburgh for the production of high-quality furnishing fabrics. After a short while, however, the connection was dissolved; at the age of sixty-five Edmund retired with Dorothea to Hampstead Garden Suburb.

A smaller craft enterprise in Letchworth was the Iceni Pottery, started by W.H. Cowlishaw in 1905 and specializing in leadless glazes; some items are on show in the Garden City Museum. Cowlishaw was an architect – the one, incidentally, who had wished to build a medieval hall for his brother-in-law Edward Garnett to live in in the woods at Limpsfield. His most notable commission was for The Cloisters, a remarkable establishment which no doubt made a large contribution to Letchworth's reputation for eccentricity. For among the pioneers drawn to the Garden City was Annie Jane Lawrence, daughter of a London ironmaster and sister of Frederick William (later Lord) Pethick-Lawrence. She moved to Letchworth in 1905 and employed Cowlishaw to build a residential college where the New Life would be practised by a small community of elected souls, apostles of the new religion. She herself lived in an adjoining house.

The main feature of this building was the Cloister Garth, a horseshoe-shaped terrace around a marble fountain, divided into sections by canvas curtains where the residents slept on flat-frame hammocks slung from the vaulting but otherwise open to the winds. In bad weather more canvas could be used to keep out the rain but heating was always a problem. At the end of the Garth was a marble swimming pool where residents and guests were encouraged to bathe daily. During the day, the hammocks and curtain were pulled up, and the Cloister hosed down before becoming a kind of open-air common room. Fresh air and water were key elements in Miss Lawrence's conception of the New Life. The architecture was symbolic as well as functional, green marble columns being chosen to give 'a strong idea of upward growth and aspiration' and the flowing fountain representing the eternal stream of wisdom. One of the jobs George Adams is known to have had as well as sandal-making was the modelling of designs for lead downpipes and gutters at The Cloisters. When half-completed in 1907 the building was dedicated to 'Eternal Reality' and the 'Perfect Inviolable Whole'.[16]

Miss Lawrence, a renowned local figure with a battered brass ear-trumpet, appears to have been a well-meaning but naïve lady whose wealth made her open to exploitation – which may be a harsh judgment on her main associate in the early days at Letchworth, J. Bruce Wallace. Wallace, whose history is incompletely known, is thought to have been an independent clergyman from Ulster.[17] He inspired the Brotherhood Church in north London in the early 1890s, and indirectly the Croydon offshoot which was responsible for founding both the Purleigh and

Whiteway Colonies, and was also a founder-member of the Garden City Association and an ardent supporter of Ebenezer Howard. He was, however, looking more for followers than leaders, and by 1906 he was engaged in a new movement called the Alpha Union, with theosophical connections, for whose residential courses and summer schools he persuaded Miss Lawrence to let him use The Cloisters. In his advertisements for customers, Wallace wrote 'It is hoped that there may in time go forth from this centre a number of strong and joyous men experienced in wholesome thought and labour to preach and practise among the masses of the people a wholesome and emancipating joyous gospel and a saner mode of living.'[18]

The permanent residents were observed between February and June of 1911 by the young David Garnett, who had been shown the building by his uncle the architect and had fallen for its owner's idealism. Space, leisure, beauty and food eaten off a pink alabaster table were provided, he recalled, for 12s 6d a week. Lodging was free for the permanent members of the little commune, among whom Garnett remembered an earnest young believer in primitive Christianity, a young anarchist named Sidney Potter who refused to take a regular job, saying that if Miss Lawrence withdrew her benefaction he would take up making sandals and rucksacks and sell them, like George Adams, to other aspirant New Lifers. There was also a sad young man who had been asked to leave a similar community in Surrey, and who, Miss Lawrence had already suggested, should soon move on elsewhere.

Although not organized as a true commune on egalitarian or Tolstoyan principles, the community at The Cloisters clearly had much in common with the agrarian groups described earlier in this book. Prospective members were told that they must be willing to work in the gardens, as cultivation was intended as a basic element in the life there. Possibly meals were only to be provided by Miss Lawrence until the community became self-sufficient in food. During Garnett's time the chief agricultural activity selected by Miss Lawrence was that of growing wheat allegedly on principles set out by Kropotkin, whereby each grain was to be given individual attention. A field at The Cloisters was accordingly cleared and sown by hand; in May a vast sea of weeds and thistles all but obliterated the thinly growing wheat-stalks.[19]

The Alpha Union summer schools were more successful, attracting many idealistic people who wished to savour the possibilities of
the 'alternative' lifestyle. Like a gathering of hippies in the late
1960s, for a limited period all was licensed lunacy, dedicated to
personal freedom, psychic growth, oneness with Nature and the
search for higher reality. One satisfied summer school student was
Albert Dawson of the *Christian Commonwealth* magazine, who
visited The Cloisters in the fine summer of 1911, and described it as:
'a centre of numerous activities, kindred in spirit and aim. The
Mutual Services Industries include sandal-making, carpentry,
joinery and agriculture, and weaving.' The pursuits mirrored those
of the permanent residents, whom he depicted as 'a succession of
young fellows dividing their time between manual toil and mental
study'. He went on:

> You can swing in a hammock under the colonnade from which
> the building takes its name or lie on a 'tocah' on the roof or sleep
> on a stretcher as I did with all the windows wide open so that you
> are all but in the open air. Next time I shall be content with
> nothing other than the sky for a roof . . . The arrangements are
> deliciously primitive . . . You dispense with nearly all the
> ridiculous toilet paraphernalia that an artificial civilisation has
> built up around you. You lie on your simple couch, inhale the
> fresh pure air, gaze at the stars and fall as I did into deep sleep.
> After six hours of uninterrupted dreamless slumber I awoke fresh
> and fit and took my morning bath in the invigorating sun-
> saturated air that sweeps The Cloisters through and through and
> in the deep cold water of the marble bathing pool . . .[20]

Then followed breakfast on the lawn – 'always in the open air'.
Looking back dreamily on his week at Letchworth, this delighted
visitor could only exclaim on the splendour he had seen. 'Just think
what life might be and what a poor stunted maimed mean thing we
make of it!' he concluded inspiringly.

The main philosophical leanings at The Cloisters appear to have
been towards Theosophy – reminiscences of Letchworth often
included the designation of the place as a centre of 'theosophical
meditation', but it is not clear how dominant this was, and it may be
confused with the later association of the Theosophical Education

Trust and St Christopher's School. In any case the Alpha Union summer schools and other activities came to an abrupt end in 1912 when Bruce Wallace married and his friendship with Miss Lawrence ceased. Remembered in the town as 'a handsome and charismatic figure' Wallace may have found his flock slipping away from him; after the War he moved (or returned) to Ireland, to offer his mediation in the civil conflict; he died aged eighty-five in 1939.

While retaining something of its alternative character, The Cloisters then became a kind of honorary community centre for the whole of Letchworth rather than for visiting cranks. Craft classes continued under the Mututal Service Industries, with sandal-making, weaving, pottery, basketwork and bookbinding. Concerts and organ recitals were held there in the absence of a concert hall in the town, and on summer Sunday afternoons residents could listen to free brass-band concerts and contests. The new teams of folkdance enthusiasts found it a suitable place for performances, and in the summer of 1913 a folkdance summer school was held there, inspired by Cecil Sharp's famous Stratford gatherings. The following year the Masque of Letchworth was performed by the whole town. During winter months a programme of lectures, adult education classes and informative films was offered, giving rise to the need for better heating and in 1926 the Cloister Garth was roofed in. The swimming pool was made available to the pupils of neighbouring St Christopher's School and to all the children of the town, whom Miss Lawrence encouraged to learn to swim by presenting each child with a fountain pen on completion of the first full length. Eventually it proved difficult to find a useful function for the amazing edifice and in 1948 it was presented to the Masons. The Cloister Garth was then walled off from the rest to make a Masonic temple – a use not altogether out of keeping with its bizarre beginnings.

No garden city would have been complete without a new school and, collectively, the pioneers had a full range of progressive ideas on educational reform. While the town's building plans were being prepared a sub-committee drew up its proposal for an ideal school. Alas, the local board of education which was responsible for providing public education facilities was not willing to finance what it frankly saw as an experiment: co-educational, craft-based and with none of the usual scholastic examinations and prize-givings.

The committee persisted and eventually won a compromise, so that in November 1905 a free school for all garden city children was opened in temporary premises, with the running costs borne by the local authority but the school organization determined by a committee of management. This meant that additional activities which in the committee's view were essential had to be financed separately, but efforts to raise extra money through voluntary rates and public appeals failed and eventually the county council took over the school completely. As a public elementary school it was nevertheless far in advance of its time both in terms of its building and its curriculum. Classrooms were deliberately made small with the aim of keeping the size of classes down to forty (the original aim had been thirty-two) so teaching would be more effective. All classrooms were built around a central quadrangle with a covered walkway, and opened on to it for the sake of fresh air, the occasional outdoor lesson and short recreation breaks. Although the curriculum consisted generally of subjects standard in public elementary schools, there were also hints of what might have been in the forty-two garden plots, cultivated by the pupils, and in the hens and bees kept by the school. Morris and country dancing were on the PT timetable and every year the Letchworth May Queen was elected by the older students. Of the 680 pupils the majority left when they reached fourteen years, except for a handful who were given scholarships to stay on for another year. As the population of Letchworth grew a second council school holding 500 pupils was opened.

The aims of the founders that all children in Letchworth should attend the same school were short-lived, for from the beginning, it seems, the offspring of the middle classes were sent to a different establishment. This is the progressive school which under the name of St Christopher's is familiarly associated with Letchworth. Under the name Letchworth School, this establishment was launched in 1905 by J.H.N. Stephenson and moved into its own building in Barrington Road, close to The Cloisters, in 1909. A contemporary prospectus outlined the educational approach:

> Every effort is made to secure thoroughly hygienic conditions Special attention is given to providing a suitable as well as liberal diet . . . expert advice is followed in catering for vegetarians.

Breathing exercises and Swedish drill are practised regularly throughout the school and no two lessons follow one another without a short interval in the open air . . . Further, in order to give the maximum time in the fresh air, both lessons and meals are taken whenever possible out of doors . . .[21]

The school and its classes were mixed, and 'teachers and taught work in a cooperative spirit'. As at Abbotsholme and Bedales the afternoons were spent in practical work – woodwork and gardening – or sports. The building was so designed that on fine days one classroom wall could be opened to give access to a paved area where lessons were carried on in the sunshine.

A second school, for girls only, was opened around the same date by a Miss Cartwright, with its emphasis on 'housewifery', practical science, gardening and morris dancing. According to the prospectus, the school gave 'due importance to work with the hands as well as . . . the purely mental faculties . . .' and stated as an accepted fact that the brain could only develop through muscular activity on the part of the hands.[22] A few years later a theosophical school was opened, offering mixed tuition and a vegetarian diet. By 1920 this was situated in Broadway, in a new building with a verandah for outdoor lessons and open-air study bedrooms.

There was also a Montessori kindergarten training school and something called the St Christopher Fellowship comprising five craft guilds which were intended as 'a contribution to the evolution of the Social-Industrial life of the New Age'. The main products were handwoven materials and 'artistic and useful articles in wood and metal' which were sold through the surviving outlets of the Peasant Arts Industries. In 1924 the *Fellowship News* described the agricultural activities in its large vegetable gardens, through which it was hoped to make St Christopher's self-supporting. All the potatoes eaten in the school were grown on site, while the poultry branch, with 1,700 hens, posed problems for the vegetarians. Seventy hives produced enough honey for everyone's breakfast. In 1928 the school, now known formally as St Christopher's, moved to the original buildings on Barrington Road and in 1930 detached itself from the Theosophical Educational Trust. As a private establishment under Lyn Harris and his son it went from strength to strength, offering an advanced education to pupils from liberally minded middle-class homes and surviving to find many of its principles adopted by the educational establishment.

Now nearly eighty years old, Letchworth has settled down into a less extraordinary town. It has seen its pioneering path followed first by Welwyn, Howard's second garden city, established in the 1920s, and then by the post-1945 new towns of Stevenage, Harlow and Hatfield all fairly close by. Northern Hertfordshire has thus become almost as Howard envisaged it, a cluster of rural-urban settlements with light industry and spacious residential areas. London has not yet decayed, but its population is diminishing, and the problems currently faced by inner city areas have prompted much debate about solutions. Country sentiment is as strong as ever, if television commercials are an index to the popular mood. The festering slums and dire proverty of the Victorian age may have been removed, but the essential issues remain. Letchworth's origins deserve to be remembered.

15

Pastoralism Rules

When it comes to being remembered, of course, success is what matters. Nor is it surprising that, despite the vigour and originality of the anti-industrial manifestations described here, they soon fell into obscurity, overtaken in the twentieth century by political and economic events of far greater significance. Only a handful of 'cranks' kept the alternative ideas alive, eating vegetarian health foods and sending their children to notoriously permissive 'progressive' schools. No longer in the vanguard, they soon came to be regarded as fossilized freaks, caught in a pre-1914 time warp. Bernard Shaw survived interminably until 1950, a living example of a bygone age.

The disregard of the whole cluster of back-to-nature and Simple Life ideas was almost total. When I first became intrigued by the subject I searched the general histories dealing with the period for accounts and references to the movement, which was everywhere visible in the literature of the time. I found virtually none, no doubt because history records only the dominant events and ideas, those that influence and determine what happens next. Back-to-the-landism failed, in these terms, and so remained unrecorded.

In other respects, it did not fail. It was directly responsible, for example, for the pastoralism of all kinds that makes up the Georgian poetry of the 1910–30 years, and for the weaknesses and strengths of

that poetry[1], as well as for the continuing bias of English verse –
recently described by Peter Porter as 'the torque which poetry has
towards nature and the pastoral' against which modern writers
struggle.[2]

There are other areas, too, where the anti-industrial influence
may be seen. The desire for a simpler life in close contact with the
earth helped to shape the rise of anthropology and its study of
isolated societies, together with the related fields of folklore and
mythology. It must have contributed, also, to the loose, popular
belief that primitive and peasant communities possess a quality now
lost to frenetic, modern, alienated and genocidal mankind. The
savage may no longer be noble, but he has a mythical contentment
not known to the rest of us. Associated with such ideas was the
bizarre belief in fairies that gripped many otherwise sensible persons
during the late nineteenth century, which seems in retrospect to
have been an attempt to deny the present world by putting on the
consciousness of an older, unlettered, superstitious time. Fairies
have declined in popularity, but interest in astrology, occultism and
various forms of Theosophy – claims to divine knowledge through
ecstasy, intuition and drugs – flourish still. These seem to like the
same soil as pastoralism, and it is no accident that the popularity of
quasi-religions was strong both in the 1890s and 1970s.

The correspondences between these two periods, which have
been remarked on throughout this book, are curious and
compelling. The realization that all this has happened before –
apparently without conscious recollection or revival – prompts the
suggestion that the ideas and activities of today's 'alternative
society' are perhaps less original than they appear, being but aspects
of a perennial reaction against technological and social change, a
form of protest/nostalgia that encompasses many contradictory
elements, holding blueprints for the future alongside blatantly
regressive obscurantism. The fate of the earlier movement may be
prophetic, for the popularity of country communes, macrobiotic
food and free schools is already on the wane.

The desire to live in the country, however, is as strong as ever. A
century ago, Leslie Stephen remarked that it was considered an
'outlying' virtue like early rising; today it is simply taken for
granted. To display a lack of affection for the countryside, to
confess to preferring city life, is regarded as perverse; love of the

country is assumed, among all classes and all ages. It is generally believed that, were it possible, nearly everyone would choose to live in a rural rather than an urban environment, and many of us regard ourselves as anchored by circumstance rather than choice to our city jobs and suburban homes. This is not often a matter of rational deliberation for, when pressed, many people can hardly define the virtues of the countryside except in terms of its not being like the city, which is overcrowded, noisy, dirty, violent, unfriendly, etc. Nor do many of us who dream of living in the country have much experience of the reality except for weekends and holidays. This does not matter, however, for the dream is firmly planted in the national consciousness and needs no justification. Hence the recurrent advertising campaigns, promoting diverse manufactured products through association with 'country goodness'.

Our collective pastoralism, it seems to me, is the most lasting effect of the back-to-the-land movement. Despite its 'failure' in economic and political terms, it has in fact triumphed in terms of popular beliefs and attitudes.[3] We firmly believe that the urban, industrial way of life is fundamentally unnatural, a chief cause of modern ills. For over a hundred years, since the city first became identified as the location of social problems such as poverty, squalor, ill health and ignorance (all of which were equally prevalent if not so concentrated in country districts) we have formulated solutions in terms of removing the place rather than the problems. Social policy in the past fifty years has largely been aimed at decimating Britain's major cities by moving people and their jobs out to peripheral estates and new towns. Thus they escape from the evil of the city but fail to reach the true goodness of the country, as E.M. Forster might have said. Now, in the 1980s, we are left with the decaying 'inner city' as the key problem.

The real problem, however, may well be our failure to work towards making the cities better places to live in, a failure that arises directly from our imprinted pastoralism. We know, after all, that the city is not a natural environment; its conditions can only be ameliorated. Given a free choice, we would all live in the country: English people belong in villages and while we stay in towns we may expect to be dissatisfied and unhappy. In 1896 the New Fellowship magazine argued against the Fabian fashion for municipal improvements. Rosewater was no cure for leprousness, it proclaimed: 'Reform or no reform, the city must go.' How far have we yet come to terms with the fact that the city is here to stay?

References

1 Beyond Industrialism

1. See, for example, G. Stedman Jones, *Outcast London*, 1971.
2. Notably the two classics of contemporary observation, Henry Mayhew, *London Labour and the London Poor*, 4 vols, 1861, and Charles Booth, *Life and Labour of the People of London*, 17 vols, 1886–1902.
3. C.S. Orwin and E.H. Whetham, *History of British Agriculture*, 1964, p.385.
4. E.M. Forster, *Howards End*, 1912, Ch.XLI.
5. Henry George, *Progress and Poverty*, 1883 edn., p.305.
6. Robert Blatchford, *Merrie England*, 1893, p.18.
7. John Ruskin, 'The Nature of Gothic', *The Stones of Venice*, Vol.II, 1853, sect.17.
8. John Ruskin, *Fors Clavigera*, No.I, 1871, p.1.
9. John Ruskin, *Fors Clavigera*, No.V, 1871, p.21.
10. E.T. Cook and A. Wedderburn (eds), *The Works of John Ruskin*, Vol.XXX, 1907, p.45.
11. *ibid.*, introduction.
12. *Pall Mall Gazette*, 8.2.1886.
13. Philip Henderson (ed), *The Letters of William Morris to his Family and Friends*, 1950, letter dated 17.5.1871.
14. William Morris, 'Art and Socialism', 1884, delivered to Leicester Secular Society, reprinted in *Collected Works of William Morris* (24 vols), 1910–15, XXIII, p.192.
15. William Morris, 'The Decorative Arts', 1977, delivered to London Trades Guild, reprinted in *Collected Works*, XXII, p.3.
16. William Morris, 'How We Live and How We Might Live', 1884, reprinted in *Collected Works*, XXIII, p.3.
17. William Morris 'The Beauty of Life', 1880, delivered to Birmingham Society of Arts, (under title 'Labour and Pleasure v. Labour and Sorrow') reprinted in *Collected Works*, XXV, p.51.

18. William Morris, 'The Decorative Arts'.
19. William Morris, 'Art and Socialism'.
20. William Morris, 'Useful Work v. Useless Toil', 1884, delivered to Hampstead Liberal Club, reprinted in *Collected Works*, XXIII, p.98.
21. *ibid.*
22. Edward Carpenter, *My Days and Dreams*, 1916, p.104.
23. Edward Carpenter, *The Simplification of Life*, 1886, p.29.
24. Carpenter, *op cit.* (22.), p.110.
25. *ibid.*, p.112.
26. *ibid.*, p.145. The hut is shown in an accompanying illustration.
27. *ibid.*
28. Edward Carpenter, *England's Ideal*, 1887, p.84.
29. *ibid.*
30. Edward Carpenter, *Civilisation: Its Cause and Cure*, 1889, pp.34–6.
31. Carpenter, *op.cit.* (22.), p.167.
32. Edward Carpenter, *Love's Coming of Age*, 1896, p.16.
33. Gilbert Beith (ed), *Edward Carpenter: An Appreciation*, 1931, p.78.

2 Love of the Country

1. See *General Report of the 1911 Census*, Cd.8491, 1917.
2. Gertrude Jekyll, *Old West Surrey*, 1904, p.viii.
3. *ibid.*
4. William Morris acted as consultant on the interior decoration of The Hill, and Burne-Jones designed fireplace tiles, stained glass and a painted frieze of St George and the Dragon.
5. *Birket Foster*, A. & C. Black, 1910, p.11.
6. Fine Art Society, March 1886.
7. Thomas Hardy, *The Dorset Farm Labourer*, 1884.
8. *The Builder*, 1888, quoted in Alan Crawford, *A Tour of Broadway and Chipping Campden*, Victorian Society, 15.9.1978.
9. *ibid.*
10. David Garnett, *The Golden Echo*, 1953, pp.17–19.
11. See William Cooke, *Edward Thomas*, 1970, Ch.1.
12. Geoffrey Keynes (ed), *The Letters of Rupert Brooke*, 1968, p.501.
13. See Ch. 2 of Kenneth Grahame's *The Wind in the Willows* for an account of an idyllic if curtailed caravan holiday. See also Gordon Stables, *Leaves from the Log of a Gentleman Gipsy in Wayside Camp and Caravan*, 1891.
14. Herbert and Agnes W. Valentine, *Tales of a Tent*, 1977.
15. Richard Jefferies, *The Story of My Heart*, 1883, Ch. 1.
16. Leslie Stephen, *Hours in a Library*, 1899, Vol.III, p.175.

3 Reclaiming the Commons

1. S.P.A.B. *Annual Report 1877–8*, pp.6–7.
2. W.H. Williams, *The Commons, Open Spaces and Footpaths Preservation Society*

1865-1965, 1965, p.3.
3. The early history of the C.P.S. was compiled by G.J. Shaw-Lefevre (Lord Eversley) in *English Commons and Forests: The Story of the Battle during the last thirty years for Public Rights over the Commons and Forests of England and Wales*, 1894, from which this account is largely taken.
4. *ibid.*, p.360.
5. *ibid.*, p.62.
6. *ibid.*, p.63.
7. *ibid.*, pp.64–5.
8. *ibid.*, p.66.
9. *ibid.*, p.119.
10. *ibid.*, p.132.
11. quoted *ibid.*, p.147.
12. *ibid.*, p.160.
13. *ibid.*, p.154.
14. *ibid.*, p.157.
15. *ibid.*, p.160.
16. *Birmingham Daily Post*, quoted in *N.F.P.S. Annual Report 1884–5*, p.19.
17. *ibid.*, p.38.
18. *ibid.*, p.30.
19. *N.F.P.S. Annual Report* 1897, p.28.
20. Limpsfield Commons Paper, BRA 1490, House of Lords Record Office, List 49.
21. *The Times*, 4.1.1901.
22. *Manchester Guardian*, 27.12.1902.
23. Undated cutting *c*. October 1901, in Stonehenge file, BRA 1490, HLRO.
24. Letter to Wiltshire County Council from C.P.S. National Trust, Kyrle Society and others, printed in *The Times* and other national newspapers, November 1901.
25. *Manchester Guardian, op.cit.*
26. National Trust, *Annual Reports* 1895–1900; *Works of John Ruskin*, Vol.XXX, p.xxxi.
27. National Trust, *Annual Report*, 1896.
28. National Trust, *Annual Report*, 1903–4.
29. National Trust, *Annual Report*, 1910.
30. National Trust, *Annual Report*, 1908.

4 The Countryman

1. Louis Mertins, *Robert Frost*, 1965, p.117.
2. G.E. Evans, *Where Beards Wag All*, 1980, p.263.
3. E.D. Mackerness (ed), *Journals of George Sturt*, 1967, entry for 27.6.1908.
4. *ibid.*, entry for 15.7.1910.
5. George Bourne, *The Bettesworth Book*, 1901, pp.178–9.
6. *ibid.*, pp.10–11.
7. *ibid.*, p.x.

8. George Bourne, *Lucy Bettesworth*, 1913, p.109.
9. Denys Thompson, *Change and Tradition in Rural England*, 1980, pp.275–80.
10. W.H. Hudson, *A Shepherd's Life*, 1905, p.168.
11. *ibid.*, p.232.
12. *ibid.*, pp.39–40.
13. D.H. Lawrence, *Selected Literary Criticism*, 1955, pp.81–2.
14. Lascelles Abercrombie to Edward Marsh, 11.12.1915, Marsh Letter Collection, Berg Collection, New York Public Library.
15. Gertrude Jekyll, *Old West Surrey*, 1904, pp.ix-x.
16. *ibid.*, p.5.
17. *ibid.*, p.159.
18. *ibid.*, p.221.

5 Folk Song Restored

1. *English Folk Dance and Song Society Journal*, Vol.VIII, 1959.
2. See W.R. Purcell, *Onward Christian Soldier*, 1957, Ch. 14.
3. Sabine Baring-Gould et al, *Songs and Ballads of the West*, 1891, preface; in 1905 this volume was musically revised by Cecil Sharp.
4. J.A.F. Maitland, *A Doorkeeper of Music*, 1929, pp.222–3.
5. *Folk Song Society Journal*, Vol.I, 1899.
6. *ibid.*
7. *ibid.*
8. *Folk Song Society Journal*, Vol.II, 1906.
9. See Maud Karpeles, *Cecil Sharp*, 1967 edn., p.38.
10. Cecil Sharp, *English Folk Songs: Some Conclusions*, 1907, *passim*.
11. *ibid.*
12. C.J. Sharp and H. MacIlwaine, *The Morris Book Part I*, 1907, pp.8–9.
13. *The Morris Book Part V*, 1913, preface.
14. Margaret Dean-Smith, 'The Preservation of English Folk Song and Popular Music', *EFDSS Journal* Vol.VI, 1950.
15. Karpeles, *op. cit.*, p.113.
16. Frank Kidson and Mary Neal, *English Folk Song and Dance*, 1915, p.164. Mary Neal was responsible for the section on dance in this volume, Frank Kidson for that on song.
17. Quoted in Karpeles, *op.cit.*, p.80.
18. Kidson and Neal, *op.cit.*, p.164.
19. Cecil Sharp, address to 1923 English Folk Dance Society Summer School, quoted in Karpeles, *op cit.*, pp.178–9.
20. Ursula Vaughan-Williams, *Ralph Vaughan-Williams*, 1964, p.402.
21. Karpeles, *op.cit.*, pp.41–2.
22. Edward Thomas, *The South Country*, 1909, p.219.

6 Agrarian Communes

1. See W.H.G. Armytage, *Heavens Below*, 1965; and Dennis Hardy, *Alternative*

Communities in Nineteenth Century England, 1979.
2. Retrospective account by M.A. Maloy, *Commonweal,* 25.5.1889.
3. Obituary of Joseph Sharpe by Edward Carpenter, *Commonweal,* 9.3.1889.
4. John Ruskin, *Fors Clavigera,* LXXVI, 1877.
5. M.A. Maloy, *op.cit.*
6. *ibid.*
7. *The Works of John Ruskin,* Vol.XXX, p.303.
8. *Commonweal,* 9.3.1889.
9. C.R. Ashbee, entry for 4.9.1886, *Memoirs,* 1938 (unpublished) Vol.I, p.31.
10. *ibid.*
11. Obituary of Joseph Sharpe, *op.cit.*
12. G.L. Dickinson, *Autobiography,* 1973, pp.69–72.
13. See H.S. Salt, *Seventy Years Among Savages,* 1921, p.78.
14. *Freedom,* September 1981.
15. P. Kropotkin, *Fields, Factories and Workshops,* 1898, p.77.
16. See John Quail, *The Slow-Burning Fuse,* 1978, p.227.
17. *The Clarion,* 22.2.1896.
18. Ben Glover, quoted in Armytage, *op.cit.,* p.313.
19. *ibid.*
20. Article in *New Order,* October 1889.
21. *ibid.*
22. *ibid.*
23. See H. Winsten, *Henry Salt and his Circle,* 1951, quoted in Armytage, *op.cit.,* p.332.
24. The 1889–90 winter season included the following lectures: 10 December, William Morris on 'How We Shall Live Then'; 25 February, Edward Carpenter on 'The Future Society'; 11 March, Herbert Rix on 'Tolstoi's Ideal and Doctrine of Happiness'. Other meetings were based on Edward Bellamy's popular book *Looking Backward,* and discussed how manufacturing and commerce would be organized after the demise of the industrial system. On the subject of the Simple Life, lectures were given on how to do without servants.
25. *Seed-Time,* October 1889.
26. *Seed-Time,* October 1894.
27. See Armytage, *op.cit.,* pp.342–6.
28. *Seed-Time,* April 1895.
29. *The New Order,* September 1897.
30. Nellie Shaw, *Whiteway,* 1935, p.227.
31. *ibid.,* pp.171–4.
32. *The New Order,* April 1898.
33. *The New Order,* November 1898.
34. Shaw, *op.cit.,* p.39.
35. Aylmer Maude, *Life of Tolstoy: Later Years,* 1910, p.546.
36. Shaw, *op cit.,* p.39.
37. Pamphlet by William Sinclair, quoted in Shaw, *op.cit.,* p.49.
38. Shaw, *op.cit.,* p.115.

39. *ibid.*, p.76.
40. *ibid.*, p.175.
41. *ibid.*, p.87.
42. *ibid.*, p.96.
43. *News Chronicle*, 14.3.1934.
44. Shaw, *op.cit.*, p.158; Foster was a former pupil of Sidney Barnsley at Sapperton.

7 Cottage Farmers

1. *Seed-Time*, October 1893; *The Cable*, 25.2.1899, 4.3.1899.
2. *The Cable*, 25.2.1899.
3. *Labour Annual*, 1897.
4. For example, *French Gardening*, 1909. Thomas Smith's other books include *The Profitable Culture of Vegetables*, 1911, and *The Book of Dry Wall Gardens*, 1916.
5. Mary Fels, *Joseph Fels: His Life Work*, 1920, p.30.
6. *ibid.*, p.51.
7. *ibid.*, p.79.
8. F.E. Green, *The Awakening of England*, 1912, p.252.
9. *ibid.*, p.254.
10. F.E. Green, *How I Work My Small Farm*, 1907, p.5.
11. F.A. Morton, *The Simple Life on Four Acres*, 1906, p.78.
12. Tickner Edwardes, *The Lore of the Honey-Bee*, 1908, pp.269–72.

8 Farm Colonies

1. J.A. Hobson (ed), *Co-operative Labour on the Land*, 1895, pp.vii–ix.
2. H.V. Mills, *Poverty and the State*, 1892.
3. H.V. Mills, evidence to the Mansion House Conference on the Condition of the Unemployed, Sub-committee on Agricultural Colonies, 26.12.1887.
4. Hobson, *op. cit.*, p.64.
5. 'Towards a Commune', *The Clarion*, 14.5.1892.
6. *The Clarion*, 29.4.1893.
7. *The Clarion*, 1.4.1893.
8. Dennis Hardy, *Alternative Communities in Nineteenth Century England*, 1979, p.114.
9. William Booth, *In Darkest England and the Way Out*, 1890, p.231.
10. *ibid.*, endpaper.
11. See W.H.G. Armytage, *Heavens Below*, 1965, p.320.
12. H. Rider Haggard, *The Poor and the Land*, 1905, p.128.
13. *ibid.*, p.131.
14. *ibid.*, p.136.
15. *ibid.*, p.132.
16. Hobson, *op. cit.*, pp.93–100.
17. W.H. Beveridge, 'The Birth of Labour Exchanges', *Minlabour*, January 1960;

see also José Harris, *Unemployment and Politics*, 1972.

18. Quoted in Mary Fels, *Joseph Fels; His Life Work*, 1920, pp.31–5.
19. Raymond Postgate, *Life of George Lansbury*, 1951, p.70; original documents, pamphlets and press cuttings relating to the Poplar Labour Colony at Laindon are held at the Greater London Record Office and the Local History Collection, Tower Hamlets Library Services, Bancroft Road, London E.1.
20. Fels, *op. cit.*, p.65.
21. See Harris, *op. cit.*, p.189.
22. Henrietta Barnett, *Canon Barnett: His Life, Work and Friends*, 1918, Vol.II, p.168.
23. See Hobson, *op. cit.*, pp.16–17.
24. Barnett, *op. cit.*, p.249.
25. *ibid.*, pp.250–1.
26. *ibid.*, p.251.
27. *East London Advertiser*, 22.5.1909.
28. *Evening Echo*, 25.6.1976; for other press reports over the years, see Tower Hamlets Local History Collection.
29. *All the World*, June 1902. This and other items relating to the Hadleigh Colony may be found in the archive department, Salvation Army headquarters, London.
30. Fels, *op. cit.*, p.53.

9 Handwork and Husbandry

1. Morris, Marshall, Faulkner and Co., prospectus 1861.
2. A.H. Mackmurdo, autobiographical notes (unpublished) William Morris Gallery, Walthamstow, quoted in Gillian Naylor, *The Arts and Crafts Movement*, 1971, pp.115–6.
3. *ibid.*
4. D.S. MacColl, *Architectural Review* 1903, quoted in Alastair Service, *Edwardian Architecture*, 1977, p.20.
5. Arts and Crafts Exhibition Society Catalogue, 1888.
6. *ibid.*
7. W.R. Lethaby, 'Art and Workmanship', *Form and Civilisation*, 1922, p.209; see also *Handcrafts and Reconstruction*, 1919, pp.1–6.
8. *Handcrafts and Reconstruction*, p.107.
9. *ibid.*
10. Walter Crane, *Arts and Crafts Essays*, 1893, p.12.
11. Curiously, they were tempted to move to the Cotswold town of Chipping Campden, where C.R. Ashbee later moved his Morris-inspired Guild of Handicraft, and also by an old silk mill at Blockley, where they found dusty notices announcing the last reduction in wages before the mill closed, some fifty years earlier, a victim of the technological advances the Arts and Crafts movement was trying to renounce.
12. By L.L. Pocock, Victoria and Albert Museum Collection.
13. C.R. Ashbee, *Memoirs*, Vol.I, p.30.

14. C.R. Ashbee, *Journal* (unpublished) quoted in D. Robinson and S. Wildman, *Morris and Company in Cambridge*, 1980, catalogue.
15. C.R. Ashbee, *An Endeavour Towards the Teaching of John Ruskin and William Morris*, 1901, p.29.
16. For a full account of the Guild of Handicraft in Chipping Campden see Fiona MacCarthy, *The Simple Life: C.R. Ashbee in the Cotswolds*, 1981.
17. Ashbee, *Memoirs*, Vol.I, p.374.
18. *ibid.*, p.383.
19. C.R. Ashbee, 'On the Need for the Establishment of Country Schools of Arts and Crafts, *c*.1905, Victoria and Albert Museum MS Collection.
20. Guild of Handicraft, Deed of Trust, 1909.
21. *ibid.*
22. According to Ashbee, the guildsmen spoke of amateur craftsmen generically as 'Dear Emily', who 'is very versatile, she makes jewellery, she binds books, she enamels, she carves, she does leatherwork. . .' She was also modest, but 'perpetually tingling to sell her work' and competed with the professional worker 'because her name is legion and because, being supported by her parents, she is prepared to sell her labour for 2d. an hour whereas the skilled workman has to sell his for 1s. in order to keep up standards and support his family' (C.R. Ashbee, *Craftsmanship in Competitive Industry*, 1908, pp.37–8). This expresses one of the chief dilemmas of the handcraft movement, but is unfair to women, who were in fact excluded from most professional craft training, including that of the Guild of Handicraft, where only three women bookbinders were ever employed. See also Anthea Callen, *Angel in the Studio*, 1979.
23. Ashbee, *Memoirs*, Vol.III, pp.293–4.
24. Mary Comino, *Gimson and the Barnsleys*, 1980, pp.13–15.
25. Unpublished letter dated 30.6.1901, quoted in Comino, *op. cit.*, p.69.
26. Norman Jewson, *By Chance I did Rove*, 1952, p.29. Jewson married Mary Barnsley, daughter of Ernest.
27. W.R. Lethaby (ed), *Ernest Gimson, His Life and Work*, 1924, p.17.
28. Arts and Crafts Exhibition Society Catalogue, 1888.
29. Comino, *op.cit.*, p.83.
30. *ibid.*, illustrations p.119.

10 Peasant Arts

1. See *Works of John Ruskin*, Vol.XXX, pp.328–30.
2. *ibid.*
3. 'The Langdale Linen Industry', *Art Journal*, 1897, pp.329–32.
4. H. Fitzrandolph and M.D. Hay, *Decorative Crafts*, 1927, p.12.
5. For a fuller account, see Geoff Spenceley, 'The Lace Associations: Philanthropic Movements to preserve the Production of Hand-Made Lace in late-Victorian and Edwardian England', *Victorian Studies*, June 1973.
6. North Buckinghamshire Lace Association publicity leaflet, quoted *ibid.*
7. K.S. Woods, *Rural Industries around Oxford*, 1921, p.157.

8. J.L. Green, *Village Industries,* 1918.
9. Godfrey Blount, *Arbor Vitae,* 1899, p.13.
10. Godfrey Blount, *The New Crusade,* 1903, p.xi.
11. *The Vineyard,* No.1, 1910, editorial.
12. More research is needed into the origins and development of these various enterprises. In 1912 Ethel Blount and Maud King claimed to have been running their 'village industry' i.e. the Haslemere Homespun Weaving Industry, since 1897, although it is not clear at what date the Blounts joined it. An unidentified press cutting in Edmund Hunter's scrapbook states that the Kings' Haslemere Hand Weaving Industry began in 1894, and the Peasant Arts Society was based at the Blounts' home, St Cross, as early as 1896.
13. Peasant Arts Fellowship Paper, no.10, 1912.
14. *ibid.*
15. Peasant Arts Fellowship Annual Report 1911–12.
16. Peasant Arts Guild Annual Report 1916–17.
17. Peasant Arts Guild Annual Report 1920.
18. Godfrey Blount, *Rustic Renaissance,* 1905, pp.13–4.

11 Halcyon Cottage and Wild Garden

1. David Garnett, *The Golden Echo,* pp.18–19.
2. George Jack, 'An Appreciation of Philip Webb', reprinted in Alastair Service (ed), *Edwardian Architecture and its Origins,* 1975, p.17.
3. *ibid.,* p.21.
4. W.R. Lethaby, *Philip Webb,* 1925, Ch.XII.
5. Mark Girouard, *Sweetness and Light: The 'Queen Anne' Movement,* 1977, p.166.
6. See W.B. Yeats, *Autobiographies,* 1955, p.113.
7. E.S. Prior, lecture to Edinburgh Art Congress, 1889 (William Morris in the chair), quoted in Service, *Edwardian Architecture,* 1977, p.24. See also H.J.L.J. Massé, *The Art Workers' Guild 1884–1934,* 1935.
8. Laurence Weaver, *Small Country Houses of Today,* Vol.2, 1922, p.20.
9. John Brandon-Jones et al., *C.F.A. Voysey: Architect and Designer,* 1978, pp.19–20.
10. *ibid.,* p.49.
11. See Ellen E. Frank, 'The Domestication of Nature' in U.C. Knoepflmacher and G.B. Tennyson (eds), *Nature and the Victorian Imagination,* 1977.
12. M.H. Baillie-Scott, *Houses and Gardens,* 1906, pp. 1,8.
13. *ibid.,* p.214.
14. James D. Kornwolf, *M.H. Baillie-Scott and the Arts and Crafts Movement,* 1972, p.454.
15. William Robinson, *The Wild Garden,* 1870. The fourth edition of 1894 was reprinted in 1977 with an introduction by Robin Lane-Fox.
16. See Anne Scott-James, *The Cottage Garden,* 1981.
17. Gertrude Jekyll, *Wood and Garden,* 1899, p.264.
18. *ibid.,* p.268.
19. Gertrude Jekyll, *Home and Garden,* 1900, p.92.

20. *ibid.*, p.284.
21. *ibid.*, p.270.
22. *ibid.*, pp.1–5.
23. *ibid.*

12 Rational Dress and Diet

1. Gwen Raverat, *Period Piece*, 1952, p.264.
2. Ada S. Ballin, *The Science of Dress*, 1885, p.160.
3. See Fiona MacCarthy, *The Simple Life: C.R. Ashbee in the Cotswolds*, 1981.
4. Raverat, *op. cit.*, p.259.
5. Viscountess Harberton, *Reasons for Reform in Dress*, p.10.
6. *Rational Dress Society Gazette*, April 1889.
7. Ballin, *op. cit.*, p.67.
8. *Rational Dress Society Gazette*, 1889.
9. Ballin, *op. cit.*, pp.197–8.
10. Gustav Jaeger, *Essays on Health Culture*, 1887 edn, p.118.
11. See Henry Holiday, *Reminiscences of My Life*, 1914, where some illustrations of healthy and artistic garments are given.
12. See Christopher Hassall, *Rupert Brooke*, 1964, p.374.
13. *Westminster Gazette*, 15.4.1897.
14. Michael Holroyd, *Augustus John*, Vol.2, 1975, p.5.
15. Henry Salt, *Seventy Years Among Savages*, pp.67–8.
16. *Hygienic Review*, 1893, p.246.
17. 'Man's Natural Food the Produce of Field and Garden', *Hygienic Review*, 1893, p.267.
18. *The Open Road*, July 1907.
19. *The Eustace Miles System of Physical Culture with Hints as to Diet*, 1907, p.103.
20. *Vegetarian Review*, March 1895, p.72.

13 New Schools

1. J.H. Badley, *Memories and Reflections*, 1955, p.53.
2. Memorandum from the New Life Fellowship dated 13.8.1886, reprinted in B.M. Ward, *Reddie of Abbotsholme*, 1934, pp.52–3.
3. See Reddie's obituary of Carpenter in *Everyman*, 11.7.1929.
4. Lecture given by Reddie at Glasgow Exhibition on 4.9.1901, quoted in Ward.
5. *ibid.*
6. *The Book of Illustrations of Abbotsholme School – the New School – Derbyshire*, 1904.
7. Memorandum by Reddie dated 1889, quoted in Ward, *op.cit.*, p.220.
8. Julian Drugman, 'First Term at Abbotsholme', *Fifty Years of Abbotsholme*, 1939, pp. 11–12.
9. Cecil Reddie, 'The Educative Value of Life in Dormitory', 1.12.1903, reprinted in Ward.

10. *The Book of Illustrations of Abbotsholme School – the New School – Derbyshire,* 1904.
11. Michael Holroyd, *Lytton Strachey,* Vol.I, 1967, pp.55–6.
12. Stanley Unwin, *The Truth About A Publisher,* 1960, Ch.4.
13. Maitland Radford, 'Hay Fever', *Fifty Years of Abbotsholme,* pp.27–9.
14. Unwin, *op. cit.,* p.55.
15. J.H. Badley, 'Some Problems of Government in a Mixed School', in Alice Woods (ed), *Co-Education,* 1903.
16. *Bedales Record,* No.4, 1894.
17. G. Brandreth and S. Henry (eds), *J.H. Badley 1865–1967,*1967, p.24.
18. *Bedales Record,* No.12, 1900.
19. *ibid.*

14 The Garden City

1. W.A. Harvey, *The Model Village and its Cottages,* 1906, p.9.
2. *ibid.,* p.10.
3. *ibid.*
4. Ebenezer Howard, *Garden Cities of Tomorrow,* 1902, p.112.
5. Dugald MacFadyen, *Ebenezer Howard and the Town Planning Movement,* 1933, p.31.
6. Raymond Unwin was a friend and associate of Edward Carpenter; at a meeting of the Society of Sheffield Socialists in August 1886, he spoke on 'Communism' together with Bob Muirhead, co-founder of Abbotsholme School.
7. C.B. Purdom, *The Garden City,* 1913, p.51.
8. MacFadyen, *op. cit.,* p.104.
9. Purdom, *op. cit.,* p.114.
10. Article in *John Bull,* quoted in MacFadyen, *op. cit.,* pp.107–8.
11. *Letchworth's Garden City 1903–1978,* Commemorative Exhibition Catalogue, 1978, issued by Garden City Museum, Letchworth.
12. *ibid.*
13. St Christopher's School magazine, 1966.
14. *Letchworth's Garden City* catalogue.
15. For fuller details see catalogue to St Edmundsbury Weaving Works exhibition shown at Letchworth and Stevenage Museums in 1981. My thanks also to Hester Bury, archivist with Warner and Sons, for additional information on the Hunter family and the weaving works.
16. V.W. Miles (ed), *The Cloisters,* 1967.
17. According to David Garnett in *The Golden Echo,* Wallace was a dissenting Scot from the New Hebrides, who ended his sermons at The Cloisters by simulating crucifixion.
18. Miles, *op. cit.,* p.20.
19. Garnett, *The Golden Echo.*
20. Miles, *op. cit.,* p.24.

21. Prospectus in Garden City Museum.
22. *ibid.*

15 Pastoralism Rules

1. See Jan Marsh, *Georgian Poetry and the Land*, DPhil. dissertation, University of Sussex, 1973, and *Edward Thomas: A Poet for his Country*, 1978.
2. *Observer*, 2.8.1981.
3. A similar point of view, outlining anti-industrial attitudes in relation to the British economy, is put forward by Martin J. Weiner, *English Culture and the Decline of the Industrial Spirit 1850–1980*, 1981.

Index

Abbotsholme School, 147, 194,
203, 206–14
Abercrombie, Lascelles
The End of the World, 67
Adams, George, 20, 21, 150, 194,
233, 238
Allingham, Helen, 29, 181
Allnut, Henry, 48–52
Art Workers' Guild, 141–2, 153,
174
Ashbee, C.R., 21, 58, 97, 98,
145–52, 153, 158, 176, 205,
209–10

Badley, J.H., 206, 214–18
Baillie-Scott, M.H., 176–9
Houses and Gardens, 177–8
Baring-Gould, Rev. S., 73–5, 81
Songs and Ballads of the West, 73
Barnett, Canon and Mrs Henrietta,
132, 133
Barnsley, Ernest and Sidney, 152,
153, 154, 156, 157, 218, 228
Barrat, W.A.
English Folk Songs, 75
Bedales School, 194, 203, 214–18

Bedford Park, 173–4
Berkamsted Common 43–5
Blatchford, Robert, 6
Blount, Godfrey, 164, 166–7, 168,
169, 170
Booth, William, 126–8, 130
Bournville, 222–4, 226
Broadwood, Lucy
Sussex Songs, 73, 75, 76
Brooke, Rupert, 31, 194

Cadbury, George, 222–3, 227
Carpenter, Edward, 17–22, 97–8,
101, 103, 145, 150, 188, 194–5,
198, 207, 209, 210, 212, 226, 228
Civilisation, its Causes and Cures,
21
England's Ideal, 19
The Intermediate Sex, 21
Love's Coming of Age, 21
Carrington, Lord, 6, 132
Central School of Arts and Crafts,
142
Chipping Campden, 147–50, 157
Cloisters, The, 238–41
Clowsden Hill Colony, 100–1

Cockerell, Douglas and Sydney, 234

Commons Preservation Society, Chapter 3 *passim*

Crane, Walter, 6, 142, 144

Dickinson, G. Lowes, 21, 97, 98, 99, 216

Edwards, T.
The Lure of the Honey Bee, 121, 122

English Folk Dance Society, 86–7

Epping Forest, 45–8

Fellowship of the New Life (New Fellowship) 102–4, 207, 209

Fels, Joseph, 116, 117, 118, 131, 132, 133, 135

Folk dancing, 82–7

Folk Song Society, 76–8, 79, 87

Forster, E.M., 21, 22, 247
Howards End, 1, 23

Foster, Birket, 28, 181

Fuller Maitland, J.A., 75–6

Furmston, W.G., 231–3

George, Henry
Progress and Poverty, 5, 116

Gimson, Ernest, 152–6, 174–5, 218, 228

Goodrich, R.K., 113–15, 198

Grahame, Kenneth, 37–8

Green, F.E.
How I Work My Small Farm, 120

Green, J.L.
Village Industries, 170

Guild and School of Handicraft, 145–52

Hadleigh Farm Colony, 127–30, 134

Haggard, Rider H., 128, 129, 130

Hampstead Heath, 42–3

Harberton, Viscountess, 189–90

Hardy, Thomas, 29, 30, 60, 84

Haslemere Crafts, 164–9

Healthy and Artistic Dress Union, 193

Hewlett, Maurice
Song of the Plow, 71

Hill, Octavia, 39, 56, 58

Holles Bay Farm Colony, 132–3, 134

Home Colonisation Society, 124–5

Houseman, A.E., 31–2

Howard, Ebenezer, 224–5, 227
Garden Cities of Tomorrow, 224

Hudson, W.H.
A Shepherd's Life, 65–6

Hunter, Edmund and Dorothea, 235–7

Hunter, Sir Robert, 41, 55

Jaeger, Dr Gustav, 191–3
Essays on Health Culture, 192

Jefferies, Richard, 33–4, 35–6, 60
Bevis, 35
Dewy Morn, 36
The Story of My Heart, 36

Jekyll, Gertrude, 28, 68–71, 169, 230
Old West Surrey, 69
Old English Country Life, 69
Home and Garden, 181–3

John, Dorelia, 195–6

Kropotkin, 99, 100, 239

Lace-making, 161–3

Laindon Farm Colony, 131, 134

Langdale Linen Industry, 159–60

Lansbury, George, 130, 131, 132, 133

Lawrence, Annie Jane, 238–9, 241

Lee, Mrs Kate, 76, 77, 78

Letchworth Garden City, 226–43

Lever, W.H. (Lord Lever), 220–1, 227

Lupton, Geoffrey, 218

Mackmurdo, A.H., 140–1, 153
Martineau, Scott
  My Farm of Two Acres, 120
Masefield, John
  Tragedy of Nan, 67
Mayland smallholders, 115–18
Methwold Fruit Farm Colony,
  113–15
Miles, Eustace
  *System of Physical Culture with
    Hints as to Diet*, 200
Morris, William, 12–17
  Kelmscott Manor, 13
  Morris and Co., 14
  Red House, 13
  The Earthly Paradise, 13–14
  News from Nowhere, 16–17,
    139–40, 144, 145, 153, 172,
    173, 188, 189, 226, 228,
    234
Morton, F.
  The Simple Life on Four Acres,
    121

National Footpaths Preservation
  Society, 40, 48–52
  merged with C.P.S., 52
National Trust, 55–9
Neal, Mary, 82–3, 85, 86
Norton Colony, 101–2, 200

Parker, Barry, 227–8, 236
Peasant Arts Society, 165, 167, 168,
  169
Poore, G. Vivian, 202–3
  Essays in Rural Hygiene, 202
Port Sunlight, 220–1, 226
Purleigh Commune, 105–7, 226

Rational Dress Society, 189–91
Raverat, Gwen, 187, 212
Rawnsley, Hardwicke (Canon), 53
  see also National Trust
Reddie, Cecil, 21, 103, 206–14
Robinson, William, 179–80
  The Wild Garden, 179

The English Flower Garden, 180
Ruskin, John, 8–12, 93–8, 139,
  144, 158, 159
  Fors Clavigera, 9

St Christopher's School, 242–4
St Edmundsbury Weaving Works,
  235–7
St George's Farm, 94–8, 210
Salt, Henry, 196–8
  Animal Rights, 197
  Humanity, 196
  Seventy Years Among Savages,
    197
Salvation Army
  see Booth, William
Sapperton, 152
Sharp, Cecil, 78–82, 84, 85, 86,
  87–8, 156, 168
  Folk Songs from Somerset, 81
  English Folk Songs for Schools, 81
Shaw, G. Bernard, 19, 193, 199,
  201, 245
Shaw, Nellie, 105, 107–11
Shaw, R. Norman, 174
Shaw-Lefevre (Lord Eversley), 40,
  41, 47, 48, 55
Smith, Thomas, 115, 116, 117, 118
Society for the Preservation of
  Ancient Buildings, 15, 40, 53,
  172
Spirella Company, 234–5
Stephen, Leslie, 34, 37, 246
Stonehenge, 52–5
Sturt, George, 4, 61–4, 98
  The Bettesworth Book, 62–4

Talbot, Mrs Fanny, 9, 56
Thomas, Edward, 22, 31, 33, 34,
  67–8, 88–9, 218
Thompson, Denys, 65
Thoreau, Henry
  Walden, 20

Unwin, Raymond, 21, 227–8, 233
Unwin, Sir Stanley, 213–14

Valentine, Herbert and Agnes,
    32–3
    Tale of a Tent, 33
Vaughan-Williams, Ralph, 87, 88
Vegetarian Society, 196
Voysey, C.F.A., 175–6

Wallace, J. Bruce, 104, 238–9, 241
Watts, Mrs G.F., 164
Webb, Philip, 13, 172–3
Whitelands Training College, 12
Whiteway Commune, 102, 105,
    107–11
Wimbledon Common, 41–2